VOL. IV
WEST COAST OF VANCOUVER ISLAND
Map Index to Chapter Locations

Chapter	Page No.
1 Cape Scott	19
2 Quatsino Sound	31
3 Cape Cook	47
4 Checleset Bay	57
5 Kyuquot Sound	69
6 Esperanza Inlet	77
7 Nootka Sound	91
8 Estevan Point	105
9 Clayoquot Sound	117
10 Tofino	129
11 Ucluelet	141
12 Broken Group — Inner Islands	153
13 Broken Group — Outer Islands	163
14 Barkley Sound — Upper Reaches	175
15 Deer Group	189
16 Bamfield to Sooke	199

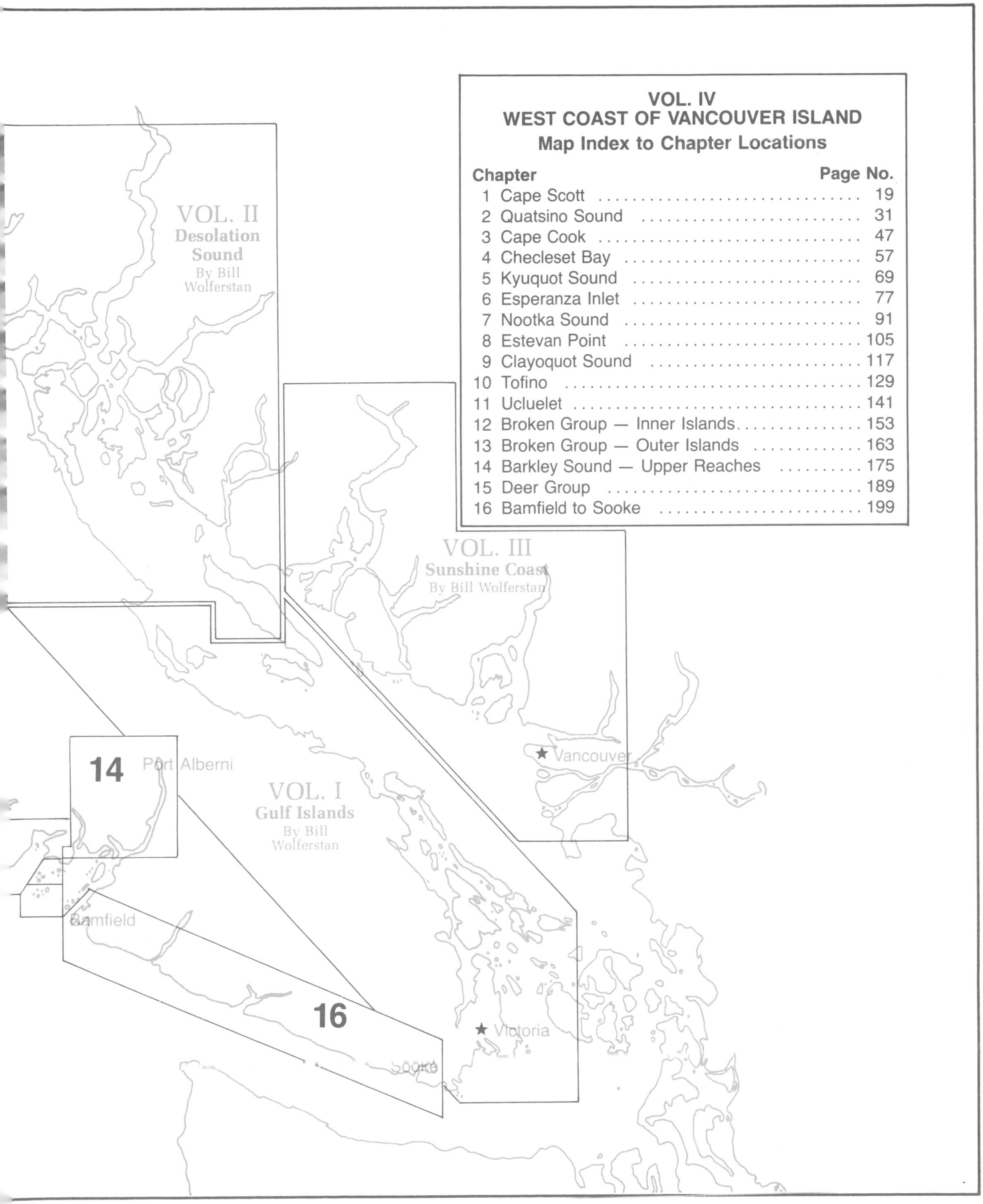

VOL. II
Desolation
Sound
By Bill
Wolferstan

VOL. III
Sunshine Coast
By Bill Wolferstan

★ Vancouver

14

Port Alberni

VOL. I
Gulf Islands
By Bill
Wolferstan

Bamfield

16

★ Victoria

500km

PACIFIC
yachting's

Cruising Guide to British Columbia Vol. IV

West Coast of Vancouver Island

Cape Scott to Sooke, including Barkley Sound

by Don Watmough

with aerial photos by George McNutt

Canadian Cataloguing in Publication Data

Wolferstan, Bill, 1942-
   Pacific yachting's cruising guide to British Columbia.
   Vol. 1 also published separately as: Pacific yachting's cruising guide to the Gulf Islands and Vancouver Island from Sooke to Courtenay.
   Vol. 4 by Don Watmough.
   Includes bibliographies and indexes.
   Contents: v. 1. Gulf Islands and Vancouver Island from Sooke to Courtenay — v. 2. Desolation Sound and the Discovery Islands — v. 3. Sunshine Coast, Fraser Estuary and Vancouver to Jervis Inlet — v. 4. West coast of Vancouver Island.
   ISBN 0-9690574-0-7 (v. 1). — ISBN 0-9690574-1-5 (v. 2). — ISBN 0-9690574-2-3 (v. 3). — ISBN 0-88896-147-2 (v. 4).
   1. Yachts and yachting — British Columbia — Guide-books. 2. British Columbia — Description and travel — 1950 — — Guide-books.* I. Watmough, Don, 1948- II. Pacific yachting. III. Title. IV. Title: Cruising guide to British Columbia.
FC3817.4.W64   917,11'34   C80-091254-3 rev
F1087.W64

Design by Ken Seabrook
Colour separations by
Mitchell Press Ltd., Vancouver
Typesetting and assembly by
Vancouver Typesetting Co. Ltd., Vancouver
Printed in Canada by Jasper Printing, Edmonton

ISBN 0-88896-147-2

PREFACE

The history of British Columbia begins with the early European explorers on the west coast of Vancouver Island. The future of British Columbia — at least for cruising yachtsmen — will be written there too. We are proud of this latest guide because, like its predecessors in the *Pacific Yachting Cruising Guide to British Columbia* series (*Gulf Islands, Desolation Sound, Sunshine Coast*), *West Coast of Vancouver Island* represents a doorway to discovery for those bold enough to accept the challenge.

As yachting has prospered as a sport in B.C. waters, the favorite and close-to-home cruising grounds have grown crowded during the busy summer season, and intrepid mariners have had to look further afield for wilderness and solitude. The "graveyard of the Pacific" — as Vancouver Island's west coast has long been known — has always represented an adventure few have chosen to face. With the publication of this guide, cruising families need no longer fear the unknown. A cruise to this vast and varied coast can now be seen as a series of comfortable day-passages, easily accomplished by any competent yachtsman with proper charts, a good weather-eye and some basic common sense.

The rewards for such a venture are manifest: the complex archipelago of the Broken Group in Barkley Sound, the stunning majesty of the Brooks Peninsula, the historic and enticing scenery of Nootka Sound and Friendly Cove, the exciting passage over Nahwitti Bar and around magnificent Cape Scott — all this can be enjoyed in the pages of this beautifully illustrated volume, and then enjoyed again aboard your own boat with this book as your faithful and reliable companion.

Readers of *Pacific Yachting* will be familiar with the work of Don Watmough and George McNutt. Don has been writing for the magazine for five years, and has cruised the west coast many times gathering material for this guide. George is responsible for the superb aerial color photographs that have become the hallmark of our cruising guides. In this new guide their broad perspective and careful attention to detail are properly presented. More than just a step-by-step guide to each and every nook and cranny of this compelling coast, this new book includes a complete introductory section detailing the history, the geology and meteorology, the flora and fauna, and the fishing spots and provisioning points from Bull Harbour to Sooke.

Sixteen chapters cover each area in detail, listing favored anchorages and popular gunkholes, pointing out uncharted rocks and reefs, relating interesting anecdotes about the natives, the early fur traders and explorers, the brave settlers and courageous mariners who first felt the spell of the west coast.

As with the other books in this series, we have assumed that the reader understands that the maps herein are not to be used for navigation, and that government charts, "sailing directions" and small craft guides are required equipment aboard any vessel undertaking a voyage on an exposed coast.

A cruising guide of this scope represents the work of a great many people who have helped to ensure that it is as accurate and complete as possible. But change is the nature of life on our coast, and we appreciate hearing from readers who have discovered errors and omissions, or who can supply new information for future editions.

October 1984

Paul Burkhart
Editor/Publisher
Pacific Yachting

FOREWORD

This is a challenging book. With this volume in your hands you might well be torn between the initial impulse to sit back and slowly savour the area page by page, and the increasing urge to cast apprehension aside and leave immediately on a voyage to the west coast of Vancouver Island. There you will find a coast of wild capes, rolling ocean swells and inspiring surroundings. The remoteness of large portions of the coast have kept it an isolated preserve accessible, until recently, only to the most adventurous pioneers and seamen.

The challenges of this coast are not understated in this book but fully described in such a manner as to instill a confidence which will guide one safely across the bar or through the narrow rocky passages to an incredible world of untouched beaches, jagged mountain skylines, historic waterways and a myriad of empty coves and serene lagoons. Don Watmough has produced a superb book, which, with the aerial photography of George McNutt, seems to capture the essence of this magnificent area.

Bill Wolferstan
Victoria, B.C.

ACKNOWLEDGMENTS

As a book begins its transition from concept to reality there is a flow of energy from a number of people that goes into the process. In the end only one name appears on the cover, even though it is a product of the accumulated talents and skills of a number of individuals. The fact that my name is the one attached to it is largely a result of my having been given the privilege of cruising this magnificent area over a long period of time, and being involved with people of great ability.

The greatest influence on this undertaking was *Pacific Yachting's* first Cruising Guide to the Gulf Islands by Bill Wolferstan. At that stage of my sailing experience I was overwhelmed by the book (and still am). My goal was then to instill that same thrill in adventurers visiting the west coast for the first time. Bill's personal help and suggestions along this path have been most valuable and encouraging.

In the conception of this book, Paul Burkhart gave me the confidence to carry out the project, and has supported my efforts towards completing this undertaking at every level, and with untiring enthusiasm. Thank you also to John Shinnick for his assistance in editing the manuscript.

My first circumnavigation was completed with the company and support of my stalwart companion Jane Herbison who helped prove that the trip can be a family adventure rather than an endurance test. On my latest circumnavigation I was the guest of Juergen and Loretta Baumann aboard *Rimsilver*. Their willingness to cruise into the furthest reaches and back waters of the coast freed me to concentrate on note-taking and photography. Thanks also to Dell McConnell and Virginia Campbell for helping on that trip.

Capturing on film this wild west coast in all its moods is a testament to the number of hours of flight time required by George McNutt to complete this mammoth task. The photos are, as you see, superb.

When it came time to take the thousands of pages of script and photos and put them into book form, it was Peter Chettleburgh and Mary Aikins who filled in where I lacked expertise — thanks for having enough faith to carry on long after closing time to get the book out. Rex Armstead, Carolyn Wells and Bill McIntyre also deserve thanks for their contributions to the guide.

Special thanks to Lisa Ferry who picked up the loose ends (of both myself and the book) whenever the task seemed too great for one person. To all those listed above, and the many others who helped along the way, I hope you're as proud as I am of *our* book.

Lastly, a thanks to my stout little boat *Coyote* which covered for me when my enthusiasm overshadowed my experience — and to all good boats that bring us safely to these wild shores.

— *Don Watmough*

This book is proudly
dedicated to my mother and father
who have always supported me in my travels
and adventures even though they would
rather I stayed closer
to home

CONTENTS

Preface vii
Foreword vii
Acknowledgements ix

Part One —   **INTRODUCTION to the WEST COAST of VANCOUVER ISLAND**

GENERAL DESCRIPTION 2
GEOLOGY 3
WEATHER and SEA CONDITIONS 5
TIDES and CURRENTS 7
NAVIGATION and SAFETY 7
NATURAL HISTORY 9
GENERAL HISTORY 10
CIRCUMNAVIGATING VANCOUVER ISLAND 13
FACILITIES 14

Part Two —   **CRUISING GUIDE to the WEST COAST of VANCOUVER ISLAND**

CHAPTER 1   CAPE SCOTT 19
     Bull Harbour, Nahwitti Bar, Sea Otter Cove

CHAPTER 2   QUATSINO SOUND 31
     Winter Harbour, Port Alice, HoLberg Inlet

CHAPTER 3   CAPE COOK 47
     Brooks Bay, Klaskino Inlet, Columbia Cove

CHAPTER 4   CHECLESET BAY 57
     Bunsby Islands, Gay Passage, Barter Cove

CHAPTER 5   KYUQUOT SOUND 69
     Tahsis Inlet, Dixie Cove, Clear Passage

CHAPTER 6   ESPERANZA INLET 77
     Rolling Roadstead, Zeballos, Tahsis, Nuchatlitz

CHAPTER 7   HISTORIC NOOTKA 91
     Friendly Cove, Gold River, Resolution Cove

CHAPTER 8   ESTEVAN POINT 105
     Hesquiat, Hot Springs Cove, Flores Island

CHAPTER 9   CLAYOQUOT SOUND 117
     Steamer Cove, Ahousat, Matilda Cove

CHAPTER 10   TOFINO 129
     Clayoquot, Adventure Cove, Pacific Rim Park

CHAPTER 11   UCLUELET 141
     Amphitrite Point, Spring Cove, Barkley Sound

CHAPTER 12   THE BROKEN GROUP — INNER ISLANDS 153
     Sechart, Pinkertons, Turtle Bay, Nettle Island

CHAPTER 13   THE BROKEN GROUP — OUTER ISLANDS 163
     Turret Island, Clarke Island, Effingham Bay

CHAPTER 14   UPPER REACHES OF BARKLEY SOUND 175
     Alma Russell Islands, Useless Inlet, Port Alberni

CHAPTER 15   DEER GROUP & EASTERN SHORES OF BARKLEY SOUND   189
     Ahmah Cove, Swiss Boy Island, Dodger Channel

CHAPTER 16   BAMFIELD TO SOOKE 199
     Cape Beale, Clo-oose, Port San Juan

PHOTO CREDITS 212

BIBLIOGRAPHY 212

INDEX 213

Introduction to the
WEST COAST OF VANCOUVER ISLAND
Cape Scott to Sooke, including Barkley Sound

INTRODUCTION

A cruise on the west coast of Vancouver Island begins where most summer cruises end. In order to make a passage along the west coast a yachtsman must negotiate the narrow, current-swept Johnstone Strait or the undulating blue seas that roll down the Strait of Juan de Fuca. These significant passages sometimes seem formidable barriers to the yachtsman approaching them for the first time. However, they should not be seen as barriers, but rather as gateways to the majesty of this magnificent coastline.

This guide is divided into two sections. In Part I we will delve into the Island's tortuous geological history; the weather and sea conditions that can be anticipated during a summer cruise and how these factors influence the ecological make-up of this biologically diverse area. As there is no official small craft cruising guide to Vancouver Island's west coast, every effort has been made to include useful information from all sources as an aid in planning and enjoying a cruise here.

We will also look into the history of man on this coast, from the early native populations and European explorers and traders to the loggers, miners and fishermen who ultimately established permanent settlements on this remote coast.

Part I also contains a summary of the more significant recreational features on the coast and lists facilities such as marinas, hospitals, parks, mooring buoys and settlements. Part I also includes a great deal of essential general information on making a passage to the west coast and should be read by anyone wishing to know the general conditions which can be expected.

Part II consists of sixteen chapters, each covering a specific section of this long and intricate coastline. (See inside cover for a map showing the arrangement of chapters.) The area covered by each chapter varies according to the complexity of the terrain and the number of anchorages available in the area. And because many west coast cruisers receive their introduction to the pleasures of the west coast by sailing first to Barkley Sound, this area has been covered in considerable detail.

The chapters begin at Cape Scott near the northern tip of the Island and progress southwards, the usual route for boats circumnavigating the Island. At the end of each chapter is a brief summary of particular cautions for the area covered in that chapter.

In addition to the general outline, the following points should be noted about this guide:

● All measurements are in the familiar Imperial units: feet, fathoms, miles, and knots. For metric conversion see table on inside back cover.

● Fuel means gasoline *and* diesel unless otherwise noted.

● Navigational instructions refer to the "new" buoyage system adopted by the Canadian Coastguard in 1983. The prudent yachtsman should make himself familiar with the symbols and structures used in the new system.

● All directions given are *true* unless otherwise stated.

● All depths given are at low water. (U.S. visitors should note that Canadian charts show depths at the lowest low water, not the mean low water level as on U.S. charts.)

● 'West coast' means West Coast of Vancouver Island unless otherwise noted.

● 'The Island' means Vancouver Island unless otherwise noted.

GENERAL DESCRIPTION

Vancouver Island is the largest island lying off the western shores of North America. It is 285 miles long and averages 60 miles wide. It lies in a northwest-southeast direction and its western shores receive the full brunt of the Pacific swells which roll in unhindered for thousands of miles. The coastline itself is rugged and uneven with five major sounds cutting deeply into the mountain range that makes up the backbone of Vancouver Island. Some of these mountains climb to over 7,000 ft and remain snowcapped most of the year.

Logging remains as one of the west coast's two primary industries. The other is commercial fishing.

The continental shelf extends westward from the shoreline an average of 40 miles at the south end of the Island to just over 10 miles at the north end. The portion of coastline covered in this guide runs from 50°47′ N/128°26′ W (Cape Scott) to 48°21′ N/123°44′ W (Sooke Harbour) and contains most geographical features from rocky headlands and curving beaches to bubbling hot springs and deep fjords. All of these features combine to make the west coast a cruisers' paradise.

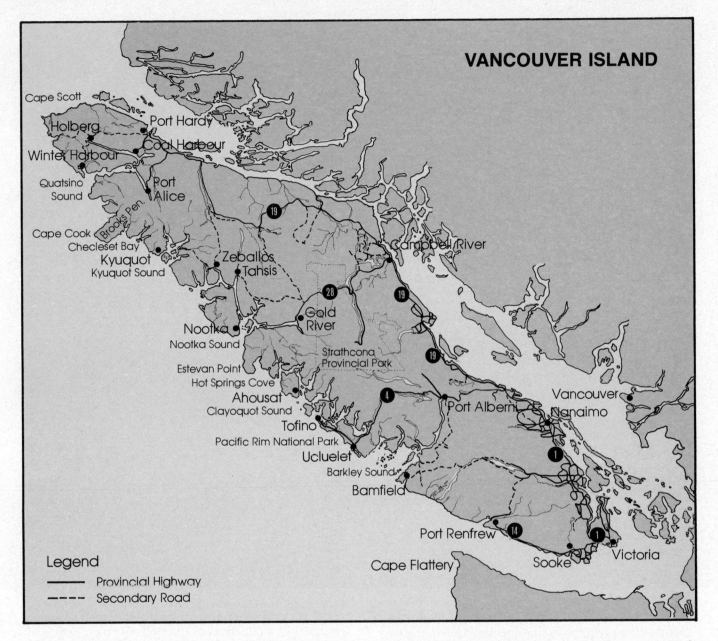

Cape Scott
Holberg
Port Hardy
Coal Harbour
Winter Harbour
Quatsino Sound
Port Alice
Brooks Pen.
Cape Cook
Checleset Bay
Kyuquot
Kyuquot Sound
Zeballos
Tahsis
Nootka
Nootka Sound
Gold River
Strathcona Provincial Park
Estevan Point
Hot Springs Cove
Ahousat
Clayoquot Sound
Tofino
Pacific Rim National Park
Ucluelet
Barkley Sound
Bamfield
Campbell River
Port Alberni
Vancouver
Nanaimo
Port Renfrew
Cape Flattery
Sooke
Victoria

Legend
—— Provincial Highway
- - - Secondary Road

Coastal settlements are resource related, with logging, fishing and mining being the most common industries along this sparsely populated shore. Roads reach the outer coast in very few places and water and air transport are essential to many settlements. Like the native people that preceded them, the present generations living on the west coast have an intimate association with the sea and the natural forces that continue to shape and reshape the landscape of the Island, as well as those who now make it their home.

GEOLOGY

In order to fully understand the origin of Vancouver Island we must go back 200 million years, when all the continents were locked together in a large mass called Pangea. When this mass fractured along the mid-Atlantic ridge it began breaking up into the continents as we see them today. The continents are floating on 'plates' hundreds of miles thick. These plates move about according to the forces exerted upon them from beneath and from the plates rubbing against one another. It is this 'Plate Tectonics Theory' which is the generally-accepted theory of how the land masses were transformed into the major continents we see today.

This is particularly significant in the area of Vancouver Island because it is a very active plate area. In fact, it is thought that Vancouver Island was formed as a result of the slow collision of the Juan de Fuca plate beneath the waters of the Pacific (just a few miles west of the land mass) and the larger North American Plate. The tremendous forces that build up as the Juan de Fuca Plate slides under the North American Plate result in volcanic eruptions along the coastline. The line of volcanoes resulting from this activity runs from Mt. Shasta in California to north of Mt. Garibaldi in British Columbia. The recent eruptions of Mt. St. Helens in this chain are evidence that these forces are still very active.

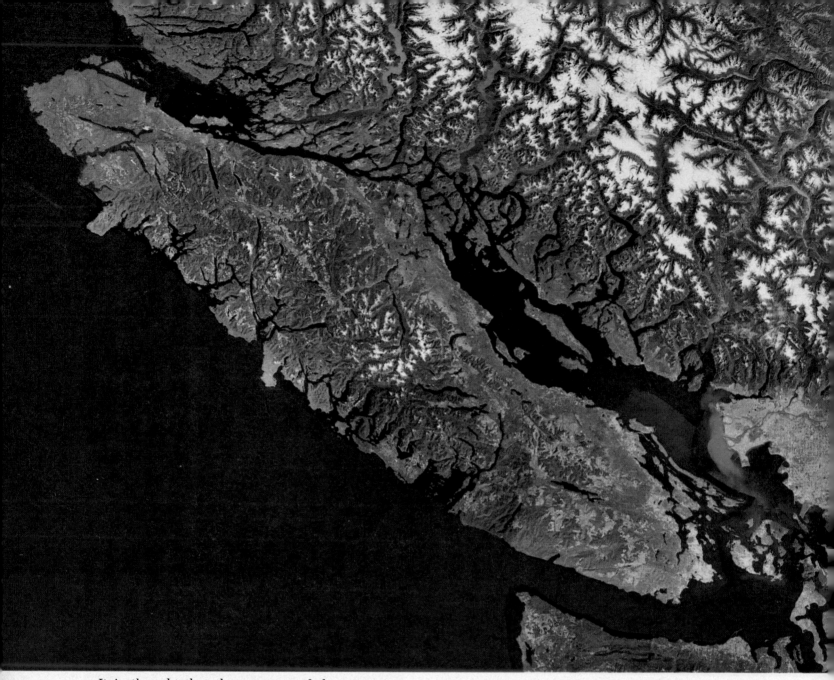

It is thought that the pressure of these moving plates also caused buckling of the land along their border subsequently forming the mountain backbone of Vancouver Island. With all these forces in action, it is not surprising to find that the rocks on Vancouver Island exhibit almost every form of deformation and change. They have been melted, eroded, transported, dumped, compressed and mashed into their present forms. As a consequence, geological maps of Vancouver Island show that much of the west coast is comprised of "undifferentiated metamorphic rocks". Such formations are found on the Brooks Peninsula, Nootka Island and in most of Clayoquot and Barkley sounds. The area from Brooks Peninsula to Cape Scott is almost entirely made up of Jurassic rocks (200 million years old) while much of the remainder is Tertiary, with the relatively recent age of 22.5 million years. These sedimentary rocks, mostly shale, sandstone, siltstone and conglomerate are clearly visible in the exposed shelves extending from the shore in places like Hesquiat Peninsula and parts of the West Coast Trail between Clo-oose and Port Renfrew.

Striking infra-red satellite photo shows ragged contours of the west coast. What appears as red is actually infrared colouring of B.C.'s coastal rainforest.

Glaciation: There have been four glacial periods in this region during the last million years, and those mighty 'rivers of ice' have been the most dominant factors in shaping the visible landforms. The deep valleys and unconsolidated sediments in this area are visual reminders of the time when glaciers hundreds of feet thick gouged their way from the interior of the province all the way across Georgia Strait and Vancouver Island. The last ice sheet was thought to have been almost ½-mile thick. When it retreated, about 10,000 years ago, the land rebounded from under the tremendous weight and, combined with the release of water formerly locked up by the glaciers, changed the water level by as much as 400 ft.

Since the last ice age thin soil has accumulated over the bedrock and glacial deposits. Waves have relentlessly pounded the rocks, eroding the softer materials and leaving the stronger materials to stand out as bold promontories. Beaches have formed and

4

Left: Seacave and surge channel in Barkley Sound were created by the pummeling of waves and currents over millions of years. Above: A lone jogger pounds along one of the west coast's many fine sand beaches.

sediments fill many of the bays and coves, making them safe and convenient for anchoring.

SUGGESTED READING

"Barkley Sound, A History of The Pacific Rim National Park Area", Victoria, B.C., 1972.

"British Columbia Geological Highway Map", Ministry of Energy, Mines and Petroleum Resources Geological Survey of Canada, 100 West Pender Street, Vancouver, B.C.

WEATHER AND SEA

Because of the exposed nature of the outer coast, weather can determine destination more than any other factor, and even the most plausible itinerary must bend to nature when she is in her wildest moods. Normally a summer cruise on the west coast (May-July) is predictably safe, though the exhilaration of surfing down a Pacific swell can be a bit overwhelming for the novice.

Weather patterns have been recorded officially on this coast for over 40 years in some places and statistical averages are summarized in the Canadian Hydrographic Service publication "Sailing Directions for the B.C. Coast, (South Portion)." This book complements the charts in giving information on passages and anchorages, but its shortcoming is that it is primarily written for larger ships such as ocean

freighters and not the cruising yachtsman. In the appendices of this book, however, is a valuable collection of weather data going back over 40 years. It provides important details on rainfall, temperatures, incidence of fog and hours of sunshine. This statistical data is averaged for each month and is the best available information for planning a west coast cruise. Of particular interest is data collected at the following stations: Bull Harbour, Quatsino, Estevan Point, Tofino, Port Alberni, Pachena Point, Tatoosh Island (Washington State) and Ocean Station Papa (Offshore bearing 50°N/145°W).

Weather forecasts are also broadcast on VHF radio but owing to the fact that conditions can change so dramatically and rapidly, the frequency and detail of forecasts are often insufficient for planning a passage. Besides having alternate destinations to fall back on, it is often useful to "be your own weatherman". One way to improve your chances of having a comfortable voyage is to plan your trip around the times of most stable weather conditions which can be done by studying the averages in the "Sailing Directions". The following is a brief outline of the general conditions which might be expected during a summer cruise to the west coast as well as a list of navigation and safety suggestions which might make the voyage more enjoyable.

Winds: The average wind speed and direction for the month of July is shown on the accompanying map. If you refer to the "Sailing Directions" you will see that the wind roses for the month of January are considerably different. Winter winds blow very hard (max. Force 11, average Force 4 on the Beaufort Scale)

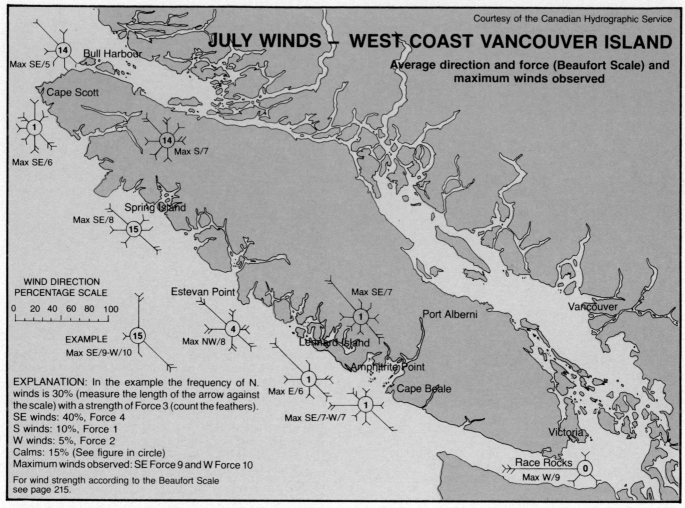

JULY WINDS – WEST COAST VANCOUVER ISLAND

Average direction and force (Beaufort Scale) and maximum winds observed

Bull Harbour
Max SE/5
14

Cape Scott
1
Max SE/6

14
Max S/7

Spring Island
Max SE/8
15

WIND DIRECTION
PERCENTAGE SCALE
0 20 40 60 80 100

EXAMPLE
Max SE/9-W/10
15

Estevan Point
4
Max NW/8

Max SE/7
1

Port Alberni

Vancouver

Lennard Island

Amphitrite Point
1
Max E/6

Cape Beale
1
Max SE/7-W/7

Victoria

Race Rocks
0
Max W/9

EXPLANATION: In the example the frequency of N. winds is 30% (measure the length of the arrow against the scale) with a strength of Force 3 (count the feathers).
SE winds: 40%, Force 4
S winds: 10%, Force 1
W winds: 5%, Force 2
Calms: 15% (See figure in circle)
Maximum winds observed: SE Force 9 and W Force 10

For wind strength according to the Beaufort Scale see page 215.

predominantly from the southeast, while in July the strength of the wind diminishes to maximum Force 8, average Force 2, predominantly from the northwest. For this reason alone it is better to cruise the west coast in the summer months. Of course local winds can funnel through the fjords to much higher velocities but, from a wind standpoint, it is best to make a passage along the coast from north to south (to take advantage of the northwest winds) in June or July.

When the "regular pattern" sets in along the coast (i.e. when the Pacific High is well established) the winds follow a predictable pattern: calm in the early morning (best for kayaks and small boats) and beginning to blow by about 10 a.m. It increases steadily in velocity as the earth warms, peaking in late afternoon, then dropping suddenly in the evening to near calm where it remains all night. Of course, when the weather is "unsettled", southeast winds, rain and squalls are the order of the day, making a southward passage difficult and often miserable.

Sea and swell: The general condition of the seas and swells for the west coast are also summarized in the "Sailing Directions". The swells are predominantly westerly year round, varying from southwest in the winter to northwest in the summer months. The swells are higher in the winter (over 12 feet 25 % of the time compared to over 12 feet 10 % of the time in July)

but you can expect the big Pacific rollers to march down the coast in an irrepressible line almost all year round. Swells present no real danger, and riding these aquamarine leviathans is a part of the west coast sailing experience that sets it apart from cruising the tamer "inside waters". In these conditions, however, towing a dinghy is inadvisable. When making longer passages on the outer coast, it is best to find some means of securing your tender on deck.

Fog: The insidious fog which pervades the west coast in summer is perhaps its most potentially hazardous weather condition. It often lies in a long bank just a few miles offshore and may remain there for several days. Moreover, it can blow in with little advance warning and completely obliterate the ragged landscape. For this reason a good dead reckoning (D.R.) plot of the vessel's position should be kept at all times, particularly during those months with a high incidence of fog. For most stations, the month of August has the most fog (10.6 days at Estevan Point, 12.8 at Pachena Point, and 14.9 at Tofino). Boatmen wishing to avoid this uncomfortable phenomenon would be better off cruising this coast in May, June or even July when the incidence of fog is somewhat less. It is, however, almost customary to expect some fog during a west coast journey, and if the fog does roll in, this area can take on an almost surreal, magical appearance. Islands drift in and out of view and the line between sky and sea vanishes. It is a world of grey where the intensity of each shade constantly changes and the nuances of viewing through this vapour curtain is an experience all in itself.

If you want to make a passage and fog is in the area, do your moving early in the morning. When the fog blows in it usually arrives with the westerlies in mid-morning. You can move to a different anchorage or get out into clear water *before* the "cat's paws" move in. But if you do get caught behind its veil there is usually some limited visibility just above the water's surface, but better yet, the fog usually dissipates by mid-afternoon. Proceed cautiously, keeping track of your position and you should have little difficulty in reaching your destination safely.

TIDES AND CURRENTS

Tides on the west coast display a mixed, semi-diurnal rhythm, similar to those on the inside waters of British Columbia. This means that there are two high and low tides of unequal heights over a period of approximately 24 hours. Tidal predictions for the west coast area are based on measurements at Tofino and appear in Volume 6 of the "Tide and Current Tables" published by the Canadian Hydrographic Service. (You will also need to get Volume 5 for portions of the inside waterways.) There are 21 secondary stations between Cape Scott and Port Renfrew which are also listed in the tide tables, all of them based on the reference port at Tofino.

Because of the large tidal range on the west coast (13.6 ft), and the number of potential hazards exposed at low water, it is important to know the stage of the tide whenever approaching shore. (Note: American yachtsmen should be aware that Canadian charts and tables measure depths relative to the *lowest*, low water level expected, not the mean low water level as shown on American charts). Overall, however, the tides themselves are less significant than the currents they generate in the narrow channels along the coast.

There are significant tidal currents at Nahwitti Bar, Scott Channel, Quatsino Narrows, Clayoquot Sound, the Strait of Juan de Fuca and, to a lesser degree, Tahsis and Alberni Inlets. Although the rate of tidal currents does not match that of some channels on the inside passages, the presence of winds opposing large ebbs or floods can create very difficult conditions for boats, and should always be considered when making a passage in these areas. Currents at Nahwitti Bar for example, can reach 5 knots and ebbs at Quatsino Narrows can achieve 6.5 knots. The current tables will tell you when to expect these extremes so you can avoid them as much as possible.

In addition to tidal currents, wind-generated currents can be created during prolonged periods of steady winds. In general, this results in a northwest-setting current of 1 knot in the winter months and a southeast current of about 1 knot in the summer

In some months fog is more of a threat than wind or waves on Vancouver Island's western shore. Cruises should be planned accordingly.

months, giving a boost to boaters heading down the coast during this time of year. Keep this offshore current in mind when plotting your Dead Reckoning position (D.R.).

Because of precipitation and snow-melt, ebb tides tend to be larger than flood tides. On a large ebb, waters flowing from the west coast's five major sounds can cause the seas to get uncomfortably steep and choppy if they meet opposing winds. For this reason it is best to try to avoid leaving any of the major sounds in the midst of a large ebb tide.

NAVIGATION AND SAFETY

With all the aids to navigation available to the modern yachtsman, this region, once dubbed "The Graveyard of the Pacific", is no longer the menace it once was. The square-riggers whose timbers once littered the shores of this rugged coastline did not have the benefits of good charts, lighthouses, radio beacons, radar, weather reports or even engines to assist them in their passages. With all the advantages provided by such aids today, shipwrecks are rare.

There have been many books written on the subject of wrecks on the west coast, but close examination of these incidents indicate that most occurred in winter months during the years when there were very few aids and when coastal currents were little understood. The stories of shipwrecks on this coast make interesting reading and are an integral part of the legacy of the west coast. (See suggested reading list at the end of this section.)

On the west coast there are 10 lighthouses and numerous other aids to navigation, all shown clearly on the appropriate charts. Yachtsmen should be familiar with the 'new' system of buoyage adopted by the Canadian Coast Guard in 1983 and available at all Coast Guard offices or by writing to Box 10060 Pacific Centre, 700 West Georgia Street, Vancouver, B.C., Canada V7Y 1E1. Light characteristics are published by the Canadian Coast Guard in a booklet entitled, "Lights, Buoys, and Fog Signals". Along with the "Sailing Directions" and tide book it is an essential aid to navigation.

In addition to visual aids, marine weather forecasts are broadcast via a VHF-FM radio network on a regular basis. In order to receive these broadcasts, your VHF radio must be capable of receiving Channel 21 (161.65 MHz). Reception can be hampered by poor weather or by proximity to mountains (VHF reception is "line of sight"), but with the powerful transmitters at Holberg, Eliza Dome and Tofino, forecasts can be heard in most anchorages on the west coast. At times, though, a yachtsman must become his own weatherman.

During times of poor visibility it's wise to have a Radio Direction Finder (R.D.F.) aboard. Radio signals transmitted from the lighthouses and radio centres can provide you with an approximate position though in some instances are accurate only to a limited degree. The signal characteristics are listed in "Radio Aids to Marine Navigation" available wherever charts are sold.

Some yachts are equipped with modern navigation aids such as radar, Loran-C and satellite navigation systems. These devices, when working properly, make navigation an easy task but are not essential to making a passage on this coast. West coast cruising is strictly coastal navigation so a sextant is also not necessary. However the open sea does give a good western horizon for practising celestial skills while still in sight of land and in a known location for checking results. Most passages are made with modest instruments such as a good handbearing compass (for taking "running fixes"), a depth sounder and a complete set of up-to-date charts.

The Canadian Hydrographic charts are of very high quality and can be relied on completely in almost all instances. Get the large-scale harbour charts for each area you intend to visit as navigation gets tricky around many of the settlements, especially Kyuquot, Tofino and Ucluelet. It is a wise idea to purchase a complete set of charts since weather can force a change of destination or keep a yacht in a limited area for days. Moreover, having detailed charts of each area provides both confidence in navigation and additional information on topography, trails, beaches, etc. (A complete list of charts is published each year, free of charge, and is available at chandleries.)

Canada is in the midst of converting all units of measurement to metric and charts are being updated to include this change meaning that some chart numbers will change as the chart is reprinted. Be careful when using charts of various scales when negotiating a passage and when changing from chart to chart, take careful note of the scale. A metric conversion scale is provided on each new chart and one appears on the inside back cover of this guide.

Other navigation and safety tips pertinent to west coast cruising are briefly summarized below:

- Besides good ground tackle (two anchors with chain and at least 200 ft of line), take along some stout mooring lines. Many convenient public mooring buoys are located on the west coast and good lines will be required.

- Take a First Aid course and carry a First Aid book and adequate medical kit. Hospitals are far apart on this remote coast.

- Know the 'diver down' flag and avoid areas where diving is in progress.

- Gillnet fish boats work extensively in channels along the coast. Learn to recognize them and how to avoid damaging their nets — or your boat. The nets, suspended from corks floating on the surface, stretch in a line as much as 1800 feet away from the boat. The best approach in avoiding these nets is to proceed slowly towards the fishboat until the net is spotted, then go around the fishboat on the side opposite the net.

- Kelp marks many submerged shoals, especially in summer months and it's wise to use this useful natural marker to locate unseen rocky shoals. Moreover, on the exposed outer coast, swells often break on offshore shoals and can then be located on the charts and used as additional aids.

- Leave an itinerary with a responsible party and report any significant delays. This will help determine if you are overdue on your trip.

- The emergency Search and Rescue telephone numbers are: Victoria (604) 388-1543; Vancouver (604) 732-4141. (Call Collect.)

U.S. Visitors: When entering Canadian waters it is of course necessary to clear customs. This formality can be undertaken at several locations on the west coast though some are located up long inlets in out of the way places which are used mostly for loading and unloading by offshore freighters.

For pleasure yachts clearing into Canada, Bedwell Harbour (South Pender Island) and Victoria on Vancouver Island are the recommended locations.

SUGGESTED READING

"Breakers Ahead!", R. Bruce Scott, Review, Sydney, B.C. 1970

"Vancouver Island's West Coast 1762-1962", George Nicholson, George Nicholson's Books, Vancouver, B.C. 1965

"Oceanography of the B.C. Coast", Richard E. Thomson, Department of Fisheries and Oceans, Ottawa, 1981

"Shipwrecks of the B.C. Coast", Fred Rogers, Douglas & McIntyre, Vancouver, B.C. 1973

NATURAL HISTORY

Still relatively untouched by man, many parts of the west coast remain well populated with species of wildlife that may be rare in other areas.

The ecosystems on the west coast of Vancouver Island are as distinctive as they are appealing in their rugged beauty. The coastline is a battlefield between the ancient spires of granite and the relentless seas and winds that pound the shores. Surviving in this battlefield are flora and fauna that have adapted to these harsh conditions and which, in fact, thrive in every backwater and habitable area of the coast.

Even on the surf-lashed shores, barnacles and sea-palms defy the elements and flourish in the clean nutrient-laden waters. When the tide is out, the table is set, and the bounty of food resources is one of this wild area's great attractions.

The nature of this coast is so pervasive that it is virtually inseparable from its history. Its economy has been tied to its natural history from the time native Indians began catching fish and using the cedar for their canoes and clothing. It continued through the fur trade and mining eras to the present time with the resource industries of fishing and forestry.

In the sea the prime source of its bounty is the result of a physical phenomenon known as "upwelling". Upwelling is a process by which the nutrient-laden deeper waters are brought to the surface by currents striking submerged ridges and deflecting upward. This phenomenon occurs along the west coast and accounts for both the colder-than-usual waters and the richness of the food supply available to the marine organisms.

According to Richard Thompson in "Oceanography of the British Columbia Coast" the fishing yields of areas where coastal upwelling occurs are at least a thousand times more productive than other oceanic regions where it does not occur. This basic food source is reflected by the abundance of the more visible wildlife such as salmon, sea lions, whales, eagles and the sea otter which has had such a pro

found influence on the historical development of this coast. Less visible, but no less important is the multitude of invertebrates such as sea urchins, crabs, abalone and shellfish which abound in the rich waters of the west coast.

Many books have been written regarding B.C.'s abundant wildlife and a list of some of the more useful ones appears at the end of this section. For visiting yachtsmen there are four principle biological zones of note:

- The intertidal area which is covered and uncovered with each succeeding tide.
- The shore zone where seaweed, barnacles and countless invertebrates have adapted to life in the restless saltwater surge.
- The backshore with its thick stands of salal and ferns.
- The coastal rainforest where access through the dense tangle of greenery is limited to wherever trails have been cleared.

One of the most significant features of the coastal ecosystem is that it is so vulnerable to change. These changes often have serious repercussions. An interesting example is the pilchard, a small herring-like fish which suddenly appeared on the west coast in vast numbers around the year 1925. Processing plants (which reduced the fish to an oil used in agriculture and manufacturing) sprang up all along the coast. By 1927 there were no fewer than 26 of these between Barkley Sound and Kyuquot. Over 1,000 people, 75 seine boats and 100 tugs were employed in catching and processing this seemingly inexhaustible supply of fish. Then, as quickly as they appeared, the fish suddenly changed their feeding habits, moving farther offshore, so the industry had to adapt to offshore methods which were more difficult and less profitable. By 1944 the pilchards were scarce indeed and by 1946 there were none at all. Today the only reminder that the pilchards were ever here are the abandoned ruins of the reduction plants scattered here and there among the coves and bays of the west coast — a monument to nature's fickle ways.

Some of the more critical biological areas of the coast are protected by the Ecological Reserves Act which sets aside certain unique biological areas for scientific study and preservation. According to the Act:

"Ecological reserves are needed to unravel and help understand some of the basic ecological processes. As genetic pools they serve the function of a nature museum. As man continues to modify the surface of the earth, some plants and animals can become extinct before they are even known to science. Used as benchmark areas against which to measure changes wrought by man, they can teach us how to soften the impact of man on the environment."

There are currently over a hundred such reserves in the province, with eight of them on the west coast. These are not parks, recreation areas or wildlife man-

Nature has designed intertidal species such as the sea palm (Postelsia) to survive in surge areas that receive the full brunt of ocean swells.

agement areas and, while casual use is sometimes permitted, they are primarily intended for scientific purposes. For further information and permission to visit these reserves, write the Ecological Reserves Unit, 1019 Wharf Street, Victoria, B.C. V8W 2Y9.

It should also be pointed out that in order to fish in B.C. waters, it is necessary to have a sportfishing licence. According to the law, "no person 16 years or older may legally fish, spearfish, or use set lines to capture fin fish (all fish excluding shellfish, crabs, prawns and sea urchins) in the tidal waters of British Columbia unless that person is in possession of a valid tidal water sport fish licence." Licences are available at many outlets along coastal British Columbia.

The "Tidal Water Sports Fishing Guide" is also available at many coastal outlets (no charge). Some of the most critical subjects covered in this booklet are to do with restrictions imposed on collection of bivalves (clams, oysters and mussels) owing to the dangerous and sometimes fatal "redtides", or paralytic shellfish poisoning (P.S.P.). Closures are in effect for the entire west coast of Vancouver Island during summer months and because the conditions causing this phenomenon are always changing, it is important to consult the local fisheries officers to find out if the closure has been lifted temporarily. Call (604) 666-3169 for information on closures before consuming any bivalves on the west coast.

Also, since the migrating California Gray whale is often seen on this coast between March and May and later, between August and November, it's important to be aware of their habits so as to avoid a collision. (The Department of Fisheries and Oceans forbids boats from going within 300 feet of these sea mammals.) Whale-watching expeditions are organized each year on the coast by Whitewater Adventures, 1511 Anderson St., Granville Island, Vancouver, B.C. V6H 3R5 (604) 669-1100.

It is the ongoing challenge of visitors to this coast to ensure that nature will not be destroyed by carelessness or abuse. It is the responsibility of each individual to ensure that his presence as an observer does not destroy the very thing he has come to see. Be conservation-minded in your actions. "Take only pictures, leave only footprints" is the byword when approaching this magnificent wilderness and the best way to ensure that it will be there for others to enjoy in the future.

SUGGESTED READING

"Oceanography of the British Columbia Coast", Richard E. Thomson, Department of Fisheries and Oceans, Ottawa. 1981

"Exploring the Seashore", Gloria Snively, Gordon Soules Book Publishers Ltd., Vancouver. 1978

"Between Pacific Tides", Edward F. Ricketts and Jack Calvin, 4th Edition, revised by J. Hedgepeth, Stanford University Press. 1968

"Guide to Marine Life of British Columbia". G.C. Carl, Handbook #21, Provincial Museum, Victoria, B.C. 1971

GENERAL HISTORY

When Captain Cook stepped ashore in British Columbia he did not find a barren land occupied by a primitive culture. Instead there was a highly developed society which had an elaborate social structure and ingenious methods of dealing with a harsh and volatile environment. The natives were hunters of whales, and fishermen adept at their craft. Moreover, they had enough time left after providing for themselves to develop elaborate dances, carvings, music and mythology. Their canoes were a marvel of technology and their massive longhouses defied the limitations imposed upon them by their lack of tools.

Linguistically these west coast people were of two root languages — the Nootka south of Cape Cook and the Kwakiutl who inhabited the northern part of the Island and adjacent mainland. They lived in a delicate balance between the aggressive Haida of the Queen Charlotte Islands and the Makah from Cape Flattery on the Washington coast.

Within the Nootka there were sub-tribes such as the Kyuquot, Ehatisaht, Moachat, Hesquiat, Clayoquot and Nitinat. They fought amongst themselves, captured slaves and raided each others' villages, but between battles lived a relatively easy existence living off the bounty of the land.

In winter the natives lived in large sheltered villages. They inhabited large communal houses that often sheltered as many as 100 members. In summer months the whole village moved (cedar planks, animals and all) to their temporary residences on the coast closer to the whales and fish that formed the bulk of their diet. In the fall they occupied the banks of the west coast rivers where the bountiful salmon appeared each season to spawn. Fish were dried and stored for winter consumption.

After European contact this fierce and proud culture quickly succumbed to disease and the "white tide" that followed the discovery of the wealth they had in luxurious sea otter furs. The culture they had developed over centuries slipped like the sun over the western horizon.

The reading list at the end of this section outlines some of the more interesting texts where further information might be found. (**Note:** Indian reserves are private and permission to visit them should be sought from local bands before entering. Reserves are protected by law and it is illegal to remove any artifact from any reserve in B.C.)

It was March 29th, 1778 when Royal Navy Captain James Cook reached the shores of Vancouver Island. On his third voyage of discovery Cook had been assigned the task of locating the elusive "northwest passage" which would provide Britain with supposedly easy access to the riches of the Orient. He had reached these shores via the Cape of Good Hope, New Zealand and Hawaii.

On this date however, Cook was in urgent need of a safe harbour in which he could repair his battered ships *Resolution* and *Discovery*. There was a break in the clouds, a favourable wind, and around 5 p.m. his ships were able to drop anchor in the mouth of Nootka Sound. The chain rattling over the bow rang the chimes of change for this remote corner of the globe.

Although Cook received distinction for being the first European to set foot on the shores of what later became British Columbia, it was only a matter of time before the Spanish (based in Mexico) and the fur-seeking explorers out of Russia would reach this area as well. In fact, four years before, Juan Perez in the corvette *Santiago* had anchored very near Nootka Sound himself. A storm sprang up, however, and he never left his ship. Thus it was that Cook became recognized for the fact that he actually went ashore and stayed in Nootka for nearly a month. Moreover, Cook later *published* his discoveries, while the Spanish government kept their explorations secret.

Cook's voyage also inadvertently sparked the rush for sea otter pelts which his men found fetched a high price on the open market in China. Sadly, Cook was killed in Hawaii before he could return to England, but his great discoveries sparked a significant chain of events for the west coast.

In the years immediately following Cook's visit there was a flurry of interest in getting more furs to markets in Macao. Traders such as Hanna, Strange, Meares, Barkley and Gray all followed Cook's maps and came to Nootka in search of the new wealth to be found there.

Trade was carried on at a rapid pace, that is until the Spanish began asserting their claim to the entire west coast and sent Esteban Martinez to formally take possession of Nootka. The feisty Spaniard seized a number of English ships and touched off the "Nootka Controversy" which nearly resulted in war between Britain and Spain — a war which neither nation could afford. Fortunately a settlement was reached by negotiation (the Nootka Convention) and Captain

Sacred sea caves were once used as burial sites by west coast Indians.

George Vancouver (once a midshipman under Cook) was sent to take back possession of lands and ships confiscated by the Spanish.

Meanwhile, trade was still continuing at a furious pace between the natives, seeking iron and brass, and a variety of English and American traders who, in search of more sea otter skins, began branching out from Nootka to discover (and name) other areas of Vancouver Island. Charles Barkley discovered the sound he named after himself and later found the Strait of Juan de Fuca which, though described by a Greek pilot in the service of Mexico in 1592, had remained unexamined for nearly 200 years.

One of the more interesting accounts of life in these transitional times was recorded by John Jewitt, an armourer on the trade ship *Boston*, which was captured in Nootka Sound by the powerful chief Maquinna in 1803. Jewitt, who then served as Maquinna's slave for two years, kept a diary (originally written in berry juice) of his time in captivity at Friendly Cove.

Following the fur trade came the slow but steady development of other resource exploration. The fur trade, which fell off after the near annhilation of sea otter, was replaced by the development of mining, logging and fishing. This development was accompanied by the efforts of overzealous missionaries such as Reverend Brabant and Reverend Moser who helped accelerate changes already crushing the natives and their traditional ways.

In order to utilize the resources here it was necessary to chart the coastline and define its safe harbours. In this way hydrographers such as Captain Richards and Captain Pender of the survey ships *Plumper* and *Hecate* became explorers in their own right, plotting the thousands of miles of coastline and thereby opening up new areas for commerce. Their efforts to bring this area into the light and the stories and names compiled by Captain John T. Walbran ("British Columbia Coast Names") give us some of the main sources of history and knowledge we have of early west coast life.

Fortunately, through all the changes this area has undergone in the past 200 years, it is nature which prevails. The "bold promontory" that Captain Cook called "Woody Point" (now Cape Cook) is still there for us to see. Not a single tree has felt the logger's axe and the climax forest stands in all its uncut glory for the voyager of today who seeks adventure in the still undulating wake of the trading ships.

SUGGESTED READING

"Barkley Sound", R. Bruce Scott
"B.C. Coast Place Names", J. Walbran
"Narrative of the Adventures and Sufferings of John R. Jewitt", John R. Jewitt
"Voyages Made in the Years 1788 and 1789 from China to the Northwest Coast of America", John Meares
"Vancouver Island's West Coast", George Nicholson

CHRONOLOGY

1492   Columbus reaches the New World

1522   The **Victoria**, under Magellan, becomes first ship to circumnavigate the globe.

1579   Sir Francis Drake lands briefly on the California coast

1592   Juan de Fuca pilots Mexican expedition north of 48°

1620   Pilgrims settle New England

1639   Russia reaches Pacific at Okhotsk

1741   Bering explores Alaska from Russia

1774   Juan Perez of Mexico reaches Queen Charlotte Islands, anchors off Nootka Sound.

1776   Declaration of Independence (American colonies)

1778   Cook's ships reach Nootka via Cape of Good Hope, Tahiti and Hawaii

1785   James Hanna reaches Nootka in Sea Otter

1786   Hanna, Strange, Meares, Dixon and La Perouse engage in fur trading

1787   Charles Barkley discovers Barkley Sound and re-discovers Juan de Fuca Strait

1788   Meares erects west coast's first building in Friendly Cove. Gray winters in Clayoquot

1789   Martinez takes possession of Nootka for Spain, confiscates Meares' ships. Captain Gray discovers mouth of Columbia River. Fall of the Bastille in France

1790   Nootka Convention signed by England and Spain averts war between them. Vancouver first circumnavigates the Island and takes possession of Nootka

1793   Alexander MacKenzie reaches Pacific by overland route

1803   Trade ship **Boston** captured by Maquinna. Jewitt made prisoner

1808   Simon Fraser reaches the Pacific Coast by river

1815   Battle of Waterloo

1837   Queen Victoria born

1855   Last great Indian battle between Kyuquots and Clayoquots

1862   Hankin crosses Vancouver Island by foot

1874   First lighthouse built on west coast at Cape Beale

1875   Reverend Brabant establishes first west coast mission at Hesquiat

1894   Rasmus Hansen initiates colony at Cape Scott

1902   Bamfield Cable Station built

1906   **Valencia** wrecked near Cape Beale (117 people perish). Lifesaving trail conceived

1924   First gold discovered at Zeballos

1952   CP steamship **Maquinna** makes last west coast run

1971   Pacific Rim National Park established

CIRCUMNAVIGATION

Sailing around Vancouver Island is often compared to sailing around the world, but on a lesser scale. The voyage will test numerous skills as one faces fog, currents, windy capes, large waves and complex navigation en route to calm lagoons, beautiful beaches and wild, unexplored shores. The delightful difference is that the voyage can be broken up into a series of exciting day trips, each one distinct from the other, with a safe anchorage available at the end of each day's run. Indeed, circumnavigating the island allows cruisers to see its entire 285 mile length without having to repeat any anchorages, all while taking best advantage of the prevailing conditions.

The usual way to circle the island is counterclockwise. This allows one to gain distance north and west (the prevailing direction of the wind and seas) while still in the relatively protected "inside" waterways. After reaching Cape Scott, the prevailing summer northwesterlies provide a following wind to whisk you down the coast — a rush that must be experienced to be appreciated. By using the winds on the outside and the powerful ebb tides to carry you up the inside passages, the entire circumnavigation can be done in three sailing weeks, provided there are no weather delays. However, six to eight weeks is preferable to allow for a margin of comfort and the pleasure of exploring the coves and archipelagos that make up this magnificent area. One would truly need years to see the west coast in all its moods, and yachtsmen who visit its shores usually return for longer, not shorter, visits.

Timing is important for a successful trip. Generally late May, June, and July are the preferred months for a circumnavigation. These months generally provide the steadiest winds, least amount of fog and the lingering twilights which give extra hours of visibility when making longer passages. If you plan to circumnavigate *clockwise*, it is best to leave in May when spring southeasterlies will get you up to and around Cape Scott before the summer pattern (mainly northwest winds) sets in. The disadvantage of this, though, is that southeasterlies are usually accompanied by strong winds and rain.

Provisions can be found in various locales along the outer coast, but it is best to get a good supply of food stocks before leaving, as some items, especially produce, might be unavailable at the more remote locations. Port Hardy on the "inside" is a good place to stock up on those last few items, although basic foodstuffs are available at all major settlements on the west coast. However, don't forget to take into account the natural resources available along the way. The west coast is famous for its abundance of salmon, cod and crab. All the same, have a good supply of canned goods in case weather keeps you in a remote area for a few days. Also, be prepared to carry your garbage to proper disposal facilities at most public floats. This is

West coast lightstations such as this one at Sheringham Point have drastically reduced piloting risks on a shore once known as the "Graveyard of the Pacific".

a beautiful, bountiful, wild and pristine cruising area — let's keep it that way.

An increasing number of adventurers are using trailerable boats to get to the wild areas of the coast. This is a great way to explore Barkley, Quatsino and Clayoquot sounds. Some boats are hauled by professional boat haulers (listed in the yellow pages of your phone book) to coastal locations and then sailed back — thus eliminating some of the more difficult passages. There are boat launches at several locations on the west coast but, since more are being constructed all the time, it is best to phone Tourism B.C. to check if there is one closer to the area you want to explore — call (604) 668-2300.

When contemplating and executing such a major undertaking as circumnavigating the island (often a cruiser's first venture into open waters) remember that the primary purpose of doing the trip is to enjoy it. By taking your time, using common sense and careful planning, a west coast cruise is both an exciting adventure and one of the most memorable vacations imaginable. In the words of solo sailor and adventurer Joshua Slocum:

"To young men contemplating a voyage I would say go. The tales of rough usage are for the most part exaggerations, as also are the stories of sea danger... Dangers there are, to be sure, on the sea as well as on the land, but the intelligence and skill God gives to man reduce these to a minimum. And here comes in again the skillfully modeled ship worthy to sail the seas... To face the elements is, to be sure, no light matter when the sea is in its grandest mood. You must then know the sea and know that you know it, and not forget that it was made to be sailed over."

West Coast Marine Facilities

Public floats, marinas, mooring buoys and medical facilities

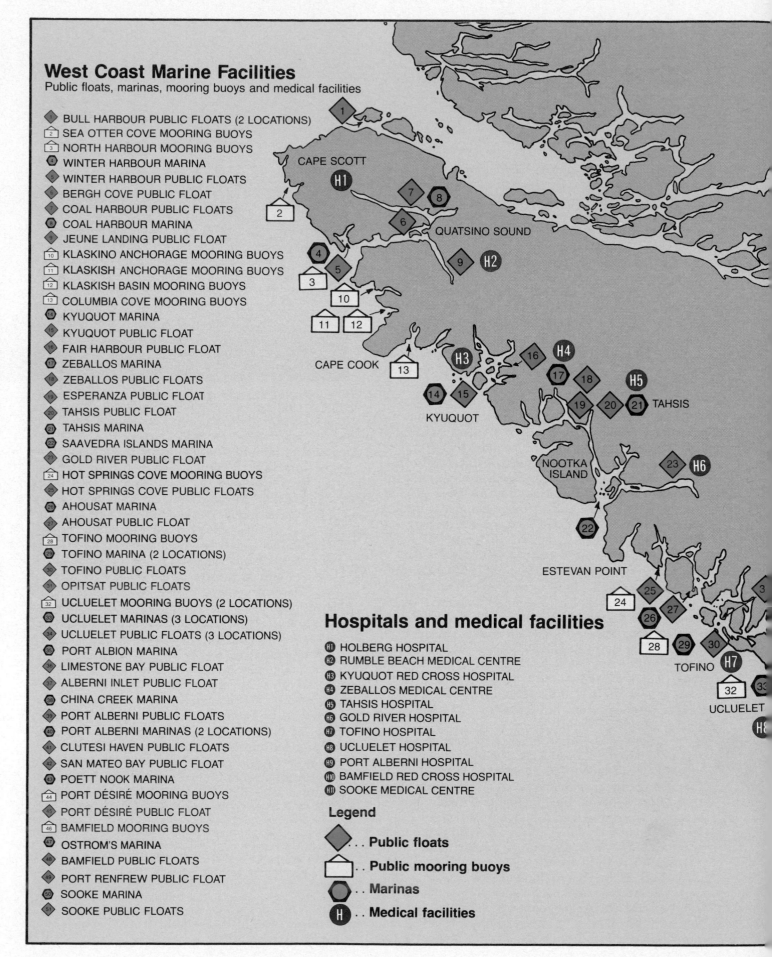

1. BULL HARBOUR PUBLIC FLOATS (2 LOCATIONS)
2. SEA OTTER COVE MOORING BUOYS
3. NORTH HARBOUR MOORING BUOYS
4. WINTER HARBOUR MARINA
5. WINTER HARBOUR PUBLIC FLOATS
6. BERGH COVE PUBLIC FLOAT
7. COAL HARBOUR PUBLIC FLOATS
8. COAL HARBOUR MARINA
9. JEUNE LANDING PUBLIC FLOAT
10. KLASKINO ANCHORAGE MOORING BUOYS
11. KLASKISH ANCHORAGE MOORING BUOYS
12. KLASKISH BASIN MOORING BUOYS
13. COLUMBIA COVE MOORING BUOYS
14. KYUQUOT MARINA
15. KYUQUOT PUBLIC FLOAT
16. FAIR HARBOUR PUBLIC FLOAT
17. ZEBALLOS MARINA
18. ZEBALLOS PUBLIC FLOATS
19. ESPERANZA PUBLIC FLOAT
20. TAHSIS PUBLIC FLOAT
21. TAHSIS MARINA
22. SAAVEDRA ISLANDS MARINA
23. GOLD RIVER PUBLIC FLOAT
24. HOT SPRINGS COVE MOORING BUOYS
25. HOT SPRINGS COVE PUBLIC FLOATS
26. AHOUSAT MARINA
27. AHOUSAT PUBLIC FLOAT
28. TOFINO MOORING BUOYS
29. TOFINO MARINA (2 LOCATIONS)
30. TOFINO PUBLIC FLOATS
31. OPITSAT PUBLIC FLOATS
32. UCLUELET MOORING BUOYS (2 LOCATIONS)
33. UCLUELET MARINAS (3 LOCATIONS)
34. UCLUELET PUBLIC FLOATS (3 LOCATIONS)
35. PORT ALBION MARINA
36. LIMESTONE BAY PUBLIC FLOAT
37. ALBERNI INLET PUBLIC FLOAT
38. CHINA CREEK MARINA
39. PORT ALBERNI PUBLIC FLOATS
40. PORT ALBERNI MARINAS (2 LOCATIONS)
41. CLUTESI HAVEN PUBLIC FLOATS
42. SAN MATEO BAY PUBLIC FLOAT
43. POETT NOOK MARINA
44. PORT DÉSIRÉ MOORING BUOYS
45. PORT DÉSIRÉ PUBLIC FLOAT
46. BAMFIELD MOORING BUOYS
47. OSTROM'S MARINA
48. BAMFIELD PUBLIC FLOATS
49. PORT RENFREW PUBLIC FLOAT
50. SOOKE MARINA
51. SOOKE PUBLIC FLOATS

Hospitals and medical facilities

H1. HOLBERG HOSPITAL
H2. RUMBLE BEACH MEDICAL CENTRE
H3. KYUQUOT RED CROSS HOSPITAL
H4. ZEBALLOS MEDICAL CENTRE
H5. TAHSIS HOSPITAL
H6. GOLD RIVER HOSPITAL
H7. TOFINO HOSPITAL
H8. UCLUELET HOSPITAL
H9. PORT ALBERNI HOSPITAL
H10. BAMFIELD RED CROSS HOSPITAL
H11. SOOKE MEDICAL CENTRE

Legend

◆ . . **Public floats**

⬠ . . **Public mooring buoys**

⬡ . . **Marinas**

Ⓗ . . **Medical facilities**

CAPE SCOTT

QUATSINO SOUND

CAPE COOK

KYUQUOT

NOOTKA ISLAND

TAHSIS

ESTEVAN POINT

TOFINO

UCLUELET

14

West Coast Marine Facilities

Public docks and floats on the west coast are available for temporary use by visiting yachtsmen. A small daily fee is collected usually based upon the length of boat. These facilities provide access to shore and often have water, power, garbage collection and derricks available for use by the public. During summer months one will usually find that there is space available. Also scattered along the west coast are the large, sturdy mooring buoys provided by the Small Craft Harbours Branch for public use. Use a strong mooring line to tie to these buoys. Marinas shown on the adjacent map are private, and usually provide repair services for boats and motors as well as petroleum products from one or another of the oil companies. Some operate on a cash-only basis, while others still accept the appropriate credit cards. Water and ice are also generally available at marinas, although propane is only available at a few locations. Chevron Marine in Tofino and Gulf Oil in Zeballos are the only locations listed in the Small Craft Facilities index in the "Sailing Directions" where reliable propane supplies are available for yachtsmen. Portable tanks can, however, be taken to shoreside service stations in several major settlements. Medical facilities vary along the coast from small Red Cross Hospital outposts to major General Hospitals such as those in Tofino and Port Alberni. Basic medical help can be found at the locations shown on the map opposite. As the map shows, there are areas of the coast which are well provided by facilities and services, while others are far more scattered. If a yacht experiences difficulty on the west coast, safe harbours and repair facilities are usually nearby. Don't be afraid to turn back if conditions become unmanageable. The Coast Guard monitors Channel 16 VHF, as do many marina operators and fishermen. People who live on the west coast are known for being particularly friendly and helpful, and will assist you whenever possible. For a complete list of facilities provided by the government of Canada (public floats, wharves and mooring buoys) please consult "Guide to Federal Fishing and Recreational Harbours" British Columbia, Department of Fisheries and Oceans, Small Craft Harbours Branch, Vancouver, B.C.

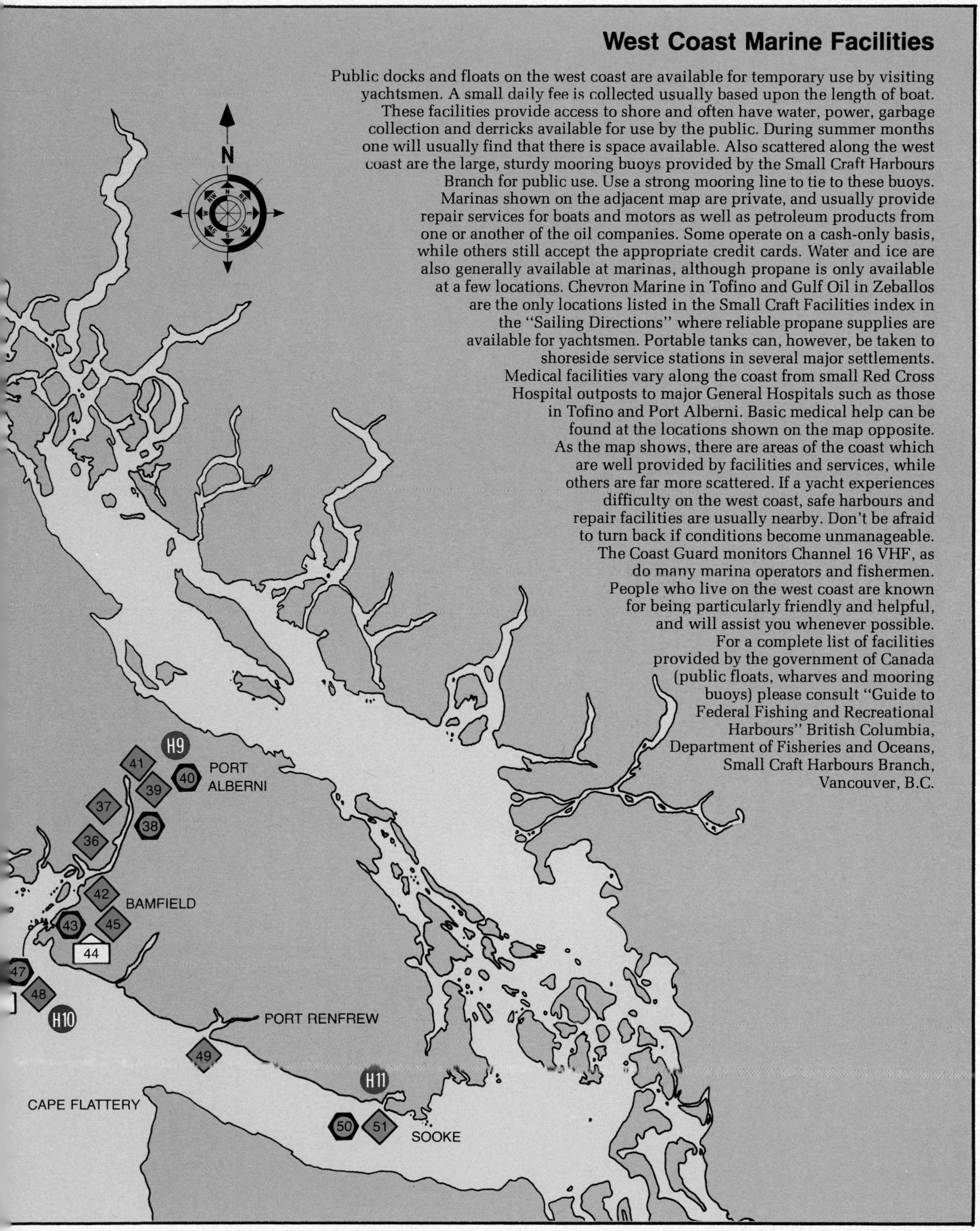

PART TWO

Cruising Guide to the

WEST COAST OF VANCOUVER ISLAND

From Cape Scott to Sooke
including Barkley Sound

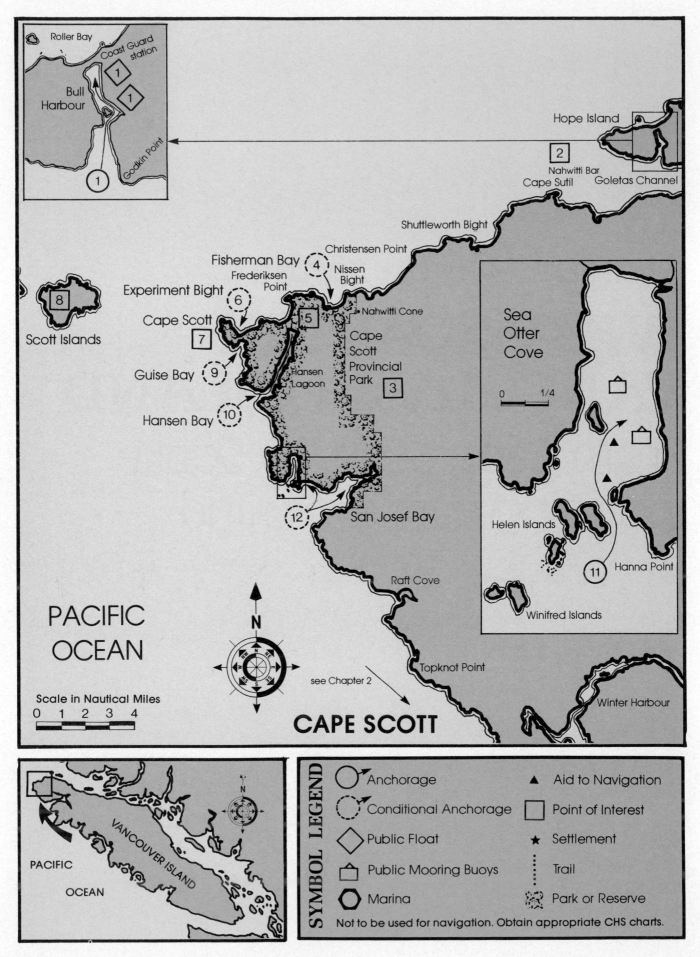

Roller Bay

Coast Guard station

1

1

Bull Harbour

Godkin Point

1

Hope Island

2

Nahwitti Bar

Cape Sutil

Goletas Channel

Shuttleworth Bight

Christensen Point

Fisherman Bay

4

Nissen Bight

Frederiksen Point

Experiment Bight

6

Nahwitti Cone

8

5

Cape Scott

7

Cape Scott Provincial Park

Scott Islands

3

Guise Bay

9

Hansen Lagoon

Hansen Bay

10

Sea Otter Cove

0   1/4

Helen Islands

11

Hanna Point

12

San Josef Bay

Winifred Islands

Raft Cove

PACIFIC OCEAN

N

Topknot Point

see Chapter 2

Winter Harbour

Scale in Nautical Miles

0   1   2   3   4

CAPE SCOTT

PACIFIC OCEAN

VANCOUVER ISLAND

N

SYMBOL LEGEND

◯ Anchorage

⬭ Conditional Anchorage

◇ Public Float

⬠ Public Mooring Buoys

⬡ Marina

▲ Aid to Navigation

□ Point of Interest

★ Settlement

⋮ Trail

▒ Park or Reserve

Not to be used for navigation. Obtain appropriate CHS charts.

CHAPTER ONE

Cape Scott

Bull Harbour, Nahwitti Bar, Sea Otter Cove

The Cape Scott area is one of the most exciting areas of the western shores of Vancouver Island and worth a lingering visit. It is an area of extremes — exceptionally beautiful beaches fight for space between rocky headlands and foam-swept reefs. Grassy meadows glisten in the sunshine in a place where the weather is notorious for being wicked and fickle. The native occupation of this area dates back a long way, and local legends tell of giants and gods that could turn tempests loose on anyone who challenged their power.

We begin our voyage on this exciting coast from the ancient refuge of the Nahwitti Indians, then travel over and around some substantial navigational obstacles, past some of B.C.'s most significant ecological reserves and anchor amidst the crumbling remnants of doomed attempts at colonizing this wild coast. Access to these attractions requires negotiating several potential hazards, so this chapter will highlight these and offer suggestions on how to deal with them.

1 Bull Harbour

Although Bull Harbour is not on Vancouver Island (it is on Hope Island, on the eastern side of Goletas Channel) it is the most convenient all-weather anchorage from which to initiate a crossing of the infamous Nahwitti Bar before rounding Cape Scott. The harbour is described in John Chappell's "Cruising Beyond Desolation Sound", an essential book for making the passage up the mainland side of Van-

couver Island. The harbour is secure with a mud bottom, but because the neck of land separating the open sea from the head of the inlet is so low, a northwesterly wind may really rip through the anchorage. The sound of high winds whistling through the rigging in such a remote spot has kept many a pleasure boat in this refuge longer than needed. Often, the outside conditions are not as extreme as they seem while anchored here. This scenic harbour was named for the large bull sea lions that frequented the shores of Hope Island in large numbers before the turn of the century. The entrance is quite picturesque and the harbour itself often yields good-size crabs.

There is a detached public float in the harbour, with 50 ft of docking space to tie up to, but there is no access to shore from here, and it is located some distance from the Coast Guard Station. There is also a public dock and float further inside the harbour with 250 ft of docking capacity, but most of the available space is taken up by the Coast Guard cutter based in Bull Harbour. Because of the favourable bottom, and adequate swinging room, most boats anchor near the centre of the basin in 12 to 18 ft, just past the public float. The mudflats extend a fair way out from the Coast Guard residences so stay near the centre of the harbour.

The seasonal fish-buying barge which moors in the harbour during fishing season is not a reliable source of gas, water or supplies. Its schedule varies from year to year, and its limited supply is primarily meant to serve north island fishermen. It is best to ensure that

you have a full stock of supplies by the time you leave Port Hardy, 23 miles to the southeast.

For an interesting shoreside excursion, row to the float and walk the 1.5 mile gravel road to Roller Bay and watch the great Pacific swells, unimpeded by islands or shoals for thousands of miles, hurl themselves upon this gravel beach, pushing huge boulders high above the tide line on Hope Island. A visit to the Coast Guard Station is also an interesting and informative experience. In this remote place, using grossly outdated equipment, a handful of men and women keep an eye on this large and desolate part of the coastline, performing tasks that range from collecting weather data to performing dangerous marine rescues. If they have time, they are happy to show you around the station, and by and large they welcome visitors.

Preceding page: Cape Scott, at northern tip of Vancouver Island is part of Cape Scott Provincial Park, was first colonized by Danish settlers in the last century.

Bull Harbour (behind isthmus) on Hope Island is the traditional jumping off point for boats rounding the Cape.

2 Nahwitti Bar

Before leaving Bull Harbour, heading towards Cape Scott, it is necessary to calculate the crossing of Nahwitti Bar, between Tatnall Reefs, and Nahwitti Point, on Hope Island. Timing makes all the difference between a dangerous experience and an easy passage. The bar, just 2 miles from Bull Harbour, is a problem because a lot of water ebbs out of Goletas Channel over a submerged sandbar which shallows up to little over 36 ft. This piled-up water can reach ebb current velocities of up to 5.5 knots, and this whole system, when meeting the open waters of the Pacific against the prevailing northwest winds and swell, can create rough and often dangerous breaking seas. There are several ways to avoid this situation and, depending on your destination for the day and the prevailing conditions, there is no need to put yourself in danger. Your basic options are:

Cross at high slack — this is the preferred option

Long Pacific swells hurl themselves ashore at Roller Bay on the northern side of Hope Island. The bay is an easy 1.5 mile walk from the public dock at Bull Harbour.

because at slack tide there will be no water flowing over the bar, and the tide will be working in your favour when you get to Cape Scott, 22 miles farther on.

Cross at low slack — this reduces the problem at Nahwitti Bar, but it means that the current which rushes through Scott Channel and around the northern side of Vancouver Island, reaching a speed of 3 knots, will be against you for the duration of the passage around Cape Scott. If the wind is north-westerly at the Cape (which it normally is in the summer), the clash between the wind and the flooding tide in Scott Channel can create a rough chop and make things uncomfortable. In this case you might consider staying awhile in one of the conditional anchorages on the north coast (see 4 and 6 below) and waiting out the peak of the flood.

Go around Hope Island — this route adds 11 miles to the trip but allows the flexibility to leave at a time more compatible for a rounding of Cape Scott. Although this option is always available, you might try one of the other options first, as conditions are not totally predictable over the bar, and the thrill and accomplishment of crossing it is a good way to start a west coast trip.

Crossing the bar takes about a half hour, and using one of the above methods, you should have no trouble. Once over the bar, you will see the result of countless waves pounding the rocky shores along the north coast. Beach after beach appears on the port side, scalloped out of the rocky shoreline, and beckoning for a visit. Unfortunately, because of the repu-

tation that Cape Scott has for bad weather, most yachtsmen quickly bypass these beautiful sandy strips and press on towards the first of the great capes on the west coast. If conditions are calm, or if the wind is south of west, a visit ashore in this area can reward the visitor with a pure sand beach where cougar and bear tracks can often be seen and the occasional glass ball still makes its way ashore from Japan. Sailing along this coast with the blue swells rolling in, on a close reach and making good time pressing toward the cape, is truly a thrilling experience.

3 Cape Scott Provincial Park

Starting near Nahwitti Cone about 6 miles from Cape Scott and continuing all the way around to San Josef Bay is one of this province's newest parks, the 37,238-acre Cape Scott Provincial Park. This spectacular and rugged park has over 40 miles of ocean frontage, including nine major beaches. Although this park preserves a large part of the shoreline, it is not primarily a marine park. Trails traverse the marshy uplands leading to the many campsites available in the park. These trails and campsites are rudimentary, and must be hiked into several miles from a parking area near San Josef Bay. This parking area is reached by a rough road from Port Hardy, and past Holberg.

Shallow waters, strong currents and incoming swells from the open Pacific make Nahwitti Bar an area to be crossed with caution; best done at high water slack.

For the cruising yachtsman, the park still offers many opportunities to explore one of the greatest features of the park: the remnants of the doomed attempts to colonize Cape Scott. In 1894, a Danish immigrant, Rasmus Hansen, was fishing on the newly-found fishing bank off the northern end of Vancouver Island in the small schooner *Floyborg*. When his vessel was anchored in Goose Harbour (now Hansen Bay)

23

he went ashore and found a great tidal meadow, with two salmon-filled streams flowing into it. He conceived the idea that this site would be ideal for a Danish colony similar to the Norwegian settlements at Quatsino and Bella Coola.

At this time the Federal Government was actively promoting colonization of the remote areas of Canada, and Hansen had little difficulty convincing the other prospective colonists of the opportunity for a successful colony here. Potential settlers, attracted by the offer of free fertile land in return for their labours, saw rivers teeming with fish and countless numbers of waterfowl nearly covering the lagoon. By 1898 there were more than enough settlers to qualify for official recognition as a colony, and a year later the population of this remote corner of British Columbia stood at 90. With the promise of a road to connect the colony with the rest of Vancouver Island, and the favourable prospect of developing a co-operative society not only capable of sustaining itself, but having enough resources to export as well, the fledgling colony looked as though it might survive its relative isolation.

The reasons why this was not to be are described in Lester Peterson's book, "The Cape Scott Story." In this book Mr. Peterson writes nostalgically from recollections of his childhood in the colony. The main reasons for the settlement's failure were a changing government attitude towards colonies, the failure to get a road connecting the colony to the rest of the population, and the lack of an all-weather harbour where supplies could reliably be landed. Remnants of the efforts of the colonists can be found throughout the Park, including trails, decaying buildings and

cleared meadows which are steadily returning to the rainforests from which they were taken with such futile toil.

4 Fisherman Bay

Continuing along the northwest coast, another sand beach opens up on the port side, this one in Nissen Bight. In the westernmost nook of this bight, a small bay provides a safe anchorage under certain conditions. It is an ideal place to wait out a southwesterly blow and a good place to wait out the peak flood at Cape Scott if the tide is against you and seas are choppy. Even in westerly winds, it is a pleasant place to visit, providing there is no great northwest swell. It has good holding ground (sand and shells), and the beach ashore is worth exploring. Anchor near the centre of the bay, close in toward shore, taking note that a submerged rock lies due north of the small islet forming the eastern shore of the bay, and that the shoal on the western side extends out into the bay. This rock is usually covered with kelp, and fairly easy

Fisherman Bay (foreground) in Nissen Bight is an ideal location to wait out a southwesterly blow, but take care when wind and seas are from the north.

to locate. Its weakness as an anchorage is that it is completely exposed to northerly winds and swells.

Since shallows prevented steamers from using the harbour at Sea Otter Cove, 14 miles to the southwest (see 11 below), this little bay had to be used as the primary supply landing spot for the Cape Scott colony. Because of the northerly swells, no dock or float could be built, and goods had to be ferried to shore using small skiffs. It also meant that supply boats serving the colony from further down the west coast of Vancouver Island had to round Cape Scott both ways in order to land machinery and goods. Because of this difficulty, reliable delivery of supplies to the colony could not be guaranteed, causing many hardships.

There is a good deal of wreckage on the shores of this bay, mainly from failures at trying to establish a

A lone eagle views his surroundings from a perch high on a treetop.

loading dock here. First a barge was anchored in the bay to facilitate the unloading of goods, but rough seas frequently prevented its use. Later it was moved farther out to serve as a breakwater but washed ashore in a winter storm in 1946 and broke up on the beach.

The Indian name for the bay was 'Beka', meaning "meeting of the spirits". The beach on the east side of the island in the bay once called 'Kechegwis' (wood drifted on the beach) is now known by fishermen as "sunset beach". Humpback whales are sometimes seen in the bay and bears visit the shores regularly.

A rough trail leads from the beach all the way to Hansen Lagoon to the southwest. Over this trail the colonists carried everything from simple staples to heavy equipment on their hardy backs. An entire sawmill was moved piece by piece to the main colony over 3 miles inland near the lagoon. It was largely this distance from a reliable all-weather harbour that spelled doom for the colony.

5 Frederiksen Point

This point of land contains a powerful blowhole, where swells rolling in from Queen Charlotte Sound are funnelled into a narrow opening and explode in a

Nels Bight east of Cape Scott has a tempting mile-long sand beach but its exposure to northwesterly swells makes it a dubious landing site.

geyser of water and spray visible a great distance from shore. Behind the point, in Nels Bight, over a mile of white sand beach beckons for a visit, but its open exposure to the prevailing northwest swell makes landing there extremely difficult. If you can't resist the urge to walk along one of these magnificent north coast beaches, press on another mile or so.

6 Experiment Bight

Immediately east of Cape Scott is another sweep of sand contained by a bight of land named after one of

the first vessels to visit the coast. In 1786 (just eight years after Cook landed at Nootka) James Stuart Strange, in the service of the East India Trading Company, came to the northwest coast in the 300-ton *Captain Cook* (Capt. Henry Lowrie) and the 100-ton *Experiment* (Capt. Henry Guise). After visiting Nootka, where he discharged Dr. John McKay (surgeon of the expedition) in order for the doctor to recover his health and study the native customs, Strange headed further north. On August 1 of that

Narrow neck of sand joins Cape Scott to the main body of Vancouver Island. Sand beaches stretch into the distance either side.

year, he arrived at what he thought was the western-most promontory of the North American continent. Off this point, he saw a chain of islands which he determined had not yet been discovered, and named them after the patron of the voyage, Mr. David Scott, who had assisted in fitting out the expedition. The cape off which the islands lie came to be known as Cape Scott, and later geodetic surveys added the names Strange Rock, Lowrie Bay, Guise Bay (9) and Experiment Bight as memorials to this early trader and explorer.

If the swell permits, anchor in the bight close to the beach and go ashore. A conical red buoy marks a dangerous sunken rock on the west side of the bight. A sand neck connects Cape Scott to the root of Vancouver Island, and a short walk over this natural bridge will take you to the other perfect crescent beach at Guise Bay. Remnants of reclamation attempts by Danish settlers can be found here as well, although the extreme weather conditions in this part of the island are quickly rendering the pioneers' work nearly invisible.

Lone footprints wend a sandy trail along Lowrie Bay north of Cape Russell.

7 Cape Scott

This infamous Cape is the most westerly point of land on Vancouver Island, and justly deserves its reputation as a place where weather conditions can suddenly change for the worse. Surprisingly, a lighthouse was not built here until 1960, and though the light keepers gather weather conditions regularly, and pass this information via the weather receiving channels, conditions can change so severely and rapidly that the frequency of their weather reports is insufficient to provide adequate advance warning for the cruising yachtsman. Winds can change direction and rise from 5 to 45 knots in less than an hour. Fortunately, these squalls blow over as quickly as they arise, and there are fairly safe anchorages within a short distance of the Cape, depending on the direction of the blow.

The winds also affect the sea conditions in Scott Channel, especially when the tide changes and the 3 knot current opposes the wind to create a steep chop. Rounding Cape Scott can be difficult when this happens, and many worthy vessels have gone down in this channel. The schooner *Louisa Downs* was wrecked here in 1868 with all hands lost; in 1892 the whaling barque *Hermit* and sealing schooner *Maggie Mac* also went down, leaving no one to tell the tale. Needless to say, rounding the Cape can be a dangerous experience when conditions are bad. It's best to exercise caution and discretion when rounding this cape, and turn back, or seek temporary shelter if the tidal stream is severely opposing the wind. A wait of a few hours in one of the conditional anchorages near the cape could make the difference between a memorable cruise, and a damaging or frightening experience.

Cape Scott once sheltered a Kwakiutl Indian summer village called "Ouchton" (foam place) where the natives fished for halibut that was plentiful nearby. On a boulder on the beach at Experiment Bight there is a depression that resembles a large footprint. According to Indian legends this is the footprint of 'Kanekelac' who it was said could step from Cape Scott to Triangle Island (a distance of 25 miles) in a single bound. During World War II a secret radar station was built at the Cape, though nature has since reduced many of the structures (including the plank road) to a pile of rotting timbers.

8 Scott Islands

These strikingly high islands, especially Cox Island (1025 ft) and Lanz Island (695 ft) are clearly visible long before you reach Cape Scott, inviting a closer look. The "Sailing Directions, British Columbia Coast" mentions temporary anchorages on the northwest side of Cox Island, the northeast side of Lanz Island, and in the bight on the northeast side of Triangle Island. However, their northern exposure rules them out as anything but temporary anchorages. The channels between them are strewn with partially submerged reefs and, though some protection from southerly winds could be found in these places, the prevailing northerly swell would make anchoring here uncomfortable. If the wind switched around to

Lighthouse on Cape Scott is located slightly inland; was built as recently as 1960.

the northwest (the prevailing summer wind) these anchorages would likely have to be vacated quickly. Local fishermen paint a bleak picture of what conditions are like if it does blow up suddenly: there is no safe place to move to. The "Sailing Directions" also warn of dangerous overfalls and tide rips around the Islands, and there is no doubt of the danger there. Attempts to set up a lighthouse at Triangle Island failed because of persistent fog, and the wicked winds which blow through here. The buildings were braced on all sides and anchored by guy wires to the rock, but a 1912 storm blew the radio towers and rigging over the cliffs, and lifted one building off its concrete foundation. The station was abandoned 10 years after it was built, and never replaced.

Because of their exposure, dangerous approaches, the barren nature of their shoreline, and their geo-

graphical isolation from the rest of the west coast cruising grounds, they are not recommended as overnight anchorages. Beresford Island, Sartine Island, and Triangle Island are all Provincial Ecological Reserves; the first two as marine wildlife refuges, the latter a seabird colony. Triangle Island is considered to be the most important seabird colony on the B.C. coast according to the Canadian Wildlife Service. There are numerous tufted puffins, Cassius and rhinoceros auklets as well as pelagic cormorants and gulls. For this reason, public access is restricted on the islands. In order to visit these reserves, written permission must be granted by the Ecological Reserves Unit of the Ministry of Lands, Parks and Housing, 1019 Wharf St., Victoria, B.C. V8W 1T6.

9   Guise Bay

After rounding Cape Scott, if conditions allow — and if you follow the chart carefully — you can anchor in Guise Bay and go ashore to the beautiful crescent beach here. If conditions do not allow landing at Experiment Bight (ie. northwest swell, or wind) then things should be ideal for a landing here. The idyllic, almost tropical beach contrasts starkly with the rugged, reef-strewn shoreline around Cape Scott. Be-

Hansen Bay (Hansen Lagoon in background) still shows signs of Danish settlers who colonized the area during last century.

cause the neck of land connecting the cape to the main part of Vancouver Island is so low, north winds can blow through the anchorage but, on a fair day (settled conditions) a yacht can find secure anchorage while exploring the ruins of colonial efforts ashore. It is not recommended as an overnight anchorage: it is exposed to southwest winds.

10   Hansen Bay

Three miles out of Guise Bay, clear of the reefs and around Strange Rock, lies Hansen Bay, which opens into Hansen Lagoon. During the settlement of the colony, smaller schooners anchored here or proceeded right into the lagoon area at high tide. Overnight anchorage here is not recommended, as the bay is open to westerlies. A visitor who is inspired by the moving saga of the Cape Scott pioneers might anchor here to seek some relic of the fated colony and empathize with the original Danes who were so inspired by the place that they abandoned everything to move here.

11 Sea Otter Cove

Nine miles from Cape Scott is a protected cove with a rock and reef-strewn entrance, and a large drying bank at its head. The safest way to enter this cove is to give the Winifred and Helen islands a wide berth, and enter the cove from the south, between the most easterly Helen Island and Hanna Point (see inset on guide map). The swells break almost all the way across the entrance in a southwesterly, but a narrow channel with a least depth of 21 ft allows relatively safe entry.

In order to get into the shelter of the Cove, it is advisable to use the enlarged inset on Chart #3624, and keep a sharp eye on it as you enter. By keeping close to the navigation marker on the starboard side as you enter, you can avoid the shoal area to the east of the eastern Helen Island. From here, the cove opens up, but shallows and an unmarked rock which lies awash at chart datum require that you continue cautiously past the 60 ft islet that lies inside the cove. From here, simply round the islet, noting the black beacon on it and either anchor, or tie up to one of the eight mooring buoys provided by the Small Craft Harbours Branch of the Federal Government. These buoys are connected to "hurricane chains" and are substantial enough to hold the largest fishboats which ply the coast. They are not like the recreational mooring buoys provided in Provincial Marine Parks and are placed at strategic places along the outer coast

Swells break across the rock-strewn entrance to Sea Otter Cove, but a narrow channel with a minimum depth of 21 ft allows relatively safe access. Once inside visitors can seek safe overnight moorage at one of eight stout public buoys within the bay.

for the convenience and safety of small craft. By using buoys instead of anchors, more boats can shelter in these small remote coves in bad weather. In Sea Otter Cove there are eight of them, in two neat rows of four, each with large rubber bumpers to protect the hulls of boats tied to them. If you prefer to anchor, pick a spot in the cove where you won't swing onto one of the many rocks or onto the drying shallows throughout the cove. The wind can really whistle through here in a southwesterly and it can get a bit rolly, so be prepared if a front is coming up from the southwest.

Once inside, Sea Otter Cove is a pleasant, interesting place to explore by dinghy or on foot. It was on the beach at the head of this cove that the writer found a glass ball. A trail leads from the head of the cove to Lowrie Bay where a beautiful and rugged west coast beach, littered with huge derelict timbers, stretches out in a smooth curve towards the headland to the north. The trail, about 2 miles long, is difficult to find, but in better condition than the one leading in the other direction towards Erie Lake. Although these trails are in the park, they are very rudimentary and require good footwear. The walk to the beach takes

you through very primitive bog and forest lands but it is marked by surveyor's tape, and well worth the effort.

The cove was named in 1786 by Captain James Hanna after his ship *Sea Otter*, a snow of 120 tons. (A snow is a ship with two masts, both square-rigged, similar to a brigantine but having an additional trysail mast stepped abaft the main mast. Most 16-19th century traders were snows.) Captain Hanna was in this area to trade for the sea otter skins which had brought such a high price when Cook's men showed them to fur merchants in Canton a few years earlier.

12   San Josef Bay

This large bay, first named St. Patrick's Bay by Captain Hanna, is open and offers little shelter except from north winds. If the north winds are harsh in Sea Otter Cove, alternative anchorage may be found far inside the bay, or close northeast of Hanna Point. **Note:** the mooring buoy shown on Chart #3624 is no longer there. Although the bay is protected in a northerly blow, it is completely open to westerlies and southwesterlies and can only be considered an anchorage under settled conditions with the wind from the north. The San Josef River runs into the head of the bay, where many old remnants of the colony can still be found.

From here to the Quatsino Lighthouse on Kains

Remnants of the Cape Scott colony can be found near San Josef Bay but seaborne visitors should exercise caution in anything but settled conditions and winds from the north.

Island, 16 miles down the coast, there is little shelter and the swells can really make for a "sleighride".

Raft Cove is sometimes used as a refuge for kayaks and other small boats, and the area is being considered as an addition to Cape Scott Provincial Park. It does not provide sufficient shelter for cruising boats however, and is not recommended as an anchorage except under completely calm conditions. If it is getting late, or if conditions look bad, it is best to "hole up" in Sea Otter Cove and wait until better conditions prevail before heading south.   ⚓

LOCAL CAUTIONS
- Nahwitti Bar should not be crossed during high tidal flows in either direction, particularly when the wind opposes the tide.
- Currents in Scott Channel can reach 3 knots. Wind opposing this current can cause steep, short seas.
- Entry to Sea Otter Cove is difficult in SW winds because waves can break across the entrance in extreme conditions. Use the inset on Chart #3624 to find the safest passage into the cove.

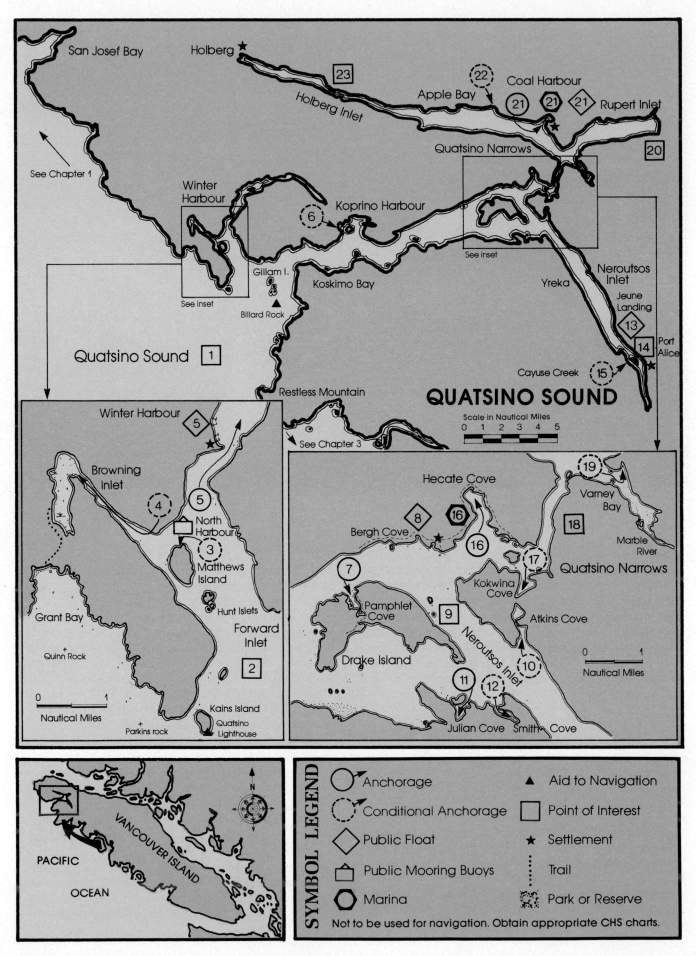

San Josef Bay

Holberg ★

23

Holberg Inlet

Apple Bay

⊙22 Coal Harbour

㉑ ⬡21 ◇21 Rupert Inlet

Quatsino Narrows

20

See Chapter 1

Winter Harbour

Koprino Harbour

⊙6

See inset

Neroutsos Inlet

Yreka

Jeune Landing

13

Koskimo Bay

Gillam I.

▲ Billard Rock

14 Port Alice

Quatsino Sound 1

Cayuse Creek ⊙15

QUATSINO SOUND

Restless Mountain

Scale in Nautical Miles
0 1 2 3 4 5

Winter Harbour ◇5

See Chapter 3

Browning Inlet

⊙4 ⑤5

Hecate Cove

⊙19

Varney Bay

North Harbour

⬚ ⊙3 Matthews Island

◇8 ⬡16 Bergh Cove

18

Quatsino Narrows

Marble River

Grant Bay

Hunt Islets

⑦7 Pamphlet Cove

⊙16 16

⊙17 Kokwina Cove

Atkins Cove

Quinn Rock

Forward Inlet

2

Drake Island

9 Neroutsos Inlet

⊙10

Nautical Miles
0   1

0   1
Nautical Miles

Kains Island

Quatsino Lighthouse

Parkins rock

⑪11 ⊙12 Julian Cove Smith Cove

PACIFIC

N

VANCOUVER ISLAND

OCEAN

SYMBOL LEGEND

⊙→ Anchorage
⊙→ Conditional Anchorage
◇ Public Float
⬚ Public Mooring Buoys
⬡ Marina

▲ Aid to Navigation
⬚ Point of Interest
★ Settlement
⋮ Trail
▨ Park or Reserve

Not to be used for navigation. Obtain appropriate CHS charts.

CHAPTER TWO

Quatsino Sound
Winter Harbour, Port Alice, Holberg Inlet

Heading south from San Josef Bay, the Vancouver Island coastline as far as Quatsino Sound is rugged and offers little protection to the passing yachtsman. To port is the twisted landscape of the Island's barren outer coast, while the starboard view includes only the glistening blue of the open Pacific, with its undulating swell. The matching peaks of Restless Mountain (2240 ft.), marking the southern entrance to Quatsino Sound, provide an unmistakable landmark to head for, and the passage along this part of the coastline seems to go quickly. Just past Lippy Point you might catch a glimpse of a few fishboats anchored in Grant Bay, but this bight offers little except, perhaps, a temporary break in the day's fishing. Once past the bay and clear of Quinn Rock, you can begin calculating your entry into the sound. There are a number of unmarked dangers lying in the entrance, so depending on your ultimate destination, it is best to prepare early for your entry.

If you are heading for Winter Harbour in Forward Inlet, it is best to round up and stay fairly close to Kains Island (once known as Entrance Island) upon which the Quatsino lighthouse is located. Be careful as you round Cape Parkins, as Parkins Rock lies nearly half a mile off, and is submerged. Once around Kains Island, the large swells normally rolling on the outside dissipate somewhat, and the route past Hunt and Matthews Islands is straightforward and clear.

If your destination is into Quatsino Sound itself, a safer course is to continue southward past Kains Island until the green can buoy on Billiard Rock is visible, then plot a course clear of South Danger Rock, and head into the sound south of the Gillam Islands. This rock-strewn group of islands in the entrance was named after Captain E. Gillam, long time master of the C.P. steamship *Princess Maquinna*, which plied the west coast for nearly 40 years. Whichever part of Quatsino Sound you choose to explore, a myriad of interesting harbours and anchorages will open up for you.

1 Quatsino Sound

Quatsino is one of the five major sounds that cut deep into Vancouver Island's west coast. Because of its remote location, and the massive resource developments throughout the sound, it is often overlooked as a cruising area by yachtsmen travelling the coast. Despite the fact that there are areas of extensive logging, a major pulp mill, a huge open-pit copper mine, and a Canadian Forces Air Base, Quatsino Sound — with over 70 miles of waterways — is large enough to offer beautiful and interesting coastal cruising.

Quatsino is an adaptation of the word Koskimo, the name of a once large and powerful tribe of Kwakiutl who occupied a village site near the south entrance to the sound. The name is thought to have derived from the *Kwiss-Kay-nohs*, who bound the heads of their babies in order to give them a high tapered forehead, considered by those who carried out the practice to give them an aristocratic appearance. Quatsino

Sound has three main arms — Holberg Inlet, Rupert Inlet, and Neroutsos Inlet, joined by the wild and beautiful Quatsino Narrows. Within these long inlets are several historic sites, as well as fjord-like reaches, and remote coves with an atmosphere of solitude which gives the impression they have been little (if ever) visited by man. If you have the inclination, or if bad weather prevents you from leaving the sound, there is no need to spend the whole time in one anchorage. Several fascinating and exciting experiences await you when you point your bow eastward, and in the next few pages we shall examine some of the beautiful faces of this "forgotten fifth sister" of Vancouver Island sounds.

Lighthouse perched atop rugged Kains Island marks the northwestern side of entrance to Quatsino Sound.

Best access to exposed shores of Grant Bay is along a rough trail from head of Browning Inlet across peninsula.

2   Forward Inlet

Once safely in the sound, a large and beautiful inlet opens up to the north, holding the promise of good shelter within. As it turns out, there are not only safe anchorages, but a beautiful and unusual settlement as well. Forward Inlet was named after the gunboat *Forward*, built 1854, with a long and illustrious career on this coast, serving a variety of functions which ranged from daring marine rescues to early law enforcement, using her big guns to back up her authority. Forward Inlet lies between Kains Point and Montgomery Point and extends for 6 miles in a northerly direction, where it shoals up and leads into a large saltwater lagoon. About midway along its length it gets very narrow, but it is deep and free of any real dangers.

3   North Harbour

About 3 miles into Forward Inlet, a small bay opens up to the west, leading into a long narrow inlet. On the west side of Matthews Island, anchorage can be found in 20-30 ft over sand and gravel. Although it is

Preceding page: View east over entrance to Quatsino Sound.

somewhat exposed to northerly winds, several fishboats use the harbour regularly, as it affords easy access to the sound. If you prefer the convenience of a sturdy mooring buoy, there are three of them just off the north side of Matthews Island. Although they are not shown on the chart for Quatsino Sound (#3617), they are mentioned in the "Sailing Directions", and are pleasantly situated within easy dinghy access to the beach on Matthews Island.

4   Browning Inlet

This inlet, along with several other features on the B.C. coast, was named for George Alexander Browning, second master of the surveying vessel *Hecate*, under Captain Richards, who surveyed this coast 1861-1862. It is a long, narrow inlet with some shoals at its entrance, and a large drying mudflat at its head (see inset map). The northwest winds find their way down the channel, but with the limited fetch, no sea really builds up. Anchor close to the head of the bay, and take a dinghy at high water to the head of the flats, where a rough trail will take you to the open beach at Grant Bay.

The trail can get very difficult when rains turn the area into a bog, but the beach is beautiful and there is a natural arch on the headland near the centre of the Bay. Beach your dinghy at the north end of the head of Browning Inlet (where the trail starts) because anywhere else means that the receding tide can put a lot of marsh between your tender and the water needed to float it.

5   Winter Harbour

Farther up Forward Inlet, about 1½ miles from Matthews Island, the channel becomes quite narrow, with shoal areas on either side. Past this point, it opens up again into a large bay which affords excellent protection from the winter south-easterlies (hence the name Winter Harbour). Its low shores are

Yachts and fishboats share dock space at Winter Harbour on Forward Inlet. The anchorage takes its name from the excellent protection it affords during "winter" south-easterlies.

Charming shoreside community of Winter Harbour (top and bottom) is a traditional victualling port for boats making west coast passages. The general store handles everything from soup to Seagrams. Other facilities include a post office, telephones and laundry. Fuel and water is available at a float below the store.

fringed with beaches and the holding ground is 33 ft - 54 ft over mud, making for a secure anchorage. However, because the harbour is somewhat open, and the settlement of Winter Harbour is so interesting and unique, most yachtsmen choose to tie up to the extensive public floats on the western shore of the harbour. The floats have over 600 ft of docking space, although they are sometimes crowded with fishing boats. A charming coastal village hugs the shore and the peaceful setting is a pleasant contrast to the jagged shoreline just over the hills to the west. A boardwalk joins the colourful houses to one another, and to the large general store which serves as the centre of "town". This store sells everything from fresh and frozen produce to hardware, fishing gear and liquor supplies, the last place to get liquor till you reach Tahsis and Zeballos nearly 90 miles away. Because provisions are so far apart on this coast it is best to stock up on essential items here. You never know when you might be held up in some harbour further down the coast where no stores are available. The village also has a post office, telephones, laundry — and showers, a rare treat on the west coast. Fuel and water are available from the float below the store. Unless you intend to explore further into the sound, Winter Harbour is the last place to stock up before Kyuquot, more than 50 miles down the coast. There is also a Regional Park (Kwaksista) in Winter Harbour with six campsites, complete with picnic tables, fire pits, toilet facilities and a boat launch. Water is available from a creek which runs across the beach and into the harbour. For a small village, there are a number of interesting characters to meet, and a short stay here will surely provide some memorable experiences.

Forward Inlet continues northeast for another 2½ miles beyond the village, but offers little for the cruiser, as shoals, piles and log booms clutter the head of the inlet. More interesting cruising lies to the east, towards Quatsino Narrows.

Just 3 miles out of Forward Inlet is Nordstrom Cove, a small bay on the north side of Quatsino Sound, which is mentioned in the *"Sailing Directions"* as being suitable for small craft. However, since the cove is small, shallow, filled with drying rocks, and open to south winds, it is not recommended as an anchorage. Fortunately, just 2 miles past the cove is a bay which is a more suitable place to anchor.

6 Koprino Harbour

The anchorage in this bay is shown by a small anchor on the chart (#3617). Bays such as this were usually called harbours because they were used in the eighteenth and nineteenth centuries by large square-riggers which came to the coast in search of wealth in furs. They were considered good harbours because they were large enough to permit maneuvering under sail, deep enough to accommodate their large draft, and easily accessible to the open ocean. Unfortunately, the same conditions which made these anchorages ideal for 200 ft ships, make them undesirable as coastal anchorages for small boats. Koprino Harbour, for example, calls for anchoring in anywhere from 48 to 84 ft of water, requiring a considerable amount of scope.

Within Koprino Harbour there are three deep, conditional anchorages: Spencer Cove, Robson Cove, and an unnamed spot behind Schloss Island. Each of these is in moderately deep water, directly adjacent to drying shoals which drop off quickly. If you manage to drop the anchor in 25 ft of water or less on one of these steep-sided shoals, you could drift onto the shoal and ground out at low tide. Conversely, you could drift off the shoal if your anchor dragged, slip into deeper water and begin drifting out to sea. Coves with sharp drop-offs are common in west coast fjords such as those found in Quatsino, Kyuquot, and Nootka Sounds; the abrupt deeps rule out a lot of otherwise beautiful coves as overnight anchorages.

However, if you don't mind anchoring in deep water, Koprino Harbour affords limited protection from both winds and swell. Spencer Cove, a Provincial Recreation Reserve, has a boat launch ramp, float, and primitive camping facilities. Robson Cove is the site of an active logging camp, and a cable crosses overhead, making this a less-than-ideal anchorage. The space behind Schloss Island gives good wind protection, if one steers clear of the 1-ft drying rock shown on the chart. There are also log booms to tie to in the harbour if you have difficulty getting an anchor to set, or simply want the convenience of boom mooring. Booms are private, so if you choose to tie to a boom you should be prepared to relocate if requested by a company operator, or if a tug arrives to move the boom.

There is no trace of Ned Frigon's fur-trading post which was located here in the 1880s. Ned was a colourful French-Canadian who came to this coast, married an Indian woman called "Long-headed Lucy", and later operated a combination store, hotel, and saloon near the village of Quatsino.

Another 2½ miles south across the sound, Koskimo Bay offers protection from most wind and waves, but is deep (72-90 ft), and offers little of interest to the cruising yachtsman. Mahatta River, located just behind the bay, is the site of a major logging camp. The wharf located there is private.

For the next 7 miles as you proceed eastward towards the other inlets of the sound, Quatsino, with its steep sides and deep water, resembles the typical fjords on the mainland shore. Winds tend to blow either up or down the inlet, depending upon the prevailing direction outside the sound. Because of the high mountains, local wind can be unpredictable, both in direction and intensity. When the Pacific High is established in summer months, you can count on the winds blowing up the inlets, increasing steadily throughout the day. If you must go against this flow, do it in the early morning before the convection wind has a chance to build up.

Recreational reserve at Spencer Cove in Koprino Harbour has launching ramp, float and primitive camping facilities – semi-protected anchorage.

Pamphlet Cove (centre and bottom) at middle of Drake Island makes a delightful overnight stop. It's protected from wind and waves from all directions and on shore provides a public recreation area with trail and open meadowland.

37

7 Pamphlet Cove

Mid-channel on the way to the narrows lies Drake Island, with a beautiful little cove on its north side (see inset map). This cove is ideal, as it offers protection from all wind and waves, and anchorage is in 12-24 ft over a mud buttom. It is a great place, with room for three or four boats to anchor (although you will rarely find that many yachts in one anchorage anywhere on the west coast). The cove has an interesting shoreline, and because 18 acres of land and 12 acres of water have been set aside as Provincial Recreation Reserve, you can go ashore and explore the meadows and shores around the cove. There is a short trail going to the south side of Drake Island, and the

The busy public dock at Bergh Cove (above) serves as the landing for Quatsino settlement a short distance to the east.

The saltwater lagoon behind Atkins Cove (below) in Neroutsos Inlet is a snug little nook protected in all conditions but only accessible at medium to high water.

flatland at the head of the cove makes an ideal site to go ashore for a picnic. From ths anchorage, you can choose to go east into Holberg and Rupert Inlets, or head south-east into Neroutsos Inlet, where Port Alice is located.

8   Bergh Cove

About 1½ miles from Pamphlet Cove is Bergh Cove, the site of the public dock and float for the Quatsino settlement. Entry to the cove is fairly straightforward if you use the expanded chart (#3687), "Plans in Quatsino Sound". You should also have this chart if you plan to go through Quatsino Narrows, and on into Coal Harbour in Holberg Inlet. There is a shoal area on the east as you enter Bergh Cove, but it is marked by a red can buoy. Anchorage is possible in the cove, but because of the intense local marine traffic to and from the public float, it is not recommended. Between Bergh Cove, and Hecate Cove 2 miles to the east lies the village of Quatsino, settled by Scandinavian pioneers in 1894. At one time the prospect of wealth in Quatsino Sound attracted many settlers; at that time the sound was being considered for the prime Pacific Coast railroad port. Extensive docks were planned, as well as the terminus for the Grand Trunk Railway. Compared with Vancouver and Victoria, Quatsino cut a full day off the trans-Pacific crossing. When Prince Rupert was later chosen as the rail terminus, the disappointed pioneers reverted to other pursuits such as mixed farming, fishing and small industry.

Today, houses in the village are scattered along the shoreline, and there is no real "town centre". Although there is a small store ½-mile east of the float, supplies are meagre, and local residents pick up their main supplies from Port Hardy via Coal Harbour.

9   Neroutsos Inlet

Directly south of Bergh Cove lies the entrance to Neroutsos Inlet. This inlet was formerly called Alice Arm, but the name was changed so as not to duplicate an inlet of that name on the mainland coast. The new name honours Captain C. D. Neroutsos, who at one time was the manager of the B.C. Coast Steamships line. Although the inlet is more widely known for the large pulp mill located at Port Alice, there are a number of interesting little coves along the way that deserve exploration, and which offer secluded shelter in a magnificent setting. It extends 18 miles southeast from Bergh Cove, and like the other inlets on this part of the coast, is high and steep on both sides, terminating in a drying mudflat.

10   Atkins Cove

On the north shore of Neroutsos Inlet, just 3 miles from Quatsino village, is a little nook, just large enough for one or two boats to anchor in. At high water, you can pass through the narrow channel and into the small lagoon behind, allowing complete protection from wind and waves. It is just a short hike across a narrow land neck to the waters of Kokwina Cove, from where you can look into Quatsino Narrows. Both Atkins Cove, and Kokwina Cove on the narrows side, have been studied as a possible marine-oriented Provincial Park, and the simple beauty of the place lends wisdom to the plan. The outer part of Atkins Cove, however, is open to southwesterly winds blowing up the inlet, and there is enough fetch to make anchoring there a bit uncomfortable. If this occurs, you can carefully make your way into the lagoon beyond the cove, or cross the inlet to the more protected anchorages on the south shore.

11   Julian Cove

This ideal little cove is protected from adverse winds and waves by a small island at its entrance, and is an ideal anchorage, with a mud bottom, an easy entry, and an attractive shoreline setting. One gets the sense here that no other people have ever set foot on this primeval green wilderness, and the haunting call

Picturesque anchorage at Julian Cove.

of the loon further enhances the feeling of this remote setting. The waters are calm, there is a small meadow, and spruce and cedar reach upwards for their place at the top of the forest greenery. There are crabs to be caught, and it's the kind of place where you feel you could stay for a long time, satisfied with watching each successive sun sinking over the timeless greens and blues of Quatsino Sound. One can empathize with the early settlers who endured many hardships trying to eke out a living in order to remain in this magnificent setting. Anchor near the meadow at the end of the cove.

12   Smith Cove

Just beyond the point forming the eastern shore of Julian Cove is another small, precious cove where good anchorage can be found. This is Smith Cove,

39

which although fairly protected, allows winds from the northwest to enter. In addition, entry to the cove is complicated by three drying rocks (keep to the southern shore) which also limit the size of the useful anchoring area. In spite of this, a yacht can find good shelter in Smith Cove, in about 18 ft of clear water, in an almost landlocked bay, adding another to the list of great small anchorages in Quatsino Sound.

Continuing down Neroutsos Inlet, there are no other coves or bays which would afford convenient anchorage for the cruising yachtsman until about 3 miles from the head. However, there are some interesting sights.

On the west side of the Inlet, about 2 miles from Smith Cove, you will see the ruins of an old wharf. The wharf once served as the supply platform for the Yreka mine, at the 1200 ft level of the surrounding range. A trio of Quatsino's early Scandinavian settlers staked claims for the Yreka mines, and in 1897 built a trail up to the mine to haul up the machinery. Although three shipments of copper ore were taken out, the mine was abandoned after two dry years when there was insufficient water in the creek to operate the compressors. The copper remains in the ground and activity in the area indicates that it may again come into production. Remnants of the old mine works can still be seen, if you can get ashore and walk around in the surrounding woods. Because of the extreme depths, anchorage is difficult, and the old wharf is not a thoroughly stable landing place. The visit would best be carried out by dinghy from a more secure location across the inlet.

13 Jeune Landing

The public wharf and float for the Port Alice settlement is about 1 mile north of the town, at Jeune Landing. There is no anchorage, but the public float has 100 ft of space. Most private boats tie up at the yacht club, a mile away at Rumble Beach. Rumble Beach is the new townsite for the hundreds of people who work at the Port Alice pulp mill. There is a modern shopping centre with a liquor store, laundromat, restaurants, and a hotel. There is also a doctor, and a small medical centre.

In order to save the long walk into town, visiting yachtsmen are invited to tie up to the visitor's space at the yacht club in Rumble Beach, provided prior arrangements are made. Since access to and from shore is normally locked, you must arrange to get the key from the wharfinger, Mr. Andy Fawcett, who can be reached by telephone at 284-3300, or 284-3331.

14 Port Alice

This pulp mill site was once the terminus of the west coast steamer run from Victoria. The 7-day round trip was maintained for over 30 years by the *Princess Maquinna* and *Princess Norah*, each with accommodation for 200 passengers, and plenty of freight. These ships were often the only link between

Rumble Beach (top) townsite for personnel working at the Port Alice mill, has full facilities including shopping centre, liquor store, restaurants and a hotel. There is also a small medical centre. The Port Alice Yacht Club (above) is usual stopping place for visiting pleasure boats.

Jeune Landing on Neroutsos Inlet, 1 mile north of Port Alice.

40

Quatsino Indian village, circa 1875.

this remote coast, and the outside world. For some, survival often depended on regular service runs by these old steamers, while for others, the beauty of the west coast could be enjoyed as a pleasure cruise from the decks of the old steamers. The ships would normally stay in Port Alice for 24 hours, loading pulp, and allowing passengers the opportunity to stretch their legs, see the sights, or go fishing in the nearby lake. In those days there was always a dance in the local hall. These days, no regular ship service is maintained along the west coast, and most freight and passengers are brought overland by roads connecting to the east coast of the Island. The pulp is now carried out by huge freighters which regularly ply the inlet.

15   Cayuse Creek

Between the mudflats of Cayuse Creek and Ketchen Island, there is a small cove used mainly by local yachtsmen. Reasonable anchorage can be found in 35 ft over mud. Although the anchorage is partially exposed to winds from the north, the large mudflat protects the bay from the chop that can build up in these long inlets. Entry requires caution, as there is a detached rock off the northwest tip of Ketchen Island, and you must locate the channel between this rock

and the drying mudflat of Cayuse Creek. Once inside, the island blocks the view of the pulp mill with its belching towers of smoke, and pleasant time can be spent in the cove away from the intrusions of industry. This anchorage is only about 2 miles from the head of Neroutsos Inlet, and makes a convenient spot to spend the night before starting the 18 mile trek back into Quatsino Sound. Neroutsos Inlet, despite the mill, offers an interesting side trip from the open waters of the west coast. Other pleasant stops are available in Rupert and Holberg Inlets, and in Quatsino Narrows itself, which we shall now explore.

16   Hecate Cove

Some 2 miles past Bergh Cove towards Quatsino Narrows is Hecate Cove, named by Captain Richards after the survey vessel of that name under his command, a paddle-wheel sloop of 860 tons. The cove is wide and offers limited shelter from all winds, and because of the limited fetch, waves do not build to any appreciable size. The holding ground is good, consisting of sand and shingles. The cove itself is ringed with houses, which detracts somewhat from the wil-

41

derness experience for which most yachtsmen make long journeys. There is no public float, but there is a boatyard and marine ways available for boats up to 28 tons.

17 Kokwina Cove

As you travel east from Hecate Cove, you can begin to feel the influence of the channelling through Quatsino Narrows. The tidal current begins to pull you towards the narrows (or push you back, if the tide is ebbing). If you want a convenient spot to wait for slack water, or just want a pretty anchorage from which to watch boats negotiating the narrows, Kokwina Cove makes an ideal spot. Although it is open to north winds, and low land surrounds it, the cove is still considered a reasonable anchorage. You must get right inside the cove before you are out of the influence of the tidal current, but once in far enough, you can anchor in about 40 ft on a mud bottom, and watch the turbulent pools at the entrance to the narrows. Across from the cove is an interesting abandoned native village. The natives must have enjoyed living in this majestic site, situated along the edge of the beautiful narrows. Eagles in good numbers circle over the tide rips, keeping a watchful eye on the restless waters, waiting for a meal to come closer to the surface. Kokwina Cove is not as pretty as it was in the days of the first settlers, as the surrounding area has been extensively logged, much of it right down to the high tide line. However, the lush growth which the Pacific coast rain forest can generate in a short time is again lending its green colours to the cove.

18 Quatsino Narrows

Through this channel, a few hundred yards wide, 2 miles long, and in places only 30 ft deep, all the tide water of Holberg and Rupert Inlets must pass. Because these inlets are both deep and long (a total of 26 miles), the large volume of water flowing through this confined space results in currents reaching 5 to 8 knots, and creates tide rips at the northern entrance. This narrow channel is plied regularly by large freighters going to the Island Copper Mine in Rupert Inlet. Ships passing through the narrows are controlled through Tofino Vessel Traffic Management Zone using 156.55 MHz (Channel 11), ensuring that two ships will not be in the channel at the same time, as it is not wide enough to permit passing.

The narrows are remarkable, and perhaps the prettiest part of Quatsino Sound. If time allows, a visit is well worth the effort. The sides are steep, and the timbers on either side make borders of uncut green to savour as the dark water rushes past the high walls of the gorge. Except for the sound of the constantly-moving water, a peaceful silence pervades the scene.

Preceding page: Tides in Quatsino Narrows often reach 5-8 knots; plan to make passage at slack water. Freighters regularly use narrows en route to copper mine in Rupert Inlet.

Then an eagle cry pierces the silence as you slip past the eyrie he is guarding. The narrows are part of the eagles' domain, and the whole area has a sense of timeless habitation. This is the Quatsino that the Kwakiutl knew, essentially unchanged, and for a moment you feel a part of that time and space . . . .

Plan to pass through the narrows at or near slack tide, especially if the wind is opposing the tide. The most difficult part of the transit is the shallow northern entrance, where tide rips and overfalls can make passage dangerous. The passage is no more difficult, however, than some in the Gulf Islands, and a yachtsman with experience negotiating those passes should encounter few problems here.

19 Varney Bay

Once through Quatsino Narrows, the waterway divides, with Holberg Inlet branching to the west and Rupert Inlet running to the east. On the south side of Rupert Inlet is the small indentation where the Marble River flows through a beautiful canyon and out

Quatsino Sound was once the domain of the powerful Kwis-Kay-Nohs who occupied a village site on the south side of the entrance.

---

into a small bay. Varney Bay is another Quatsino delight, as it is protected from most winds (if you get inside the nook formed by Kenny Point) and has a good mud bottom. The Marble River is a truly remarkable place if you can get your dinghy upstream far enough to get right into the canyon itself. Crab traps are abundant throughout the bay, and on the small island at the entrance to the bay there are weasels, deer, and a family of river otters. Only its exposure to northwesterly winds and the large drying rock in the small cove behind Kenny Point make this anchorage less than ideal. If you have a chance, go talk to Mrs. Varney, an old-timer whose house is at the head of the bay.

20 Rupert Inlet

This 4-mile-long inlet is totally dominated by the huge open pit Island Copper Mine. The mine is a major operation, employing hundreds of people in the nearby area, with large trucks and equipment operating almost continuously. The mine is literally

Coal Harbour in Holberg Inlet was once one of the few whaling stations on this coast. Earlier endeavours included a coal mine opened in 1891.

changing the face of the inlet, as the company has been permitted to dump the overburden and tailings from the mine into the inlet itself. So, while a bigger and bigger hole is dug out of the hillside, Rupert Inlet is being filled in. Unfortunately, hopes that the tailings and sediment would be contained within the inlet have proven false, and contamination from the mine has spread throughout Rupert and Holberg Inlets, and even out through the Narrows — something engineers thought would never happen. Because of this, recreational use of Rupert Inlet is limited, and it appears that this will be the case for some time to come.

21 Coal Harbour

Just 2 miles from the narrows lies the only all-weather anchorage in Holberg Inlet. Coal Harbour has served as the location for a great number of human endeavours in its checkered past. Its name arises from its first function, when a mining syndicate opened up the ground in 1881. Later it was a supply centre for Quatsino Sound colonies, and subsequently served as

an aerodrome for amphibious planes during World War II. At one time it had the dubious distinction of being one of the few whaling stations on this coast. The whaling ramps still occupy the shores of the harbour, but today they serve as a boat launch and marine ways. Logging is now the main industry in the area. Anchorage is available throughout the bay, with depths ranging from 72 ft in the centre to 18 ft nearer the shores. Stephens Creek, at the head of the harbour, pushes a mud shoal hundreds of feet out into the harbour, so keep clear of it.

The public float at Coal Harbour is connected to the shore by a long and well-kept dock. There is over 300 ft of docking space on the floats and the road to Port Hardy, just 11 miles away on Vancouver Island's east shore, lies at the head of the wharf. Because of the close proximity to the excellent supply centre at Port Hardy, there are limited supplies available for purchase in Coal Harbour. There is a restaurant, but the town's general store listed in the "Sailing Directions" is not open on a regular basis. There is a post office, and water and fuel are available at the wharf. The old landing ramp for the amphibious aircraft which operated here during the war is now used as a marine ways, capable of hauling boats up to 50 ft in length. A boatbuilder rents space in one of the old hangars, and by taking a short walk from the end of the wharf you can stand beneath the huge arched jawbones of a whale.

22. Apple Bay

Another 3 miles up Holberg Inlet past Coal Harbour there is a small bight where there is just enough shelter from the prevailing wind and waves to afford limited anchorage in 9-12 ft of water over a mud bottom. Stay clear of the east part of the bay, as the shoal extends out for a quarter-mile. This bay has been studied by the Provincial Parks Branch as a possible marine access point, complete with a boat launch, camping facilities, and picnic sites.

23 Holberg Inlet

This inlet stretches 18 miles in an east-west direction towards the small settlement of Holberg at its head. Because this inlet is a classic fjord (i.e. shallow entrance, deep water, steep shores) there are few opportunities for convenient anchorage. Because the round trip from Quatsino Narrows to the head is over 36 miles, with little refuge in between, few pleasure boats venture very far up the inlet. There is no public wharf at Holberg for visiting yachtsmen, but there is a private wharf (owned by Rayonier) to which you could tie temporarily if you wanted to visit the town. Holberg, named after the famed Danish historian and dramatist, was another of the early Scandinavian settlements on the north end of Vancouver Island. At one time a floating village anchored by pilings, today it is the main residential settlement for a large Canadian Armed Forces base. There is a post office, and an

acute-care hospital available for emergency treatment.

The head of Holberg Inlet is deep, then shoals up rapidly. Because of this, and the completely open exposure to southeast winds, anchorage is not recommended. ⚓

Coal Harbour settlement showing launching ramp in foreground and public float centre left.

LOCAL CAUTIONS
- When large ebbtides out of Quatsino Sound meet opposing westerly winds the sea around the entrance to the sound can get confused and choppy. It is sometimes best to enter or leave the sound at slack tide.
- There are many unmarked rocks in the entrance to Quatsino Sound — be sure to use Chart #3618 carefully and follow the aids to navigation.
- Currents in Quatsino Narrows can reach 5 to 8 knots; overfalls and rips can occur at the northern end.

Holberg is the main residential settlement for Canadian Armed Forces base nearby. Wharf shown is private.

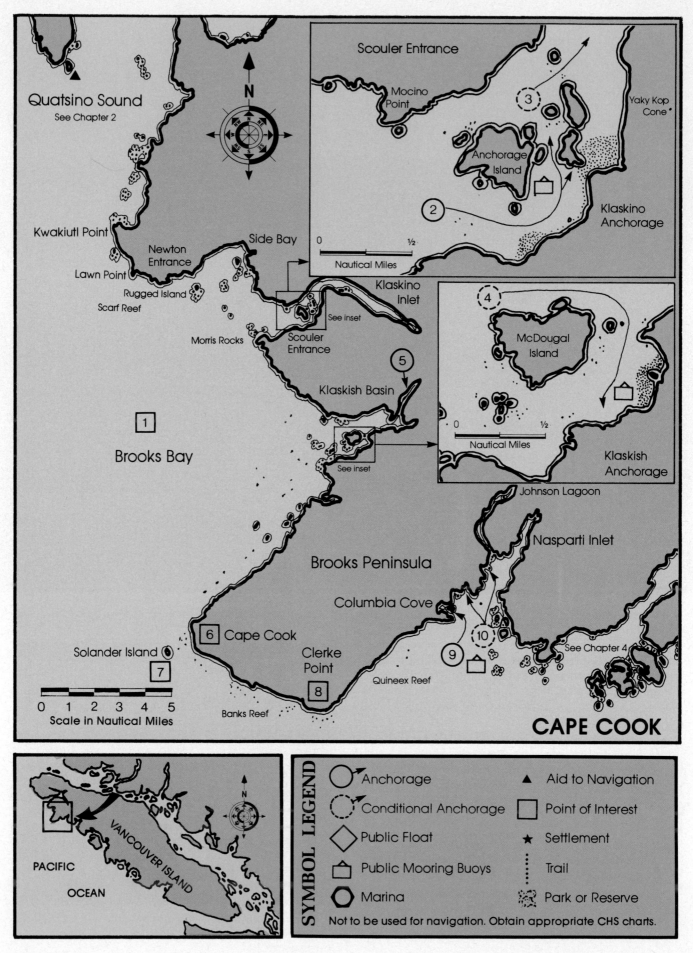

Quatsino Sound
See Chapter 2

N

Scouler Entrance

Mocino Point

③

Yaky Kop Cone

Anchorage Island

②

Klaskino Anchorage

Kwakiutl Point

Newton Entrance

Side Bay

Lawn Point

Rugged Island

Scarf Reef

Morris Rocks

Scouler Entrance

Klaskino Inlet

See inset

0   ½
Nautical Miles

④

McDougal Island

Klaskish Basin

⑤

See inset

0   ½
Nautical Miles

Klaskish Anchorage

1

Brooks Bay

Johnson Lagoon

Nasparti Inlet

Brooks Peninsula

Columbia Cove

See Chapter 4

⑩

6 Cape Cook

⑨

Solander Island

7

Clerke Point

8

Quineex Reef

Banks Reef

0 1 2 3 4 5
Scale in Nautical Miles

CAPE COOK

PACIFIC

OCEAN

VANCOUVER ISLAND

N

SYMBOL LEGEND

⊙ Anchorage

⬭ Conditional Anchorage

◇ Public Float

⌂ Public Mooring Buoys

⬡ Marina

▲ Aid to Navigation

□ Point of Interest

★ Settlement

⋮ Trail

▨ Park or Reserve

Not to be used for navigation. Obtain appropriate CHS charts.

CHAPTER THREE

Cape Cook

Brooks Bay, Klaskino Inlet, Columbia Cove

From Quatsino Sound the high mountains of the Brooks Peninsula loom ominously in the distance — beckoning and at the same time threatening. Many cruising yachtsmen launch their "assault" on Cape Cook, the western tip of Brooks Peninsula, from the base of either North Harbour or Winter Harbour. Cape Cook, the "Cape of Storms", can be a challenging obstacle, but in trying to get over this barrier quickly, yachtsmen often pass by two of the prettiest — and safest — anchorages on the entire outer coast. So, if you can take the time to "smell the flowers along the way", Brooks Bay offers an opportunity to enjoy the unique experiences of a tropic-like waterfall, and a sheltered inlet bound by a gorge-like entrance.

When leaving large sounds, such as Quatsino, it is safest to do so when the tide is slack, or close to it. A considerable amount of water ebbs out of all the sounds on the west coast, and when this water flow meets the prevailing wind and currents at the entrance to the sound, the seas become shorter and steeper than those out of the influence of the ebb. This condition is nowhere as serious as at Nahwitti Bar, but still requires an extra measure of caution and preparation, especially if the ebb tide is a large one.

Once clear of Kains Island, a southerly course will take you past Restless Bight and Kwakiutl Point, marking the extreme southern boundary of Quatsino Sound. Three miles beyond this point is another small peninsula called Lawn Point, which is unusual because of its appearance. This flat grassy field is a stark contrast to the rocky rain forest setting in which it is found. Although the grass is too high to actually serve as a "lawn", it is a remarkable geographic anomaly. An automatic wind indicator located here provides weather information which is part of the weather broadcast on VHF Channel 21 (157.050 MHz). When rounding Lawn Point on the way into Klaskino or Klaskish inlets, keep clear of Scarf Reef. Although there is a minimum of 15 ft over it, the "Sailing Directions" warn that the reef breaks in heavy weather. In summer months, kelp can be seen growing on the reef.

1 Brooks Bay

This is a large open bay on the northwest side of Brooks Peninsula between Lawn Point and Cape Cook, 12 miles south. It is cluttered with small islets, rocks, and reefs, most of which are not marked with aids to navigation. Within Brooks Bay are two major inlets and innumerable small beaches. The panorama includes peak after peak, many well over 2000 ft, which rise abruptly from the ocean floor. The bay and the peninsula were named by Captain Richards after the title which Captain Charles Duncan of the trading sloop *Princess Royal* gave to what is now known as Klaskish, an inlet in the bay. Duncan had anchored in "Port Brooks" (Klaskish Inlet) in 1788 on his way south from the Queen Charlotte Islands. There is no indication of just who Brooks was. A visit to the bay's mountainous inlets will reveal features which are unique on this wild and rugged coast.

Buoys in Klaskino Anchorage provide safe moorage for visitors to the river and waterfall on shore.

2   Klaskino Anchorage

The seaward side of Klaskino Inlet is encumbered by numerous rocks and reefs, most of them unmarked and submerged. The safest way in is through Newton Entrance on the northern side of the inlet. Keeping north of Rugged Islands will give you a clear channel into Scouler Entrance, as buoys mark the passage between the reefs (see inset map). Nearby, Side Bay has some small beaches, but is open and exposed to the large north island swells which roll into the bay. Anchorage there is not recommended.

Once clear of the rocks and reefs which are marked by the navigation buoys, you can use the large scale Chart (#3651) for Scouler Entrance (if you plan to go into Kyuquot farther down the coast, you should already have this chart). The chart indicates the clear passage into Klaskino Anchorage, as well as the entrance to Klaskino Inlet.

Carefully following the charted route around Anchorage Island will lead you to several interesting and exceptional features. This sheltered spot is pleasantly situated and surprisingly beautiful. There is a grassy midden on the western side of the anchorage, and a clear stream cuts through a gravel bar and spills into the little cove. The sun seems to shine especially bright on the green shores, accenting the golden blossoms of the buttercups. You can anchor behind An-

Preceding page: Cape Cook and the Brooks Peninsula jut out almost 6 miles from the main body of Vancouver Island. It's been called the "Cape of Storms", though Captain Cook first named it "Woody Point" in 1778.

chorage Island in 44 ft of water, or take one of the four large public mooring buoys provided for the convenience of small craft. Once secured, a trip ashore is in order.

On the southern shores of this anchorage a stream has pushed a gravel bar out into the bay. If you follow this stream into the rainforest a few hundred feet you will come across a small waterfall, tumbling from pool to pool as it makes its way down the slope. The final drop to the pool at the base of the falls is reminiscent of a view you would expect to find in a more tropical setting — like a small piece of the South Pacific here on the west coast.

3   Klaskino Inlet

A few hundred yards past Klaskino anchorage, a narrow pass leads into another beautiful west coast inlet. Scouler Entrance is narrow and rocks appear on both sides of the channel, but a beacon and spar buoy mark the safe way through. You will again need to use Chart #3651. These rocks form part of the sill that classifies Klaskino Inlet as a fjord. Its walls are steep-to and once inside, the waters are deep and milky. The southern shore is dominated by a distinctive mountain which has the intriguing name "Yaky Kop Cone". The inlet terminates in a small basin about 3 miles southeast of the entrance. Anchorage is possible at the head of the inlet in about 42 ft over mud if you keep clear of the shoals formed by the creek fans. The best anchorage in this area is still the one behind Anchorage Island.

The narrow, curving entrance to Klaskish Basin leads to a peaceful sanctuary protected from the severest weather.

4 Klaskish Anchorage

Outside of Scouler Entrance, once clear of Morris Rocks, a southeasterly course will take you further into Brooks Bay, and into another sheltered west coast refuge. Along the way a frightful number of submerged rocks require careful navigation since most are unmarked. However, nature here on the west coast often provides her own method of locating submerged hazards. Buoys are not necessary because rocks, reefs and even shoal areas are quite visible when a 10-15 ft Pacific roller breaks over them in a fury of white foam. When navigating, simply locate these "white markers" on the chart, and set a course clear of them.

Once inside the waters of Klaskish Inlet, you will find the swells somewhat abated by the obstructions in the bay. The safest route into Klaskish Anchorage is around the north side of McDougal Island (see inset map). Anchorage is possible here, but the waters are deep, and the winds whistle down the steep slopes of Brooks Peninsula at wicked velocities. Instead, secure to a public mooring buoy (there are four of them) and pass the day between brooding peaks which, in former days, marked the edge of the Kwakiutl domain. If you want even more shelter, press on another two miles into the ancient sanctuary of the Kwakiutl through a curving narrow gorge into Klaskish Basin.

Entrance to fjord-like Klaskino Inlet with Klaskino Anchorage centre right and Heater Point on the lower right.

5 Klaskish Basin

Twisting into the side of the impenetrable green of the outer coast is a confined channel with steep sides leading to a sheltered lagoon. Not even a hint of the Pacific swell reaches this inner sanctuary. Finding the entrance to the gorge is difficult until you are right onto it because the channel curves, and there is no open view into the lagoon. The channel itself is deep (minimum depth 42 ft) but relatively narrow, being only 60 ft wide in one place. The narrowness is further exaggerated by the cliffs which loom over the channel, especially on the eastern wall. At the last part of the curve, just before you enter the lagoon, someone has taken some white paint and put a single word, "welcome", on the rock face to guide you.

Inside, the basin opens up to reveal another eight public mooring buoys standing out against the backdrop of the uncut green of the Pacific Coast rainforest. Anchorage is possible in the basin as well (15-30 ft) but keep clear of the drying flat which fills half the basin at low tide. The wind can find its way into this refuge, but this only seems to accentuate the timeless serenity of this enchanted place.

51

6 Cape Cook

Foreboding presence of Brooks Peninsula is heightened under a low ceiling of grey west coast clouds.

This cape is described in the "Sailing Directions" as "a conspicuous wooded bluff" and its appearance has changed little since Captain James Cook, R.N. described this "bold promintory" in 1778 and named it "Woody Point". Captain Richards later named it Cape Cook to honour the great sailor and navigator. It juts out over 6 miles southwest from the prevailing Vancouver Island coastline, and has a reputation for bad weather. Although it pushes its rock-strewn reefs further from shore than any other point on the Island,

Beaches and lagoon on west side of Brooks Peninsula are usually only visited by adventurous kayakers. Larger craft keep clear.

there is strangely no lighthouse marking it. In fact, Brooks Peninsula — upon which the Cape is situated — also has no roads, no logging scars, no buildings or development of any type. Because of offlying dangers, you cannot get as close as you would like to view its primeval nature, but you are struck by the tremendous number of beached logs littering its shores. A tangled mass of timber has been bashed against the rock, year after year, into a complex maze of interlocked pieces. These obstacles, combined with the heavy growth and the salal growing right down to the beach, helps one understand why so many sailors — who somehow survived a shipwreck — perished trying to find their way to safety through this impenetrable mass. Experienced kayakers who negotiate the "Cape of Storms" are often rewarded for their skill and effort when this least accessible part of the coast yields its treasure of Japanese glass floats.

Winds often strike Cape Cook before any other part of the west coast. When the winds hit they produce a cloud bank around the area known as the "Cap on the Cape". According to local fishermen, when the cap appears, strong west-northwest winds will soon develop. Seas around Cape Cook often build up higher than wind conditions in the area would seem to call for. For this reason it is often advisable to turn back and wait for better conditions.

Brooks Peninsula, with its unusual upland vegetation and remote setting is being considered as a possible site for wilderness recreation and preservation by the Parks and Outdoor Recreation Branch of the Provincial Government, along with Klaskish and Klaskino anchorages. Such proposals deserve our

Storm ravaged shores of treeless Solander Island off Cape Cook is inhabited only by seabirds and sea lions.

support; opportunities to reach these untouched portions of our natural heritage will increase, while at the same time the number and size of pristine wilderness areas shrink on an almost daily basis. Seeing Cape Cook in the same state as the intrepid navigator himself saw it over 200 years ago is a moving experience that modern day adventurers can still share. It would be a credit to our wisdom if that primeval view could still be seen 200 years from now.

7 Solander Island

Lying a mile southwest of Cape Cook is a strikingly barren mass of rock which curiously resembles Cape Horn, the southernmost part of the Americas. Captain George Dixon (who was with Cook on his historic visit here in 1778) called it "Split Rock" because of its shape; the name remained until Captain Richards renamed it after the famed Swedish botanist, Dr. Daniel Charles Solander. Dr. Solander accompanied Cook on his first voyage of discovery to the South Pacific but apparently this island's namesake never visited this coast.

Solander Island is striking. Because of numerous rocks and reefs between the island and the cape, most yachtsmen take the safer route around the outside of Solander. This rock gives mute testimony to the power of the sea and the storms which can ravage this part of the coastline. No trees grow on the island. The bleak terrain is the home of thousands of seabirds, and scattered colonies of sea lions. Its steep shores rise to over 300 ft in a very short distance. Shrubs and moss cling to its precipitous leeward sides, giving a pale greenish tinge to the black rock. A small un-manned light crowns its peak, flashing defiance to the elements every ten seconds. Its meagre effort is dwarfed by the majesty of its surroundings.

So severe are the storms here that the *Princess Maquinna*, the "old faithful" of the Canadian Pacific Steamship Company, after leaving Quatsino Sound southbound was sometimes forced to turn back — something she never had to do on any other part of the west coast in the 40 years she plied these waters. The seas in this area can pile up to frightening heights during storms, so it is best to tackle the Cape in relatively settled weather, or take shelter in one of the refuges in Brooks or Checleset Bay.

Solander Island is an Ecological Reserve (#14) set aside to preserve marine wildlife, especially the

A 15 ft swell crashes against the barren cliffs of Solander Island.

tufted puffins which seem to thrive in such desolate environments. It is interesting to note that an undefined part of the outer coast of Brooks Peninsula also marked the geographical division between the Nootka whalers of Vancouver Island, and the Kwakiutl of the northern Island and mainland coast. It also marks the end of the long exposed passages on the outer coast; much of the journey south from this point is in relatively protected waterways. If you are circumnavigating the island from the port of Vancouver, you are half way home.

8 Clerke Point

Between Solander Island and Clerke Point, 5 miles to the southeast, the shore is littered with rocks, reefs and shoals; many extend over a half mile from shore and deserve good offing. Banks Reef (13 ft high) 4 miles southeast of Solander Island dries and breaks heavily, making it easy to locate even when visibility is obscured. Between Banks Reef and Clerke Point there is a relatively rock-free part of the shoal where fishboats sometimes anchor temporarily in northern winds. The local name is "Shelter Shed", but anchorage here is not recommended. Clerke Point marks the southern tip of Brooks Peninsula, and shallows extend almost a mile from the high tide line. It is best to give it a wide berth as rocks and kelp appear a considerable distance from shore. The Point was named after Commander Charles Clerke, second in command on Cook's third and final voyage, one that proved fatal to both men. Clerke took command of Cook's voyage of discovery (when the famed navigator was murdered in the Hawaiian Islands) but died only six months later of tuberculosis while exploring the waters off Alaska.

9 Columbia Cove

Once clear of the outer shores of Brooks Peninsula, you can duck into the waters of Checleset Bay and get a bit of shelter from the large swells. If you stay close

Snug anchorage in Columbia Cove (left and above) has three public buoys and intriguing shoreside possibilities for boatweary crews. Cove was named after Captain Robert Gray's American fur trader of the same name which visited here in 1791.

to the eastern shore of the peninsula, you will be able to keep clear of the majority of rocks which clutter the bay and comprise the aptly-named Barrier Islands. The exception is Quineex Reef, which stands about half a mile from shore and dries at an 8 ft tide. Because of the ever-present swell, this reef is usually visible as breakers comb its jagged back.

About 5 miles from Clerke Point a small point of land (Jacobson Point) extends out from the shore, forming the southern boundary of a beautiful anchorage, which until recently was un-named on hydrographic charts. In this cove in 1791, an American, Captain Robert Gray, master of the 220 ton fur-trading ship *Columbia Rediviva* first anchored. As John Hoskins, the ship's mate of the *Columbia* describes their arrival in the cove: Captain Gray "sent the boats ahead to tow [the ship]; at noon came to anchor with the small bower; moored ship with a hawser out astern to the trees, and another to the rocks on the larboard bow ... we are entirely landlock'd in an excellent harbour on the west side of the Sound (sic); this harbour was named Columbia's Cove". The name for this cove was subsequently lost by cartographers until revived by the combined efforts of John Frazier Henry and the Toponymy unit of the Provincial Ministry of Environment in 1983, almost 200 years later. It is known locally as Peddlar's Cove.

Columbia Cove is an excellent harbour and a beautiful place to visit. Captain Gray returned to this snug cove the following year to secure more furs for the Chinese market. Unfortunately, this time large numbers of natives approached the ship one moonlit night and had to be repelled by the force of cannon and shot, with the loss of several Indians.

According to Gray, he held fire until he feared that an attack was imminent, although there is some conjecture that the natives were not after the ship itself, but an anchor that was above high water mark. In any case, the cove was used again in subsequent years by other ships without further problems. The methods used by Gray and other sea captains in acquiring furs were, however, to have serious repercussions for other ships such as the *Boston* and the *Tonquin* which later visited the coast.

Captain Gray and his stout little ship continued to make history on this coast, and worldwide. He spent the winter of 1792 in Clayoquot Sound (near Tofino) where he built Fort Defiance and the second ship ever built on the coast (north of Mexico) which he named the *Adventure*. After leaving Vancouver Island, he sailed south, and discovered the great river in Oregon which he also named after the *Columbia*. At the end of May he returned to this coast collecting furs for another six months (see also chapters 6 and 10). When the ship returned to Boston in 1793 it had circumnavigated the globe — the first American ship to do so.

Today you can anchor in the same spot as the *Columbia*, or you can take up one of the three public mooring buoys in the cove. If you anchor, be aware that there are rocks in the cove and that the head of the cove dries completely at low tide. Enter on the southern side of the island protecting the cove; there are submerged rocks in the northern entrance.

Once secured, a very interesting shoreside venture awaits you. Check the tide book when dinghying ashore; a 1-2 ft drop or rise can put a lot of water or mud between you and your tender. There is a squatter's cabin in the cove, and a trail leads to a beautiful beach on the seaward side of Brooks Peninsula. Because humans are still a curiosity on this remote part of the coast, eagles will circle closely over you in the lagoon, keeping a watchful eye. Cougar tracks crisscross the sand surrounding the cove, and the silence of this remote place is almost magical.

The trail to the beach is fairly easy to walk on but difficult to locate. It commences from the southernmost of three small tributaries which empty into the head of the cove. It takes only about 15 minutes to reach the log-strewn grey sand beach where driftwood and debris from around the Pacific Rim have washed ashore. Having made it to the vicinity of Cape Cook (if not around it) you deserve to spend a day lounging on the beach enjoying the experience which only the west coast of the island, with its rugged peacefulness, can offer.

10 Nasparti Inlet

A few miles beyond Columbia Cove, Nasparti Inlet offers two conditional anchorages, but neither are as attractive or protected as Columbia Cove. The east shore of Brooks Peninsula is indented with small bights which could be used if the wind is steady from the northerly sector.

The first of these, only about a mile beyond Columbia Cove, is completely open to the south. The next is a mile beyond this, well inside the inlet. Although it is more protected from winds, the anchorage is somewhat deeper (60 ft) until you are close to shore. A stern line would be useful here.

Johnson Lagoon, just beyond the latter anchorage cannot be penetrated safely by large boats, and the currents through the chasm at its entrance can run quite strong. If you are in the area, safe observation of the tidal falls could prove interesting and exciting. The remainder of Nasparti Inlet offers little refuge for the cruising yachtsman, although its steep sides make it visually interesting.

Nasparti is an adaptation of the Indian name for the tribe residing there during the days of the fur trade. It appeared on Robert Haswell's early chart as "Chickleset", or "Bullfinch's Sound". Heading south and east from Nasparti Inlet, the complex array of navigational hazards in Checleset Bay will require extreme caution if you hope to leave your bottom paint where it belongs — on your boat. Your "crash" course in west coast navigation will begin in the next chapter. 🐚

LOCAL CAUTIONS
- Winds opposing the ebb tide out of Quatsino can cause steep short seas, especially at the entrance.
- High seas are common in the Cape Cook area. Use discretion when passing around this cape, and be prepared to turn back if conditions warrant.

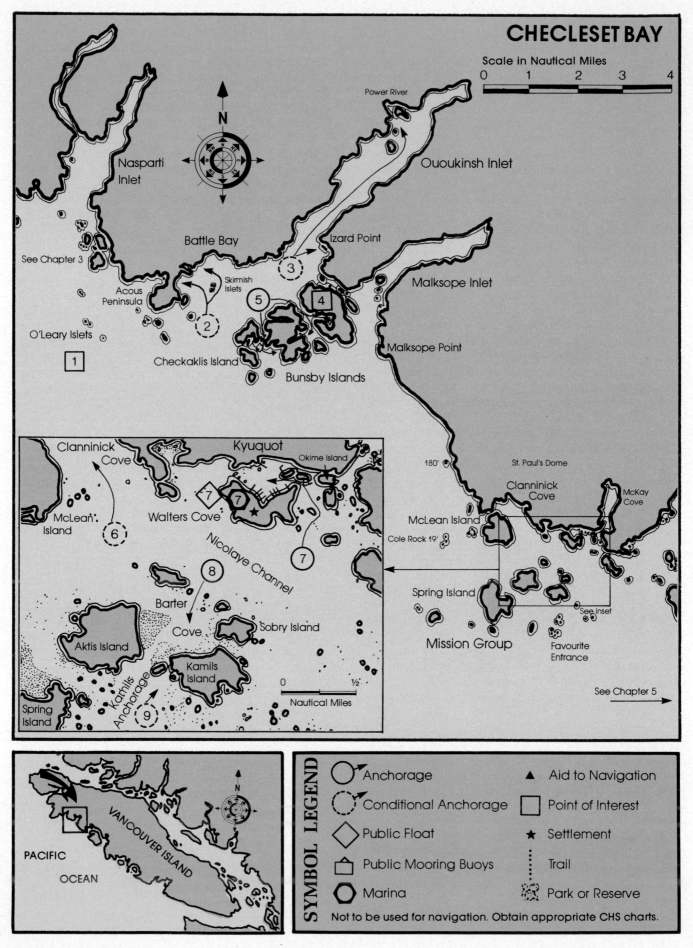

CHECLESET BAY

Scale in Nautical Miles

0   1   2   3   4

Power River

Ououkinsh Inlet

Nasparti
Inlet

Battle Bay

Izard Point

Malkscope Inlet

See Chapter 3

Acous
Peninsula

Skirmish
Islets

③

⑤   ④

Malkscope Point

O'Leary Islets

②

①

Checkaklis Island

Bunsby Islands

180'   St. Paul's Dome

Clanninick
Cove

Kyuquot

Okime Island

Clanninick
Cove

McKay
Cove

McLean Island

Cole Rock 19'

McLean
Island

◇⑦   ⑦

Walters Cove

⑥

⑦

Spring Island

See inset

Nicolaye Channel

⑧

Barter

Cove

Sobry Island

Mission Group

Favourite
Entrance

Aktis Island

Kamils
Island

See Chapter 5

Spring
Island

Kamils Anchorage

⑨

0   ½

Nautical Miles

PACIFIC

OCEAN

VANCOUVER ISLAND

N

SYMBOL LEGEND

○→ Anchorage

▲ Aid to Navigation

⬠→ Conditional Anchorage

☐ Point of Interest

◇ Public Float

★ Settlement

⌂ Public Mooring Buoys

⋮ Trail

⬡ Marina

▧ Park or Reserve

Not to be used for navigation. Obtain appropriate CHS charts.

56

CHAPTER FOUR

Checleset Bay

Bunsby Islands, Gay Passage, Barter Cove

Checleset Bay, located between Clerke Point and the Mission Group of Islands 15 miles away, is filled with rocks, reefs and islets which form part of the beautiful and treacherous Barrier Islands. From Brooks Peninsula to Walters Cove there are two safe routes: one is to go outside of all the ragged pinnacles and reefs and follow the aids to navigation into Kyuquot. The other (and more interesting) is to take the extreme inside route, navigating carefully between the reefs and islets while indulging in the thrill of the challenge, enjoying each new piece of nature as it expresses itself in the collision of rocks, sea and sky. The sights and cruising opportunities in Checleset Bay are rivalled on the West Coast only by Barkley Sound. The attractions here include sea lion colonies, totem poles, abandoned village sites, aquatic moonscapes, and a pet harbour seal named "Miss Charlie". Because of its remoteness, and complete lack of road access, the interface between man and the coastal waters is ever-present. It offers an array of cruising highlights for the experienced yachtsman, and a mesmerizing labyrinth of navigational hazards for the uninitiated. Making a safe passage through this maze is reward enough, but for those who can linger long enough to savour its delights, Checleset Bay offers much more.

Throughout this section of coastline, there are several conditional anchorages. When conditions are right, a prudent yachtsman can set his ground tackle behind almost any of the bay's hundred islands and be in relative safety within close range of many secure anchorages. In this chapter we will focus on the more significant, or particularly interesting destinations in Checleset Bay. In a place with such a bounty of cruising attractions, there will always be a special anchorage that lies waiting to be discovered.

1 O'Leary Islets

One of the appealing aspects of cruising the west coast of Vancouver Island is the variety and profusion of its wildlife. When you see a group of wild creatures thriving in its struggle against relatively hostile elements, it is a truly moving experience. When you can return to the same spot years later and again see the spectacle unfold as vividly as it had in your memory, it is beyond words. Such a place is the wild group of essentially barren rocks and reefs known as the O'Leary Islets. Sea lions rule these forsaken crags of offshore granite with the pomp and ceremony of Renaissance kings. That is, until you get close enough to hear them braying in a most uncivilized manner! The islands are not big enough to provide sheltered anchorage for a cruising yacht, and the swell can roll in quite forcibly in this area, but if you are cruising by, take a second look at the driftwood logs that appear to be on the rocks. If they bellow and smell like fish, they're probably one of the many colonies of sea lions which thrive on this part of the coast. Be careful as you navigate this area, you could get carried onto the rocks by the swell if you stray too close when your attention gets diverted.

Also, it goes without saying that you shouldn't

Surf-swept rocks are part of the O'Leary and Cuttle Islets in Checleset Bay. Sea lions are the principal residents.

coast. Hopefully any yachtsman who has made it to this remote area will have gained enough respect and appreciation for nature and man's role in it that he will allow the otter to exist in its natural habitat without further disturbance.

2   Battle Bay

By carefully skirting around the O'Leary and Cuttle islets (keeping them to the north) you will come upon one of the rock-strewn entrances to Battle Bay. The safest way into this historic place is to first locate the Skirmish Islets, and choose which side of the bay you wish to visit. The most secure anchorage is the more westerly one, and although it has several drying rocks within it — most of which are covered with kelp — it is closest to the attractions of the area. Holding ground is mud, in about 36 ft close to Acous Peninsula. Use your depth sounder to find the best spot. This anchorage makes an excellent home base from which to explore both the surrounding aquatic area

Light patches reveal dangerous rocks in the otherwise inspiring anchorage of Battle Bay, site of many ancient Checleset tribe potlatches.

disturb these creatures in an effort to get too close to them. A naturalist at Pacific Rim National Park suggests that if the seals and sea lions start sliding off the rocks and into the sea, you're already disturbing them. Try to get a photo of the beasts relaxing in the safety of their rookery, rather than diving in fright. With an increase in cruising yachtsmen over the years there is a fear that excessive disturbances may cause the "critters" to move even further away. If it is calm enough to explore the islets by dinghy, be advised that sea lions are territorial animals and are therefore protective of their domain. If an inquisitive visitor came too close, a 1000 lb bull could easily overturn a small boat, putting its occupants into the element where the irate sea mammal would have a distinct advantage.

These islets, as well as most of Checleset Bay, are protected under the Ecological Reserves Act (Reserve #109) established to protect marine wildlife such as the sea lions and more importantly, the sea otter colonies which have begun to re-establish themselves here. After being hunted to near extinction on this coast, a small group of about 70 of these creatures has found a new home in these offshore islets. If you are fortunate you may see a family of these mammals with their inquisitive eyes and glistening fur lounging in the kelp beds feeding on sea urchins. It is against the law to disturb them in any way, so give them a chance to gain a foothold here and we may see many more in the future. Sea otters have played such an important role in B.C. history, and the price paid by these gregarious creatures was their near annihilation on this

and the shoreside attractions, which are plentiful here.

Acous Peninsula is the location of an ancient Indian village which has been long reclaimed by the coastal rainforest, and because it is an Indian Reserve, you cannot remove or deface any of the structures. If you follow the shoreline of the peninsula, between the main shore and the nearly-connected island to the east, you will be able to tramp the semicircular beaches of the once powerful Checleset tribe. When you come to one that is overlooked by a large flat grassy area, you have found the former village site. (It is almost certain that Indians from this village were the ones who confronted Captain Gray in Columbia Cove in 1791.)

What a place! From the hill you have a commanding view of the complex of rocks and reefs protecting the shores from the swells and waves rolling in. In the

Preceding page: The Bunsby Islands, part of the Checleset Bay Ecological Reserve, are the site of a project to re-establish sea otters on the west coast.

days when transportation was by canoe, this area offered an unending array of channels, beaches and coves to explore. Mussels, oysters and clams abound on the rocks, and in the sand and mud. Salal grows along the shore, and a small stream of clear water bubbles away behind the village. Careful exploration of this site will reveal the remains of an ancient longhouse, toppled by time and the ravages of winter storms. Deep in the bush, a totem pole contemplates the scene through the mute wooden eyes of beaver and killerwhale figures. Another pole has yielded its features to the elements and leans over the surrounding ferns in final surrender.

If you row your dinghy to the north of Battle Bay, you will find a summer potlatch site with all the amenities needed for a good party: a long, sweeping beach, with a grassy upland behind it, and a fairly substantial river (the Battle River) pouring from the woods through meadows, across the beach and into the sea. You could spend hours watching the river push sand into the Bay, only to have the waves push it back. The first citizens of this land certainly had a good setting to stage their large potlatches.

Getting in and out of Battle Bay in a cruising boat requires careful piloting but it is not as difficult as it first appears on the chart. The islets choking the bay, though small, are quite high (some over 80 ft) and easy to identify. Use the Skirmish Islets as a reference, and take bearings from these and other significant landmarks such as Byers Cone in order to get in and out safely. The swell in this area is more dissipated, and consequently does not always break on the shoals, marking them as it does on the outer reefs.

Battle Bay is another of our beautiful west coast destinations that is being considered as a possible location for a Provincial Recreation Reserve. A protected status for this remarkable area would certainly be a good move.

Sea lions blare their territorial warnings from jagged rock haulouts in the O'Leary Islets.

3   Ououkinsh Inlet

It is almost as difficult to find a good anchorage here, as it is to pronounce "Ououkinsh". (Try the local way, oo-kinish). This 5-mile-long inlet is deep, with steep sides which stand out because the timber (as it is in most of this region) is uncut. There are two conditional anchorages here, one just south of Izard Point at the entrance to the inlet, and another at the mouth of Power River, another 4 miles up the inlet where the occasional steelhead has been caught. Both of these anchorages have satisfactory holding ground and are relatively protected, but since there are more scenic and better sheltered anchorages nearby, these spots are seldom used. Head up to the Power River anchorage if you want a remote setting, out of reach of the swells which predominate on the outer coast.

Looking west along Ououkinsh Inlet, a fjord as difficult to pronounce as for anchoring.

4 Gay Passage

This channel, between the two main Bunsby Islands is the most convenient "inside" route from Brooks Peninsula to Kyuquot. Piloting this passage, however, requires the utmost in caution; the way is blocked by partially and totally submerged rocks. It is a good place to clearly see the difference between a 1 ft high drying rock, and a rock that dries at a 1 ft tide. In case you don't know, a number in brackets [i.e. (1)] beside a rock coloured yellow, has a *minimum* height of 1 ft above high tide. A number in brackets with a line under it [i.e. (1)] indicates that this rock will dry when the tide drops to the height indicated by the number in brackets. In this example, the rock would dry when the tide dropped to 1 ft. If you don't know the difference between these two chart symbols, you will have a difficult time discerning the safe passage through this channel, and throughout the Barrier Islands.

Chartmakers sometimes inadvertently add to the confusion by printing the height of pinnacle rocks which are always above high water in smaller numerals, eg (1); while drying rocks, (although lower) are printed in large numerals, eg (1). If you understand these symbols you will have an easier time negotiating passages which have close quarters, and you may be able to refine your definition of what constitutes a "navigable channel".

Gay Passage in the Bunsby Islands is the most expedient route through this area, though innumerable rocks test even the most seasoned skippers. Excellent anchorages, however, are left centre and right centre of photo.

Mist hangs in the trees behind the Battle River where many potlatches were held.

62

Although Chart #3683 shows rocks throughout the channel, closer observance shows that a safe passage is possible by hugging first the north shore, then the south, as caution dictates. With all its hazards, it is a safer route than going around the outside, where literally hundreds of rocks await your error or lapse in attention. Besides, inside Gay Passage are some of this area's best all-weather anchorages.

5 Bunsby Islands

These beautiful islands just 2 miles from Battle Bay take their name from a character in the Charles Dickens novel "Dombey and Son". Cuttle Islets, Clara Islets, Gay Passage and Cautious Point are all geographical features in this area which receive their names from the same source. Captain Richards in the survey vessel *Hecate* is responsible for naming these features in 1862.

A visit to the Bunsbys (sounds like going to visit friends of the family, doesn't it?) is likely to provide some memorable experiences. The islands are the center of the sea otter relocation project, and a few are sometimes seen in this area. The islands themselves are "other worldly" and different from most west coast islands. They are long and low, windswept and reefstrewn. Two of the good anchorages among them are on either side of Gay Passage, while a third lies between the southern-most Bunsby Island, and Checkaklis Island. The best (and most frequently used) anchorage is the one on the eastern Bunsby Island, tucked inside the small cove in 36 ft over mud bottom. There is a slight influence of the offshore swells here, but not enough to adversely affect the anchorage.

The second anchorage, on the west side of the passage is a bit more open to southeast winds, but is secure and pleasantly situated. The other anchorage requires careful entry from the north, but once inside offers shelter from winds and waves, protected by the reef-ridden Checkaklis Island. Anchoring here offers the advantage of being close to the exposed outer shores of these islands where the surf hurls itself on the shoals in its endless battle with the rocks. Storm petrels nest on these islands by the thousands, and a towering solitary rock rules over the landscape. The Bunsby Islands offer a unique west coast experience which is truly wild and exciting.

If you would like to experience this area, but do not have a boat to get there, a course through Khoyotan ("Raven of the Sea") Marine Laboratory offers mini expeditions to the west coast at a reasonable cost. These tours, run by marine biologist Dr. W.C. Austin operate marine educational programs on the west coast as a means of expanding knowledge and experience regarding our coastal environment. Trips last 3-4 days, and are "involvement oriented" with participants gaining hands-on experience by actually playing a role in the logistics of the expeditions. For further information, contact Khoyotan Marine Laboratory,

R.R.#1 Cowichan Bay, B.C. V0R 1N0. (604-748-5020) or in Vancouver call the UBC Centre for Continuing Education (604-222-2181).

A small cove is formed by the north Bunsby Island and the Vancouver Island mainland. It borders a small Indian Reserve with the auspicious name of "Hollywood". Under calm conditions it would be possible to anchor close to shore and visit the former winter trapping station and perhaps find one of the few small totems rumoured to be there amongst the overgrown fruit trees. Malksope Inlet opens up north of here but its steep shores and deep waters offer no refuge for the yachtsman. Between Malksope Inlet and Kyuquot a further navigational challenge awaits you. The easiest way to get through the hazards is to head over to the steep shores of Vancouver Island near Malksope

Deep waters of Clanninick Cove near Kyuquot provide good temporary anchorage though skippers should be wary of two rocks near the entrance.

Point, and hug the shore (keeping inside of all the dangers) running a course towards St. Paul's Dome, which is very conspicuous. When near the small wooded island marked '180', a careful course right up to Cole Rock (19 ft high) will put you within sight of the beacons which will guide you into Nicolaye Channel, and ultimately into Kyuquot.

6 Clanninick Cove

Once safely inside the channel between McLean Island and Spring Island you will have to follow the buoys carefully in order to get safely into Walters Cove (Kyuquot). If visibility is poor, it may be best to wait for better conditions. You can wait out fog or darkness while anchored in Clanninick Cove. The anchorage is deep (54 ft) until you get right into the northwest corner, but the bay is relatively free of dangers. There are two rocks to watch for — one submerged, and one 2 ft above high water, but these are marked clearly on the chart, and there is a clear channel between them. The anchorage is exposed to the southeast wind and waves, making it less than ideal if those conditions prevail, but it is a good anchorage to keep in reserve if bad weather catches you in the Kyuquot area.

7 Walters Cove

Entry to this cove is hazardous without the large-scale chart (#3651) and careful observance of navigational aids. The channel takes a couple of 'S' turns, leading to a very narrow (120 ft wide) channel just before the cove opens up (see inset map). Fortunately all dangers are marked, and the prudent mariner should have little problem negotiating the entrance. (Note that most buoys on the west coast of Vancouver Island have been changed over to the new system of colours and shapes so be familiar with these before entering.) After transiting the channel, your eyes are treated to a view of the most interesting and unique village on the coast. Kyuquot (pronounced Ky-you-kit) with its totally protected harbour, pleasant boardwalks, colourful houses, and well-stocked general store, makes an interesting stop in a cruising yachtsman's itinerary. Because there is no road access to this village, the interaction between the people and the sea is paramount. Kyuquot is a quintessential fishing village, and small outboards buzz across the cove at all hours transporting everything from lumber and supplies to school children. A beautifully-alive Indian village decorates the north shores of the cove, and a simple but efficient group of boat-oriented services occupies the south shore at Kyuquot Marina. A general marine hardware store is here as well. There is a public wharf extending from Walters Island, with two floats attached, giving a total of 340 ft of docking space. Fuel and water can be obtained from the float just south of the public dock, and a pleasant bush-lined boardwalk connects the rustic village houses. A marina with limited repair facilities is also located here.

In Kyuquot time ticks to the throbbing beat of the marine diesel, and the pace is easy and slow. A general store at the base of the public float is the center of "town", and goods of all sorts are sold at reasonable prices. The supply boat brings fresh produce once a week (Sunday), and mail from the post office leaves by float plane a few times per week, depending on the weather. Since Kyuquot is the only settlement between Winter Harbour and Zeballos, it is an important

View west over hazardous entrance to Walters Cove and Kyuquot village. Most hazards are well marked.

The enchanting fishing community of Kyuquot is the sole provisioning and repair port between Winter Harbour and Zeballos, though one item not available is liquor; Kyuquot is a "dry" village.

supply port for both yachtsmen and the remote logging and fishing camps. One important item which is unavailable here has far-reaching effects on the entire community — Kyuquot is a "dry" village. No alcoholic beverages of any sort are sold here. Although this may cause some dismay to the thirsty traveller, a quick look around the tidy little village with its happy mix of native people and local fishermen makes this omission in the grocery list much more tolerable. The picturesque setting seems to spawn the biggest smiles on the west coast.

The villagers also have a world-famous mascot — "Miss Charlie", a small harbour seal that was befriended by a local when she was an orphaned pup that has taken residence in Walters Cove. This friendly seal has grown up thinking she is the village's guardian watchdog, and swims freely throughout the harbour, looking for fishy handouts. Locals who clean their salmon off the end of their floats have more than once been caught in a tug-of-war with this precocious pup who simply assumes it's being offered to her. Once a killer whale came right into the cove, causing Miss Charlie to shoot out of the water and all the way up the float and ramp onto the front lawn of her adopted parents, yelping the whole way like a frightened puppy. Miss Charlie is getting older now, and she's less frisky than she once was, but nonetheless is still available for handouts, if you're in the neighbourhood and have a spare salmon or two. She's just one of the many interesting characters you might meet in this coastal Eden.

Walk south along the boardwalk and you will find a beautiful tree-lined path leading to an exposed gravel beach overlooking the rugged islands south of Walters Island. For another interesting side-trip, dinghy

into the sheltered waters of McKay Cove a mile away; but take the mosquito repellant; the calm waters of this lagoon are paradise to this insect as well.

Along with a fish-buying barge, the cove has a new barge complete with showers, laundry facilities and accommodations for yachtsmen in the summer months. A restaurant has just opened which provides good seafood dishes in a remote island setting. If you wish you can fly into Kyuquot on the resort's floatplane, where you can stay in a very natural and isolated section of the coastline. For further information, contact Kyuquot Marina and Fishing Resort (604-332-5219).

Just outside the cove on Okime Island is a small hospital building which flies the Red Cross flag. Like most of Kyuquot, it is reached by boat, and sports its own small float. Clearing out of Walters Cove is sim-

The now peaceful waters of Barter Cove were the site of a gruesome nineteenth century battle between Kyuquot and Clayoquot tribes.

ply a matter of re-tracing the route in, again following the course marked by the spar buoys and beacons until you enter the clearer waters of Nicolaye Channel. From here you can proceed eastward towards Kyuquot Sound, or travel a short distance into history and visit the site of the last major Indian battle fought on the west coast, across the channel in the Mission Group.

8   Barter Cove

Here, in one of the most peaceful settings one could imagine, one of the last (and one of the most devastating) Indian battles on the west coast was fought. The arch-enemies of the Kyuquots were the Clayoquots, fellow Nootka who occupied the sound that now bears their name near present-day Tofino. After years of raids, plundered villages, enslavement of captives and clan rivalry, aggression reached its peak in 1855. In order to settle the question of tribe superiority, a surprise attack was planned by the Clayoquots — a plan that was to have dire consequences for the powerful Kyuquots, who were then the most populous tribe on the coast.

Aktis Island in the Mission Group is site of a now nearly abandoned Indian village. Barter Cove is in foreground.

Right: Overview of the Mission Group. Spring Island in foreground, Kyuquot village centre left.

Favourite Entrance is the preferred route into Kamils Anchorage in the Mission Group, a delightful area for exploration by dinghy.

The Clayoquots sent messengers to the Hesquiat, Mo-achat, Ehatisaht and Checleset, asking chiefs of those tribes to be prepared to join forces and with their combined might to crush forever the power of the Kyuquots. The tribes joined one another as they paddled up the coast, forming an allied armada of warriors. Somehow the plan was kept secret. On the night of the attack the large group assembled on a small island (probably Sobry Island) adjacent to the two main islands (Kamils and Aktis) where the main Kyuquot villages stood. By doing this, the presence of the large armada of canoes went undetected by the Kyuquots. The raid had been timed for midnight when, besides having the element of darkness, the tide was very low, allowing the attackers to quietly cross the sandbar which connected the assembly island to the islands where the sleeping villages were situated. The surprise was complete, and before the Kyuquots knew what was happening, many had already met their death under the knives of the combined forces of their enemies. Canoes were destroyed to prevent any counter-attack, and the villages put to the torch, leaving an utterly gruesome scene for the survivors. The attacking warriors took various prizes (including the scalps of the hapless victims) and vanished into the night with scarcely a man lost. The Kyuquots, on the other hand, had suffered the loss of many warriors — estimated between 60 and 70. The Kyuquots were unable to launch a reprisal and never again reached the heights of power they once held.

This former battlefield is a mile south of Walters Cove, and its peaceful appearance today is in stark contrast to its gruesome history. In order to visit the site, first get permission from the natives in Kyuquot, then cross Nicolaye Channel and carefully make your way into Barter Cove — between Sobry and Ahmacinnit Islands — taking care to avoid the reefs off Sobry Island. Anchor in 18 ft over a sand bottom near Kamils Island (now called Cemetery Island locally) taking care to avoid the sand shoals throughout the cove. This anchorage is totally protected from the seas which break on the outside of the island group. Although the wind can get into the cove, the holding ground is good, and the anchorage a secure one. The remains of the battlefield are on Kamils Island, while a nearby abandoned village site occupies the west shore of Aktis Island, facing the island of the graves. (The main native settlement is now located north of Walters Cove.)

9 Kamils Anchorage

If you approach Kyuquot from seaward, and if the weather conditions and your navigation are good, you can take Favourite Entrance and make your way into Kamils Anchorage. This rugged spot is situated in an archipelago literally peppered with rocks and reefs which, though a danger, are its main attraction. The anchorage itself is protected from all except southwest winds and provides secure holding ground in 35 ft. It is mainly used by native fishermen, but the wildness of the setting makes a spectacular backdrop to any boat. Although it can get a bit "rolly" if the swells are from the south, it makes an excellent spot from which to base a dinghy exploration. ♚

LOCAL CAUTIONS
- Throughout Checleset Bay a number of charted and uncharted rocks require extra-careful navigation. Fog can make this area hazardous — always have a nearby alternate anchorage when making passages in this area.
- Entry to Kyuquot Harbour, behind Walter's Island requires careful navigation around the buoys. Learn how to identify the markers and how to follow them correctly.

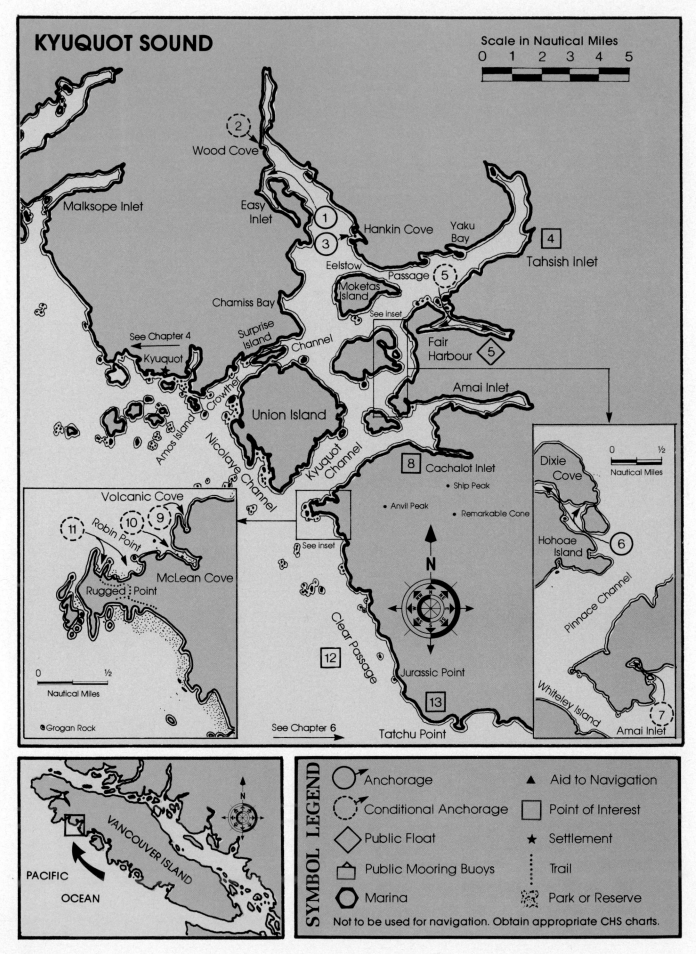

KYUQUOT SOUND

Scale in Nautical Miles
0 1 2 3 4 5

Wood Cove ②

Malksope Inlet

Easy Inlet

① Hankin Cove Yaku Bay ④ Tahsish Inlet

③ Eelstow Passage ⑤

Chamiss Bay Moketas Island

Surprise Island

See Chapter 4 ←

Kyuquot

Channel

Fair Harbour ⬠ 5

Amai Inlet

Crowther

Amos Island

Nicolaye Channel

Union Island

Kyuquot Channel

⑧ Cachalot Inlet

• Ship Peak

• Anvil Peak

• Remarkable Cone

N

0 ½ Nautical Miles

Dixie Cove

Hohoae Island ⑥

Pinnace Channel

Volcanic Cove

⑪ ⑩ ⑨
Robin Point

McLean Cove

Rugged Point

Clear Passage

⑫

Jurassic Point

⑬

Whiteley Island

Amai Inlet ⑦

0 ½ Nautical Miles

● Grogan Rock

See Chapter 6 →

Tatchu Point

PACIFIC OCEAN

VANCOUVER ISLAND

N

SYMBOL LEGEND

- ◯ Anchorage
- ◌ Conditional Anchorage
- ◇ Public Float
- ⬒ Public Mooring Buoys
- ⬡ Marina
- ▲ Aid to Navigation
- ☐ Point of Interest
- ★ Settlement
- ⋯ Trail
- ▦ Park or Reserve

Not to be used for navigation. Obtain appropriate CHS charts.

CHAPTER FIVE

Kyuquot Sound

Tahsish Inlet, Dixie Cove, Clear Passage

Kyuquot Sound, the second of the five great sounds that carve into the outer coast of Vancouver Island, is surrounded by mountains rising to 3000 ft. Entry into the Sound is made through either Crowther or Kyuquot Channels, these being separated by the rocky shores of Union Island. Kyuquot gets its name from the Indian tribe residing at the head of the sound, near the 'Ky-u-kwc' river which flowed into the inlet. Hence the natives were the 'Ky-u-kwe-ahts' ('aht' meaning "people of the...").

When entering the sound from Walter's Cove via the northern channel (Crowther) you must choose your entry carefully; a maze of rocks and reefs marks the entrance. The clearest channel in, though narrow, is the one between Amos Island and the 26 ft rock to the south of the island. This route avoids the submerged and partly submerged rocks in the wider channel further south, but the water flows through at a rate which can impede or assist your progress into the sound. If the tide is a large one, be prepared for the effects while transiting this channel.

Once clear of this restriction and back into the open water of the sound, the scars of recent logging dominate the immediate view. Kyuquot Sound is one area where the practice of hand-logging is still carried out, and this method — combined with the usual clear-cut procedure of the larger companies — has had quite an impact on the otherwise beautiful landscape. Hand-logging involves a handful of woodsmen who — operating usually with one boat and a couple of chain saws — cut timber close to shore, then gather the

fallen timber into small booms right on the spot. Since it is only practical to hand-log the steep shoreline, the effect as you pass these islands — denuded right down to the high tideline — is quite sobering. Fortunately the other attractions of the sound are enough to overcome the visual deterioration which has recently overcome this area.

Proceeding north along the western shores of the Sound, Chamiss Bay appears on the port side. This bay once housed a pilchard reduction plant and served as the main supply dock for the village of Kyuquot in the days when the *Princess Maquinna* still plied the coast. Today it is the site of a large and active logging camp. Before the advent of modern logging trucks, timber was hauled out of the bush by rail. Apparently tracks are still visible at British Creek just south of Chamiss Bay. The local Indians gather "winter berries" (blackberries) and make a dish they call chamiss which probably accounts for the name. Northwards another 2 miles from here is the entrance to the long, steep-sided Kashutl Inlet, which has two very sheltered anchorages.

1 Easy Inlet

This 2-mile-long inlet, curving between the steep green bluffs, offers everything you might want in an anchorage: shelter from all winds and waves, good holding ground, and a nearby lake. Unfortunately, timber in this area is more important than tourists so the shoreside has been completely logged off, and trucks rumble along dusty roads, unloading down

Logged-off hillsides like the one in background at Easy Inlet are all too common in Kyuquot Sound.

skids directly into the clear waters. The contrast is even greater because the peninsula on one side of the inlet is still emblazoned with proud green timber while the 180° view is one of utter devastation. Boomsticks going from one shore to the other often block access to the inner sanctum at the head of the inlet. With luck the logging will soon be completed and the tremendous regenerative powers of the Pacific coast rainforest can again come into action, weaving its green cloak over this barren land and making Easy Inlet an easy place to stay.

2 Wood Cove

A mile north of Easy Inlet, where Kashutl Inlet begins to narrow, there is a small nook just right for one boat. The anchorage in Wood Cove is subject to northerly winds, but the limited fetch should prevent any major problems with seas. This snug anchorage, notched into the side of Vancouver Island is a perfect setting though is sadly spoiled once again by the swath of the woodsman's chainsaw. It appears however that this little Cove has at last been left to nature and will begin her climb back to forest status amid a profusion of salmonberry and foxglove. In time it will again be a beautiful place to drop anchor, offering complete solitude for the yachtsman visiting this remote cove.

3 Hankin Cove.

Four miles southeast of Wood Cove, on the eastern side of Kashutl Inlet is a cove listed in the "Sailing Directions" as offering shelter to small craft in depths of 42 to 54 ft. On the chart this spot looks ideal. It is: it has a straightforward entry, is protected from all winds and waves, with two small streams flowing into the head of the cove. Hankin Cove is exceptionally beautiful, with a backshore that rises over 2000 ft, and a rugged rocky shoreline. A small temporary logging camp has been set up on the peninsula forming the northern shores of the cove. When the marketable

Opposite: Kyuquot Sound, one of five sounds that cut deep into Vancouver Island is also one of the last strongholds for B.C.'s hand-loggers.

timber from these areas has been removed, and left to recover, Kashutl Inlet and its special enclaves will be a haven for yachtsmen seeking the beauty and solitude found only on the wild west coast. Hankin Cove (locally known as God's Pocket) was named for Lieutenant Philip James Hankin, R.N. (Royal Navy) whose story appears below.

4   Tahsish Inlet

The north shore of Kyuquot Sound takes a sweeping turn through Eelstow Passage (where a dangerous 15 ft drying rock lies mid-channel) and leads to another long, steep-sided inlet terminating in a drying flat. Tahsish Inlet is not to be confused with Tahsis Inlet, farther down the coast, although their names are derived from the same source. The word comes from the native "tashee" meaning trail or passage, and refers to the fact that trails led from these long inlets overland to the east coast of Vancouver Island. Hence, trails were constructed to connect the waterways wherever an inlet cut deep into the shoreline (such as Tahsish and Tahsis inlets) and land communication established. It was from Tahsish Inlet that one of the first major surveys of Vancouver Island by land was undertaken.

In June, 1862 Lieutenant Hankin (Hankin Cove) and Surgeon-Lieutenant Charles Wood of the survey ship *HMS Hecate,* on instructions from Captain Richards, set off to gather information regarding the interior of Vancouver Island about which little was known. They were to rendezvous with *HMS Hecate* at Fort Rupert (Port Hardy) on the other side of the Island on the fifteenth of the month.

In order to carry out such a feat it was necessary to enlist the services of native guides familiar with the area, and take enough equipment to make the arduous journey and record the findings as part of the coast survey. The trio set out from Kyuquot village, where the young but powerful chief Clan-ninick (Clanninick Cove) supplied them with all the goods needed for the trip as well as seven of his best guides. For their services in conducting such an arduous journey each received a small sum of money, three blankets and a shirt.

Six hours paddling from Kyuquot brought the expedition to the mouth of the Tahsish River where they spent the night. After paddling as far as they could up the river (about 4 miles) they began the trek following animal trails, often having to wade waist-deep through streams in the pouring rain. When the rain continued, passage became first difficult, and then impossible. The troupe returned to Kyuquot to reorganize.

The second attempt, less lavishly appointed (Dr. Wood's collecting and sampling equipment being left behind) set out the next day with different guides who knew an easier way (and thus were offered an additional blanket) via a chain of lakes, terminating at the Nimpkish River. The journey put all members through extreme hardship, and after running out of

Public dock at Fair Harbour is regularly used by kayakers, yachtsmen and coastal residents coming to the west coast from other points on Vancouver Island and beyond.

food (game being scarce), Hankin named one stream the Famine River. When the group finally reached the Nimpkish village they hired canoes to take them to Fort Rupert where they most thankfully made their rendezvous with Captain Richards in the *Hecate*. Today, paved roads make a crossing of the Island a pleasant journey through what is called "scenic wilderness", and so much is taken for granted. A trek such as Lt. Hankin's across the Island would be considered a daring adventure, even today.

There are no convenient anchorages in Tahsish Inlet (Yaku Bay being deep and exposed to easterlies) but it is nonetheless endowed with scenic beauty, and the river has an exceptional salmon run. This area too may be logged, although the Kyuquot-Tahsish Committee is trying to save this fine watershed from being cut.

5   Fair Harbour

There is an opening into the Vancouver Island shoreline on the east side of Kyuquot Sound which leads to a public float and wharf. From here a road leads to other settlements, connecting the sound to the major settlements on the eastern side of the island. Entry to Fair Harbour is made between Karouk Island and the Markale Peninsula. Beacons clearly mark the entrance which is relatively free of hazards.

Within Fair Harbour two conditional anchorages — both of them deep (minimum 54 ft) — are open to easterlies. Most yachts calling here use the area mainly as a supply access point, using the broken-down public wharf and floats to load and unload cargo and passengers. Many canoe and kayak expeditions (including the Khyotan Marine Laboratories expeditions) are launched from this point, allowing the paddlers and students to begin their trip into Kyuquot Sound via its protected inner waters. There are no stores, marine supplies or fuel here. Water in small quantities may be obtained from the private mobile home here by asking the permission of the occupants. The area at the head of Fair Harbour is simply a parking lot for residents who live in roadless settlements such as Kyuquot, 15 miles away. Residents use their vehicles to bring supplies from Campbell River via logging roads through Zeballos.

Fair Harbour is a B.C. Forest Service recreation site which is being considered as a possible provincial

Though only within a few miles of the open Pacific, swells never find their way into the placid confines of Dixie Cove.

recreation area. With any luck this status will come about and facilities will be upgraded. The area receives a considerable amount of use, considering the dilapidated condition of the wharf and floats. Fortunately, yachtsmen seeking better moorage can proceed southwest 2 miles to an ideal land-locked anchorage that offers a view of a range of mountain peaks that reach into the clear blue of the west coast sky to heights of over 3000 ft.

6   Dixie Cove

This completely protected cove on Hohoae Island is perfect for one or two yachts; the waters are not only clear and calm, but relatively warm. It's about 5 miles to the open Pacific from here, but no trace of the swell is felt in the sanctum of the two anchorages. A narrow channel leads between Copp and Hohoae Island to the first of these, which in itself is nearly perfect. If you take the narrow channel at the westerly end of this anchorage, an even more isolated cove opens up. Both anchorages have good holding ground (mud) but the inner one, besides being more sheltered, is shallower (30 ft). The narrow channel has a minimum depth of 24 ft at low tide, so don't let the narrowness of the entry keep you out.

7   Amai Inlet

Two miles south of Dixie Cove, via Pinnace Channel two inlets open up on the eastern shore. You might miss them as your gaze is distracted by the multitude of peaks towering above the sound, with

Remarkable Cone (3100 ft) and Ship Peak (3265 ft) and Anvil Peak (3495 ft) grabbing much of the view. Amai Inlet, once known as Deep Inlet, is long and deep, with little to offer the cruising yachtsman except magnificent scenery. If this is enough to attract you, there is a small, unnamed cove just inside the entrance to the inlet on the west side where limited anchorage can be found. The cove is open to easterlies (which can blow quite fiercely in this area of the coast due to the funnelling effect of the mountain ranges) and has a narrow entrance, but if the prevailing summer westerlies are well established, this cove could provide a solitary haven. A gold mine was located in this inlet in the 1930s but no significant amount of ore was removed from here.

8   Cachalot Inlet

As the name of this inlet implies, this site is endowed with a bounty of marine resources. The "Sailing Directions" indicate that there are "ruins of a former cannery and wharf". Major George Nicholson in his historical overview of the west coast "Vancouver Island's West Coast" indicates that, in fact, for several years Cachalot served as a whaling station. Between 1908 and 1926 the station employed up to 80 people. Today the whale oil and ambergris are no longer needed and whale numbers are on the rise. The ruins are no longer visible, and the inlet does not make a good anchorage due to the depths and the fact that southeast squalls rip through here. These winds funnel down the valleys between the peaks, and both Cachalot and Amai Inlets are considered unsafe as anchorages in strong southeast winds, though they appear protected on the chart.

9   Volcanic Cove

About 3½ miles southwest of Cachalot Inlet, via Kyuquot Channel there is a small indentation in the Vancouver Island shore which is ideal for one boat seeking shelter from the prevailing summer westerlies in 27 ft over a gravel bottom. The cove provides protection from all winds except northerlies, but is so small that a stern line would be advisable to prevent swinging into the rocky shores. The number of volcanic cones in this locality (over 50 of them) suggest that this was once an extremely active site.

10   McLean Cove

This small bay immediately adjacent to Volcanic Cove is larger, but is less protected from westerlies, and the omnipresent west coast swell penetrates far enough into Kyuquot Sound to affect this anchorage. If the prevailing conditions were southeast or southwest, both McLean Cove and Volcanic Cove would afford good protection.

11   Rugged Point

Between Rugged Point and Robin Point, ¼-mile to the east, is a series of four beaches scalloped out of the broken shoreline. Rugged Point is aptly labelled, and because the bay behind it is unnamed, the anchorage has become known as "the beach behind Rugged Point" (see inset map).

This area is very popular with yachtsmen for many reasons, among them the magnificent "inside" beaches behind Rugged Point and the wild and beautiful beaches on the exposed *outer* shores. This anchorage is completely open to the north, but provides good protection from all other quarters. The holding ground is pure sand in 21 ft of water, but the anchorage has one small drawback — the incessant rolling swell — which though dissipated, can reach around the point just enough to remind you that you're still on the west coast.

On shore there is a small trapper's cabin which is used, repaired and maintained by the transient visitors who stay there. These visitors include yachtsmen, canoeists, kayakers and local loggers and fishermen. The trail leading to the outer beach winds through a stand of Douglas firs, which are as tall and straight as any in the province.

On the exposed outer coast the beaches curve inward between rocky headlands. Mussels and gooseneck barnacles cling to the rocks in a display of sapphire defiance. The back shore of the beaches (the largest being over ½-mile long) is littered with driftwood which occasionally yields a glass ball to the

A mottled west coast sky is a perfect backdrop for a yacht anchored off the beach behind Rugged Point.

patient beachcomber. A mile and a half southeast, Kapoose Creek cuts across the beach and empties into the sea. This is a good spot to go for a swim and a cool freshwater rinse.

12   Clear Passage

Heading south out of Kyuquot Sound there are two routes. One is to head out to sea southwest for 2½ miles past Rugged Point, where a buoy marks the outer extremity of the shoals and reefs of the lower portion of the Barrier Islands. From here it is a straightforward southeast course towards Esperanza Inlet. The other route involves more navigation, but takes you past some curious and interesting sights.

Clear Passage (so called because in such a maze of rocks and reefs there is a safe fairway), offers some striking views and some interesting geological features. Although there are many rocks and reefs throughout the passage, most are well above the high tide line, quite visible and easy to distinguish. Grogan Rock, at the entrance to the passage, is easy to distinguish; it is a 23 ft pinnacle shooting like a black tower out of the white foam surrounding its base. The rest of the wave-lashed rocks in this group also deserve cautious exploration. They are home to thousands of birds, including storm petrels, pigeon guillemots and tufted puffins which make their home amidst the black, sharks-tooth-rocks, or on the low green islets sprinkled amongst their jagged neighbours. The group of islets around Grassy Islet are impregnated with fossils of shells which were laid down in pre-

historic times. The names surrounding these islets reflect their geological history: Volcanic Islets, Brecciated Point and Jurassic Point. There are several breaks in the Barrier Islands which you can cut through to reach the open sea, depending on which islets you might want to pass near. Kayakers often paddle out here to savour the small powdery beaches.

The safest exit from Clear Passage is to skirt the outside of McQuarrie Islets, about 4 miles southeast of Rugged Point. From here it is only another 3 miles to Tatchu Point, near the entrance to Esperanza Inlet.

13 Tatchu Point

From this point, the shoreline turns sharply to the east, into the various arms and channels which indent deeply into the shoreline of Vancouver Island. Stand clear of the point, however; a kelp-covered shoal area extends over ½-mile from shore. Tatchu Point gets its name from the Indian word "tatchtatcha" which means, literally, "to chew". It refers to the local beach where a great deal of fish and shellfish were con-

Rugged Point attractions include curving sand beaches, a small trappers cabin and a stand of uncut Douglas fir.

sumed by members of the Ehatisaht Band in feasts and ceremonies. The rocks, shoals and reefs surrounding this area provided bounty of such great quantity that it gained a reputation among the natives for good local dining. Tatchu Point at one time was probably British Columbia's finest shoreside dining place, specializing in seafood and good times.

South and east from here there are two ways to proceed — either take a break from the outer coast and visit the inner protected waterways of Esperanza Inlet, or continue down the outer coast around Nootka Island, the largest off Vancouver Island. 🦑

LOCAL CAUTIONS
* Seas off the entrance to Kyuquot Sound can get rough when large ebb tides meet opposing westerly winds.
* Easterly winds can funnel to high velocities in Amai and Cachalot Inlets.

75

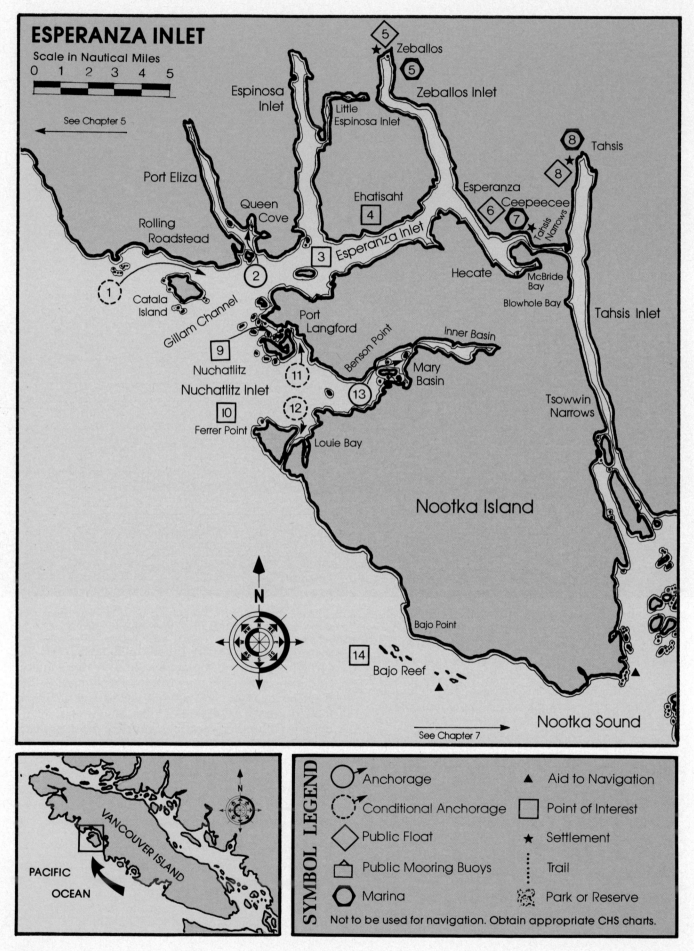

ESPERANZA INLET

Scale in Nautical Miles
0 1 2 3 4 5

See Chapter 5

Espinosa Inlet

Little Espinosa Inlet

⬙5 ★ Zeballos
⬡5

Zeballos Inlet

Port Eliza

Queen Cove

Ehatisaht

⬙8 ★ Tahsis
⬙8

Esperanza

⬡6 Ceepeecee
⬡7

Rolling Roadstead

☐4

☐3 Esperanza Inlet

Tahsis Narrows

① ①

② 2

Hecate

McBride Bay

Catala Island

Blowhole Bay

Tahsis Inlet

Gillam Channel

Port Langford

Benson Point

Inner Basin

☐9

Nuchatlitz

(11)

Mary Basin

Nuchatlitz Inlet

(12)

(13)

Tsowwin Narrows

☐10
Ferrer Point

Louie Bay

N

Nootka Island

Bajo Point

☐14

Bajo Reef

Nootka Sound

See Chapter 7

VANCOUVER ISLAND

N

PACIFIC

OCEAN

SYMBOL LEGEND

○→ Anchorage

◯⃝→ Conditional Anchorage

⬙ Public Float

⬠ Public Mooring Buoys

⬡ Marina

▲ Aid to Navigation

☐ Point of Interest

★ Settlement

⋮ Trail

▨ Park or Reserve

Not to be used for navigation. Obtain appropriate CHS charts.

CHAPTER SIX

Esperanza Inlet

Rolling Roadstead, Zeballos, Tahsis, Nuchatlitz

In 1778, Captain Cook was sailing along the outer coast, desperately seeking a break in the inhospitable shoreline where he could safely pull in to rest the crew and repair his ships. When the weather cleared, he saw a large bight which seemed to offer the prospect of a good harbour. He named the bight, between Cape Cook and Estevan Point, Hope Bay. (He found safe moorage the next day, in Nootka Sound and made history by being the first European to set foot on these shores — more in Chapter Seven.) The name on Cook's chart was translated into Spanish by Captain Alexandro Malaspina while investigating this area, and Hope Bay became Esperanza Inlet. In 1791, Malaspina explored most of the inner channels which make up Esperanza, accounting for the predominance of Spanish names in this area.

In his description of Esperanza as being a likely place to find secure anchorage, Cook was not mistaken; many fine and secure anchorages can be found in this region of the coast. If you are approaching Esperanza Inlet from the north, there are two entrances — one choked with rocks, but offering an interesting and exciting passage; the other deep and wide, and navigable by even the largest freighters. Depending on the weather conditions, you can choose either of these routes.

1 Rolling Roadstead

At first glance, the entry into Rolling Roadstead from the west seems like a difficult task, but closer examination reveals a clear channel if you feel confi-dent with your navigation. If you've successfully negotiated the Barrier Islands to the north, you will probably have no trouble negotiating this passage. The "Sailing Directions" warn that there are "numerous above-water, drying and sunken rocks to the southwest of Catala Island, and between it and Tatchu Point. The named ones of these dangers are Halftide Reef, Obstruction Reef, White Rock, and High Rocks which are connected to Tatchu Point by a reef that dries in places. The channels between these dangers are narrow and intricate; they require local knowledge for safe navigation." With such an ominous description, it's a wonder anyone could get through, but in fact, the way in is relatively straightforward under normal conditions. By taking hand bearings on Catala Island, High Rocks and Peculiar Point, most hazards can be easily identified and circumvented. Enter between High Rocks and Obstruction Reef, (after locating the dangerous rock ½-mile south of High Rocks) heading for Peculiar Point until it is clear to turn eastward past White Rock, and into Rolling Roadstead. The reward for negotiating this tricky passage is the immediate reduction of the swells, and a view of the beautiful inside shores of Catala Island. A word of caution, however: if there is a large tidal change, and the wind opposes the tide over the shallows in the roadstead, the water could get very choppy. I would not recommend this entrance in rough or foggy weather.

The anchorage for Rolling Roadstead lies between Catala Island and the mountainous backshore of Van-

couver Island. As an anchorage it is aptly named, because the west coast swells reach into the anchorage from both directions. This fact notwithstanding, Rolling Roadstead offers a great deal as a stopover; it has all the other ingredients that make for a good anchorage. The bottom is sandy, ranging from 12 to 24 ft depending on your distance from shore. Catala Island itself is wooded, and blessed with sandy beaches and sea caves to explore. It is easy to hike around, and attracts a good number of kayakers and canoeists who venture from the protected waterways to camp in safety, close to the wildness of the exposed outer coast. It is also a very common anchorage for fishermen under settled conditions, and the entire shallow bank might be dotted with boats collecting geoduck clams ("gooey-ducks") off the bottom. If you enter the area when the diver's flag is shown, proceed cautiously and look for air bubbles. Often the boat operators will point out where divers are located, and by following their directions you can get safely through the maze of air hoses and boats. The island was named for the Reverend Magin Catala, a Franciscan monk who worked for over 40 years as a missionary on the Spanish American coast, including a year at Nootka during the Spanish occupation. The island is being considered as a possible Provincial Recreation Area, and is well worth protecting.

If conditions are obscured or rough, you may choose to take the "outside" route into Esperanza Inlet. After the "moment-by-moment navigation" through the Barrier Islands, the relatively clear passage through Gillam Channel can be not only a relief, but a thrilling experience in its own right. First, locate the mid-channel marker 2½ miles south of Catala Island. This will get you safely past the offlying dangers surrounding the entrance to the inlet and help you locate the channel markers which guide you in. Once on a northeasterly course, the channel is clear, and often you will have the wind on the beam, with the waves behind you, creating surfing conditions. Besides being a thrill, surfing makes for a fast trip into the inlet.

If you wish, you can enter Rolling Roadstead from this channel, by turning eastward past Black Rock, and going around Entrance Reef, which is marked. Or you can press on for 2 miles into the inlet, and anchor in one of the safest anchorages on the west coast.

2 Queen Cove

By taking Birthday Channel, which runs northeast from Esperanza Inlet, you can get completely out of the swells of the outer coast, in one of the most serene settings imaginable. Queen Cove, one of the ancient village sites of the Ehatisaht Band is virtually landlocked, and provides a very secure anchorage in 36 ft over a good mud bottom. Access is via a narrow channel marked by cliffs on the western shore. The wharf

Preceding page: Catala Island (Rolling Roadstead on left) at the entrance to Esperanza Inlet.

The 65 ft totem at Ehatisaht (the finest on the west coast) is all that remains of the summer village that once occupied the shores of Graveyard Bay.

which used to be there has deteriorated beyond use, as have most of the old cannery buildings on the shoreline. Aside from the small Indian settlement on the eastern shore, none of the buildings are occupied. Take a dinghy at high water and explore the small branch of the cove which takes you to the mouth of the Park River. Queen Cove is usually glassy calm, regardless of any tempest raging on the "outside" and is a good spot to spend a few relaxing days in the midst of an often challenging passage.

Port Eliza stretches for 4 miles northwest past Queen Cove; though it is beautiful to explore, it offers no convenient anchorage, and is completely open to southeasterlies. As such, it is not recommended as an anchorage. It has been reported, however, to shelter a good number of oysters and a day trip here might reap a good harvest.

From Queen Cove or Rolling Roadstead there are two totally different routes you can take southwards to Nootka Sound. The outside route around Nootka Island (the largest island off the west coast) is much like the other outside passages on Vancouver Island, with its wild shores and rolling swell. The inside route consists of high mountain peaks, abandoned village sites, and side trips to either a goldmining frontier town or a bustling mill town with all shoreside facilities. Because each route offers such different experiences, you will have to decide which passage offers the attractions you're most interested in, and head that way. The inside route will be discussed first.

Tufts of fair-weather cloud hang over mountains at entrance to Esperanza Inlet.

3 Esperanza Inlet

This 10-mile-long channel separates Nootka Island from the main shores of Vancouver Island, and cuts deeply into the coastline through a series of deep inlets and channels. As a result of Captain Alexandro Malaspina's voyage of 1791, when he examined these inner channels, his lieutenants on the voyage, Espinosa and Cevallos (Zeballos) have their names perpetuated on present-day charts.

Espinosa Inlet, another 2 miles past Queen Cove as you head inland, branches out due north from Esperanza Inlet, and terminates 6 miles later in a drying flat, typical of the long inlets on the mainland coast. Little Espinosa Inlet, which branches off from the main arm, is blocked by rocks and not navigable by cruising yachts. Neither of these inlets offers convenient anchorage. Two miles past the entrance to Espinosa, on the north side of Esperanza Inlet is Graveyard Bay, and just beyond this bay is the abandoned Indian village of Ehatisaht.

4 Ehatisaht

The powerful Ehatisaht tribe which once occupied villages at Queen Cove, and Tatchu Point, also inhabited this small cove notched into the steep shoreline. A small clear mountain stream pushes a gravel bar out into Esperanza Inlet. There is little secure anchorage here, except off the eastern side of the gravel bar in settled weather. However, if you can't land you can still get close enough to shore to see the finest totem pole on the west coast. The 65 ft Ehatisaht pole thrusts its intricately carved features out of the underbrush and stands in supreme command of this once busy village. Natural dyes still colour many of the features of this magnificent pole, the detail of which renders this carving among the best ever made. No other structures remain at the site, although the meadow which supported the village is still lush, and wildflowers cover the midden. The quiet trickle of the stream and the humming of countless honeybees are the only sounds that break the silence of this enchanted place.

5　Zeballos

From Ehatisaht it is just a few miles eastward to a junction of channels. One, Hecate Channel leads to Tahsis Inlet, and the other dog-leg waterway leads to the old wild west town of Zeballos. If the wind is westerly, you can probably go the entire 14 mile length of Esperanza and Zeballos Inlets with the wind and waves pushing you from behind. Zeballos is a "character town", and worthy of a visit, even if on the chart it appears to be out of the way.

Settlements are few and far between on the outer coast and supplies can run out quickly on a boat, making this small community an important supply stop. Zeballos affords no anchorage, but there are two docks, and three public floats, which provide over 1500 ft of good overnight moorage. To get fuel and water, call on VHF channel 68, CB channel 14, or tie up to the Gulf Oil float and walk into town and phone #257. The fuel dock is a fair distance from town, so a call by radio will give you more convenient service. Frequent float plane service is also available from here. At the head of the public dock there is a restaurant, and a good store with fair prices, as Zeballos is connected to the rest of Vancouver Island by road. In the town there is a post office, liquor store, restaurant, and there is also a small hotel, with a real wild west type saloon (pub). Although the town is only about 50

Zeballos is popular west coast provisioning port. Its history goes back to the 1930s when gold was discovered nearby.

years old, the quaint houses with their porches and picket fences give the impression of being much older.

In 1931 some unemployed fishermen pulled their boats out of the water at the head of the inlet and built cabins on the shoreline. They spent their summers prospecting, and their winters trapping, and were the only residents of the area. About 6 miles up the river they finally uncovered a rich vein of gold, and began the arduous task of hauling the ore out. There were no roads at that time, so all ore had to be taken out on their backs, over bear and elk trails along the riverbank. It was a day's walk each way. Still, the effort paid off and mines sprung up throughout the area, and many of these hardy pioneers retired in wealth and comfort on the mainland. Over $11 million worth of gold bricks was taken out of this area. This west coast gold rush went on until 1948 when the price of gold was pegged at $35.00 per ounce, making much of the mining unprofitable.

After the decline of gold mining, the lumber industry dominated the scene for 10 years until mining once again became the economic base of the area — only this time it was iron ore. The huge wharf for

Esperanza public float affords access to nearby Mission school (red roof) and Outreach centre.

The name for Ceepeecee at the entrance to Tahsis Narrows comes from the initials of the Canadian Packing Company (CPC) spelled out.

loading the concentrates still serves Zeballos, although the heyday of mining is long past.

One feature of this part of the coastline which deserves mention is the tremendous amount of rain which can fall over a relatively short period of time. The moist Pacific air being pressed against these high-walled inlets can cause a lot of precipitation. A Ministry of Transport sign on the public dock states that "A charge will be levied for pumping sinking boats" — a rather ominous indication of the amount of rainfall that can collect in an unattended open boat, even overnight. Our visit provided us with enough evidence to support the locals' claim that Zeballos is the "Rain Capital of the west coast". George Nicholson, author of "Vancouver Island's West Coast", was a longtime resident and the principal authority in Zeballos for many years.

6 Esperanza

After back-tracking the 6 miles of Zeballos Inlet, the waters of Hecate Channel appear on the port side. Within this 5-mile channel are no less than three village sites, although these habitations today are almost vacant. The first of these is the settlement of Esperanza, which is now a non-denominational mission, operated as a school and outreach centre. There is a public float with 120 ft of mooring space, and the friendly people at the mission will likely offer you tea and snacks if you take the time to visit them. **Note** — The fuel supplies listed in the "Sailing Directions" are not available on a reliable basis, so if you require fuel, Zeballos and Tahsis are the closest guaranteed fuelling stops. Many of the people in Esperanza now

live in the settlement of Hecate, a mile across the channel on Nootka Island. Hecate (named after the survey vessel of that name) was at one time a pilchard (herring) reduction plant, one of five in the area. Today the buildings and sheds serve solely as residences for the Esperanza Mission school.

McBride Bay, just east of Hecate, is too deep to be used as a convenient anchorage for small craft, and booms occupy the head of the bay. An abandoned sawmill, and an old wreck appear on the south shore of the bay, but have almost completely disintegrated.

7 Ceepeecee

Just at the entrance to Tahsis Narrows is a small settlement with a curious name. Actually the name is the initials "C.P.C." spelled out — C.P.C. being the initials of Canadian Packing Company, which established a pilchard-reduction plant at this location in 1926. The local name for the place was accepted by the post office, and Ceepeecee was on the map. There is no anchorage, and the floats there are all private, but there is a marine ways capable of handling boats up to 44 ft in length, and repair facilities are available. This is also the location of the hospital which was so small it was called the "Doll's House". Incredibly, it once was the only medical centre for over 1500 loggers, fishermen and cannery workers.

Tahsis Narrows, just past Ceepeecee, is over a mile long and in one place only a few hundred feet wide. It connects the waters of Esperanza and Tahsis Inlets, both significant bodies of water, and one would expect tidal streams in the area to be quite significant. Surprisingly, the tidal change has little or no effect on

currents in the narrows and they are listed as being weak and variable. The water is deep, and there are no navigational hazards to avoid in the passage.

8   Tahsis

Just over 3 miles north of the narrows, the bustling sawmill town of Tahsis dominates the view, visible because of the tall smoke stacks which occupy the shoreline at the head of the inlet. Tahsis Inlet runs about due north, and the winds tend to blow up the inlet regardless of whether the wind on the outer coast is northwest or southwest, although the latter generates a stronger blow. This can create a miserable chop at the head of the inlet, and make docking at the public float extremely bumpy and uncomfortable. In a strong southeasterly wind it is advisable to leave the public float and find a slip in one of the private wharves further up the inlet, where breakwaters reduce the chop to tenable levels.

Fuel and water are available at Nootka Sound Marina, where hull and engine repairs are also made. There is a marine railway for haul-outs, and a good marine chandlery for boating supplies. There are a considerable number of small, privately-owned boats (mainly runabouts) in this area, so a good stock of supplies and services are available here.

Space at the public wharf is limited, and the main use of the dock seems to be the loading and unloading of supplies, as the main shopping centre and liquor store are closer to here than the private marinas. The stores are well-supplied, and prices are reasonable. There is a post office, hotel, bank, several restaurants, and a laundromat in the town area, ½-mile from the public floats. Large freighters regularly ply these waters taking out lumber produced in large quantities at the sawmill.

This beautiful setting, surrounded by high peaks on all sides was once the summer residence of Chief Maquinna, the powerful Nootka chief who met Captain Cook when he landed in Nootka Sound in 1778. It was at the head of Tahsis Inlet, where the town is now located, that Captains Vancouver and Quadra (along with Maquinna) met to continue the discussion of the terms of the Nootka Convention. On a sunny day, in September 1792, at this site George Vancouver named all of present day Vancouver Island "The Island of Quadra and Vancouver", in order to acknowledge the respect he had for the Spanish Captain, with whom he had become good friends. Only the latter part of the name remains today.

The first sawmill to be operational at Tahsis was built in 1945 by the enterprising Gibson brothers. Seven years later they sold this and other interests to the Tahsis Company, a subsidiary of East Asiatic Company Ltd., a world-wide corporation headed by a Danish prince. Today the population is just over 2000, by far the majority of which works at the mill

At the head of Tahsis Inlet lies the town of Tahsis, centre of local sawmilling activity.

producing over 2 million board feet of lumber per day. Although facilities for visiting yachtsmen are somewhat limited, the people are friendly, and the backdrop of the mill is quite astounding. Another feature of this area, similar to Zeballos, is the amount of raincloud caught in the high mountains surrounding the town. In its description of facilities and services available to the large freighters loading forest products, the "Sailing Directions" makes a simple statement: "Unlimited fresh water is available". A friend who lived in Tahsis for several years said that

Tahsis public float is primarily used for loading and unloading. Exposure to southerly winds can make it uncomfortable for overnight moorage.

when he first moved there, he never saw the sun for 10 months. It is unlikely that Tahsis will become the next west coast summer resort, but it is a good place to stock up before continuing along the coast.

The remainder of Tahsis Inlet is steep-to and offers little chance for anchorage along its 12-mile length. There is a small logging camp on the west side of the inlet at Blowhole Bay, but the wharf and float there are private. The only real navigational hazard along the route is through Tsowwin Narrows, where the Tsowwin River pushes a gravel bar out into the channel. Here the width of the channel is reduced to just over 600 ft and currents can run up to 3 knots. Tugs with booms and large freighters regularly run at good speed through the narrows. A wrecked barge is rusting away on the eastern side near the narrows, close to shore. Two miles beyond the narrows the waterway opens up into Nootka Sound (to be covered in the next chapter). You should also beware of log debris in the

inlet. Although this is a common phenomenon on the inner coast, it is the exception on the exposed outer shores, and the hazard might be overlooked by the unwary cruiser.

9 Nuchatlitz

If you choose to stay on the outside of Nootka Island, there are a few interesting anchorages and sights worth exploring along the way. Nuchatlitz Inlet cuts deeply into the side of Nootka Island, creating some interesting pockets where good protection from the elements can be found, along with some fascinating geographical features. The first of these is the Indian village of Nuchatlitz, accessible only by a tortuous rock-strewn entrance through a maze of reefs and islets. If conditions are good, and you are confident of your navigation, you can enter this seldom-visited active native fishing village. From Gillam Channel, go around the north and east sides of Rosa Island. Hug the shore of Nootka Island, until south of Rosa Island, avoiding the drying rocks shown on the chart. Once abeam of the small un-named islet (marked 145) find the buoys which mark the channel into the village, keeping both of these close on the starboard hand while entering. Once clear of the last buoy a small cove opens up, providing secure anchorage in 20 ft over a mud bottom. Native fishing boats use this anchorage year-round, and a small village here houses the Indian families. The view is quite moving, but only cautious mariners, canoeists or those with local knowledge can safely enter this isolated and placid anchorage. An old woman there still weaves weed baskets, and there are many ancient burial caves in the area. Get permission from the local people before exploring any of these; several are considered sacred to the tribe. To leave the village, you must carefully re-trace your route in, taking note of the tidal height in order to identify the navigational hazards.

The Indian village of Nuchatlitz (above and right) promises a quiet, intriguing stopover but great caution is required in navigating the rock-spattered entrance.

86

10 Nuchatlitz Inlet

In order to get to the anchorages in Nuchatlitz Inlet it is necessary to negotiate your own passage through such hazards as Blind Reef, Pin Rock, Nuchatlitz Reef, and Danger Rock. Perhaps the safest way in is to run a course from the mid-channel marker eastward between Pin Rock and the almost totally submerged Nuchatlitz Reef, taking a bearing on Cameron Rocks. This way the 15 ft drying rock east of Pin Rock can be used to identify the eastern extremity of the dangers. Once inside the inlet, there are several fine, safe anchorages to choose from. One of the most commonly used of these opens up on the north side.

11 Port Langford

After clearing the dangers as you enter Nuchatlitz Inlet, simply round Colwood Rocks and head straight into the bay that appears on the port side. This is a good anchorage in a westerly, or northwesterly, but is open to the southeast, and is not recommended if a low pressure area is advancing on the coast, bringing winds from that quarter. The "Sailing Directions" warns that it is no good in a southeasterly because the holding ground is poor, but small craft often shelter here with little difficulty in the summer months. If a blow comes up, there are two other anchorages in close proximity where more secure shelter can be found, the first just 4 miles across the inlet at Louie Bay. If you have time to explore, the remains of an uncharted shipwreck are reported to be on the small islet northwest of Ensenada Islet, near the entrance to Pt. Langford.

12 Louie Bay

If the wind is from the southern quarters, shelter can be found in shallow water behind Tongue Point in Louie Bay on the south side of Nuchatlitz Inlet.

Mary Basin beyond Lord Island (centre) affords secure all-weather protection.

Although there is good protection from northerly winds, the swells — which build up when the weather is steady — roll into the inlet, around Tongue Point, and into Louie Bay. Still, the bay is close to the outer coast, and makes a convenient stopover for west coast yachtsmen with limited cruising time. For those who have time to delve deeper into the more out-of-the-way places on the outer coast, a secure, seldom used anchorage with some interesting side trips lies waiting just 4 miles east.

13 Mary Basin

Proceeding further into Nuchatlitz Inlet, just past Cameron Rocks, you must cross the relatively shallow bar which protects the entrance to the inner basin from the Pacific swells. In westerly gales, these swells could pile up on the bar, but conditions would have to

Sea caves near Mary Basin in Nuchatlitz Inlet.

be extreme before the waves would break. Once over the bar, the inlet curves northward, providing even more shelter to the inner basin past Lord Island. The all-weather anchorage formed behind Lord Island, at the inner part of the inlet is known as Mary Basin.

Here the waters are calm and smooth, and the shallow water over mud bottom provides perfect holding conditions. Besides this, the anchorage is quite scenic, usually deserted, and surrounded by various cruising attractions. The basin is a good area for crabs, and there are large sea caves to explore just outside the anchorage, west of Benson Point. You can take a dinghy to the narrows leading to the inner basin, and watch the water rip through the tidal falls.

14 Bajo Reef

If you are continuing down the coast on the outside of Nootka Island, there is no shelter until you get to Nootka Sound, 22 miles to the southeast. After rounding Ferrer Point the coast is exposed the entire

Spinnaker set and drawing, Domani *sails down the wave-chopped waters of Esperanza Inlet.*

length of the Island, and lying as much as 3 miles outside the high water mark is one of the most dangerous hazards on the outer coast. The Spanish called the reef "Bajo", which signifies "beneath, or below", especially in reference to dangers — hence, "danger below". Captain Cook made a point of skirting around this dangerous reef before he sailed into Nootka Sound in 1778. The crew of the British ship *King David* were not so lucky, when the ship hit the reef in 1905. The story of her demise is written in Fred Rogers' book "Shipwrecks of British Columbia". Apparently her master, Captain Davidson lost track of his exact position after going through thick weather off the Washington Coast; a lookout reported seeing breakers on the lee bow according to the Captain's report:

"We weren't sure of our position, so the anchors were let out in only eight fathoms of water. Suddenly the weather cleared and we could see the dangerous reef. On the 13th, the wind increased to the point where the strain was so great that the windlass broke and she was swept onto the rocks. Soon after, she started to break up. A large portion of the bow broke off and was carried by enormous waves high on the rocks. There was little we could do but hold out until the wind and sea subsided and pray that the ship didn't fall to pieces under our feet."

As Rogers reports:

"When the crew reached shore in lifeboats, they found themselves in a remote place with no sign of habitation. After the storm, some of them returned to the ship for food and other necessities. An abandoned fish camp provided them with shelter. Large fires were kept burning day and night, but the days passed into weeks with still no help in sight. Like the men's morale, the food supply was almost depleted. In a last suicidal bid for help, seven crewmen under First Officer A. Wallstrom, a New Zealander, set out on December 23 in one of the lifeboats on the long and dangerous trip to Cape Beale. More anxious days passed for the crewmen left behind, but their shipmates never returned. No trace of them was ever found.

"The remaining 18 men now faced starvation. One of them, an old sailmaker who was in critical condition, went insane on January 14 — the very day on which a passing vessel, the *Queen City*, turned about to investigate the fires. The sailmaker died soon after they were rescued and landed in Victoria on January 19.

"The *King David* became a total loss and nothing was salvaged."

Needless to say, the reef would show little mercy to a yacht which inadvertantly ran up on its jagged back. A red buoy, over 3 miles from shore marks the edge of the danger, and yachtsmen should give this kelp covered hazard a wide berth. The Nootkas had a trail running south along the shoreline from Ferrer Point, and ambitious hikers can still walk the rugged shores of this wild coastline all the way to Friendly Cove, in the more protected waters of Nootka Sound.

LOCAL CAUTIONS
- There are numerous rocks and reefs in the western entrance to Rolling Roadstead. Enter from this direction only in settled weather.
- Geoduck divers often work the shallows of Rolling Roadstead. If "diver-down" flags are flying, proceed with caution, a diver using scuba gear may be below your boat.
- Entry to the village of Nuchatlitz is hazardous. Enter only in settled conditions.
- Driftwood and log debris, uncommon on most of the west coast, is prevalent in Tahsis Inlet. Keep a close watch for deadheads in this area.
- There is a good deal of freighter traffic in Tahsis Inlet — use caution when in the area of Tsowwin Narrows.

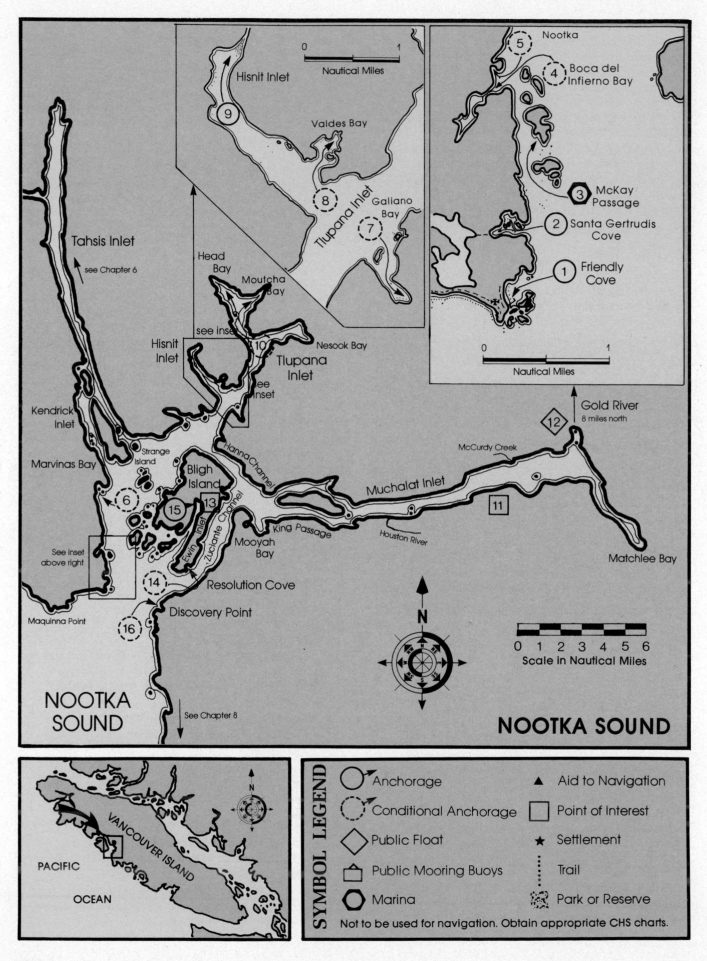

Hisnit Inlet

0   1
Nautical Miles

⑨

Valdes Bay

⑧

Tlupana Inlet

Galiano Bay

⑦

Nootka

⑤

Boca del Infierno Bay

④

McKay Passage ③

Santa Gertrudis Cove ②

Friendly Cove ①

0   1
Nautical Miles

Tahsis Inlet

see Chapter 6

Head Bay

Moutcha Bay

see inset

Hisnit Inlet

⑩

see inset

Tlupana Inlet

Nesook Bay

Gold River
8 miles north

◇12

Kendrick Inlet

McCurdy Creek

Marvinas Bay

Strange Island

Bligh Island

Hanna Channel

Muchalat Inlet

⑥

□13

⑮

Zuclante Channel

Ewin Inlet

□11

King Passage

Houston River

Mooyah Bay

⑭

Resolution Cove

Discovery Point

Maquinna Point

⑯

Matchlee Bay

N

0 1 2 3 4 5 6
Scale in Nautical Miles

NOOTKA SOUND

See Chapter 8

NOOTKA SOUND

VANCOUVER ISLAND

N

PACIFIC

OCEAN

SYMBOL LEGEND

○→ Anchorage

◌→ Conditional Anchorage

◇ Public Float

⬠ Public Mooring Buoys

⬡ Marina

▲ Aid to Navigation

□ Point of Interest

★ Settlement

⋮ Trail

Park or Reserve

Not to be used for navigation. Obtain appropriate CHS charts.

CHAPTER SEVEN

Stained glass window at Friendly Cove depicts the transfer of local power from Spanish to British hands in 1790.

Historic Nootka

Friendly Cove, Gold River, Resolution Cove

The history of British Columbia begins at Nootka, and no writer — even one concerned primarily with coastal exploration by boat — can overlook the significance of this place in the chronicles of time. The list of names affixed to geographical features in Nootka Sound reads like a "who's who" of early exploration and trade: Cook, Hanna, Bligh, Quadra, Strange, Eliza, Valdes, Galiano, Jewitt, and Maquinna are some of the names prominent in this sound. Each of these individuals is associated with events that shaped the course of history on this coast, and in some cases, the world itself. Even the name of the sound is a story.

Several books have been written about Nootka Sound, and the incidents which brought this remote part of North America into such prominence worldwide. Each book views the events from a different perspective and, depending on your interests, reading about the sound can heighten the excitement experienced when in the precise location where an event occurred. These pages will be concerned primarily with the marine aspects of these events which might interest the modern day explorers who visit Nootka. As you will see, the sound offers much more for the yachtsman who ventures out of the anchorage at Friendly Cove (see also the history section in Part I).

Our voyage through history begins in March of 1778, with Captain James Cook, R.N., in search of the elusive Northwest Passage thought to connect the Atlantic with the Pacific — a route that would bring prosperity to any country discovering and controlling it. After being stormbound for weeks, he was anxiously seeking shelter so he could repair his damaged ships and replenish his water supplies. In late March, he was off Cape Flattery looking for the Strait of Juan de Fuca, but fog and rain squalls (typical weather for this coast in March) kept him from locating the entrance to the "inland sea" which was thought to exist there. Three days later the weather cleared enough for Cook to see a "bold promontory" which he called Woody Point (now Cape Cook). The bight between here and the peninsula to the south he called "Hope Bay" (now Esperanza) because of the prospect of finding a safe anchorage. Owing to the ruggedness of the coast, he was obliged to sail for several hours before an opening appeared in the shoreline large enough to accommodate his ships *Resolution* and *Discovery*. He named this opening "King George's Sound", which he believed was an indentation in the continent of North America. Later, in an effort to use what he thought was the native name, he mistakenly called it by a name which the natives kept chanting — "Noot-ka, Noot-ka". It was much later that it was discovered that this word was an imperative advising Cook to "go around" (the island), and was not as he thought, the local name for the place. However erroneous it was, the name Nootka stuck, and came to refer generally to all the natives occupying this section of the west coast of the Island as well.

If the mis-christening of Nootka Sound was an inauspicious beginning for the site of such contention a few years later, the fact that Cook landed at this pre-

cise location at all was just as haphazard. Except for the whims of March weather, Quatsino, Kyuquot, or Barkley Sound might have held the place in history now held by Nootka. If Cook had found the Strait of Juan de Fuca, the history of such cities as Seattle and Vancouver would have surely been quite different. However, it was Nootka which opened her arms to welcome Cook, while her stormy sisters had to wait a decade or more for discovery.

The wind died just outside the entrance, so Cook lowered the boats and towed the ships towards the shelter of the sound. They came to rest in a nook on the west side of a peninsula just 2 miles inside the sound, in a place Cook called "Ships Cove". Today's

Rainbow's end glistens over light station on San Rafael Island, Friendly Cove.

charts show the small bay on Bligh Island as Resolution Cove, named after his great ship.

When Cook's ships came into the outer harbour, the natives did not know what the strange vessels were, so a chief sent out some of his warriors to investigate. They got close enough to the ship to see one man with a long hooked nose, and another who was a hunchback, and identified them in turn as the dog salmon and the humpback salmon, thinking that Cook's ships were manned by "fish-come-alive-as-people". Later investigations revealed that these "fish-people" were in fact humans not unlike themselves, and the natives referred to them as "Mamathni", meaning "their houses move over the water". From that point on, the course of history for both cultures took a radical turn, and neither would ever be the same.

1 Friendly Cove

The natives who visited Cook on his arrival were "Moach-ahts", or "people of the deer", numbering about 1500 and occupying their summer residences at

Preceding page: Spectacular view over Nootka Sound to Vancouver Island range in background. Friendly Cove is on the left.

Yuquot ("the village exposed to the winds"). The village later came to be called Friendly Cove because of the good disposition of the natives toward the traders who followed Cook. Even though this cove was a much better anchorage, Cook remained in "Ships Cove" in order to complete the repairs to his ships, unhindered by the curious natives. When he later visited Friendly Cove he recorded the event in his journal.

"Having now finished most of our heavy work, I set out the next morning to take a view of the sound. I first went to the west point, where I found a large village, before it a very snug harbour, in which was from nine to four fathoms of water over a bottom of fine sand."

Today you can set your anchor in that same sand and imagine the rows of longhouses which were once on the shore, with hundreds of dugout canoes pulled up on the beach in front of them. Your imagination will have to do the work, however, because today the prehistoric culture of the place is represented by a lone totem which peers out of the bush over the few rude buildings that remain there, lit up by the sweeping arc of a modern lighthouse.

The anchorage here today is protected by a rock breakwater which joins San Miguel Islands, and the higher San Rafael Island on which the light station is located. This breakwater prevents the surge of the Pacific from rolling into the cove, improving the anchorage considerably. There is a public dock but no float, so a beach landing is necessary to visit the shoreside attractions, of which there are plenty. However, since the entire area (except for the light station) is Indian reserve, the first place you should visit is the blue house on the shore, where Mr. Ray Williams and his family act as caretakers for the reserve. Ray will advise you where you may or may not go, because much of the land is sacred burial ground and unmarked graves are everywhere. A small fee may also be charged for landing dinghies on shore.

In the village, the fine totem pole — with its interesting history written on the back of it — is worthy of close examination. The most conspicuous building is a contemporary Catholic church with two exceptionally fine stained-glass windows, a gift from the Government of Spain. The scenes depict two significant events associated with the temporary Spanish occupation of Friendly Cove — one shows a Franciscan monk preaching to the natives, while the other depicts the transfer of the cove from Captain Quadra of Spain to Captain George Vancouver of Great Britain.

Behind the church is a long pebble beach which is exposed to the best and the worst of the tempestuous Pacific weather. A trail running behind the village leads past a series of cemeteries to a freshwater lake, site of the ancient pre-hunt rites of the Nootka whalers. The trail continues along the shore for 2 miles, where a small river interrupts the path which then carries on as far as Maquinna Point. It is not uncommon to see the recent tracks of a bear, deer, cougar or

wolf. Nootka, even in this century, is still a very wild place.

Besides the natural shoreside attractions, you can get permission from the light-keepers to ascend the light tower where the huge light and foghorn that signal the entrance to Nootka Sound are located. The view from the tower is breathtaking. From here you can look out over the sound, with its precipitous backdrop, myriad of coves, and to the foreboding Hesquiat Peninsula looming on the southern horizon. The tidy manicured residences around the lighthouse contrast starkly with the wild overgrown nature of the surrounding area. You can also visit the two nearby cairns that denote significant events associated with the cove. One commemorates the discovery of the sound by Cook, its later occupation by the Spanish, and the Nootka Convention of 1790 which averted war between Spain and England by having Spain relinquish lands taken from the British on this coast. The other commemorates the meeting of Vancouver and Quadra to sort out the specific terms of the Convention.

As if all this were not enough, Friendly Cove is also the site where Captain Meares built the first ship ever constructed on the coast — suitably named the *Northwest America*. This little schooner, 48 ft on deck, was built and launched from these shores Sep-

The natives of Friendly Cove (named after their friendly disposition) were the first to greet Captain Cook upon his arrival in Nootka Sound.

tember 10, 1788. Today a converted minesweeper, the *Uchuck III* brings foot passengers to this historic site from Gold River, further up the sound (see 12 below).

2 Santa Gertrudis Cove

Directly north of Friendly Cove, another very beautiful, protected anchorage is available that offers even more protection from the Pacific swells. There are two rocks at the entrance to the cove, both above water, and fairly easy to locate. Once inside, you have two options: carefully skirt the rock on the north side of the entrance and take the northern branch of the cove, or carefully make your way further west into the cove and settle into the peaceful anchorage which occupies its inner reaches. A covered rock lies on the way in but it is clearly shown on the chart and easy to avoid. Both anchorages offer safe moorage, though the more northerly one is deeper, requiring more scope.

There is a provincial recreation reserve in this cove, because it is seen as an excellent site for a future marine park. This status allows you to go ashore on the small islets in the cove, and along the 1¼ miles of

95

shoreline surrounding it. From here you can make your way through the bush to the lake located just behind the anchorage. The cove was named after the ship (actually Meares' *Northwest America*) which was confiscated by the Spanish and renamed *Santa Gertrudis*. The Spanish believed that they had pre-empted the entire west coast of North American when Balboa reached the Pacific at Panama and claimed the land for Spain. They were disturbed by the increased activities of the British on this coast, and consequently they sent ships to Nootka Sound in 1789 to occupy all British possessions and confiscate all British ships in Nootka by force. This act nearly triggered all-out war between England and Spain but through negotiation and the signing of the Nootka Convention major conflict was avoided. The number of Spanish names in Nootka Sound reflects their occupation here between 1789 and 1792.

3 McKay Passage

For large ships, the main channel northwards further into Nootka Sound is Cook Channel. Smaller craft can get more protection, and a more interesting view taking the channel between Nootka Island and the Saavedra Islands. This passage is relatively free from hazards, except for the reef extending northwest from the 6 ft drying rock at the southern entrance to the passage. On the largest of the Saavedra Islands there is a private resort (marked by a small float and several large storage tanks) where accommodation and limited amounts of fuel are available.

4 Boca del Infierno Bay

In this bay, just outside the lagoon, is an anchorage which is good in all but strong northeast winds. The lagoon itself is inaccessible by yachts, but can be explored by dinghy at high slack when the waters are relatively calm. At other times the tide rushing through the narrow entrance creates a torrent of frothy water which the Spanish aptly named "mouth of the inferno". If you climb the bluffs above the rapids you can get a great view of both the lagoon and the smoky rapids at the entrance. The foreshore of the lagoon and 43 acres of the upland area are protected by a Recreation Reserve, as the possible site of a future marine park.

5 Nootka

The former settlement and pilchard reduction plant at Nootka today lies in total disrepair. The boilers of the plant lie on their sides, leeching rust onto the rocks around them. Modern trailers can be found on the flat land, serving as temporary residences for a nearby logging camp. The crumbling dock can no longer be used safely, and beware of submerged piles

Public dock at Friendly Cove lacks a float so beach landings here are standard procedure.

Santa Gertrudis Cove offers secure anchorage and a recreational reserve ashore with access to a small lake inland.

Spanish names given to such anchorages as Boca de Infierno Bay (above) are evidence of early Spanish presence in the area.

The small settlement of Nootka was once site of a thriving pilchard reduction plant. In more recent times it's been used as a temporary logging camp.

on the north side of the small peninsula in the cove. The best anchorage is directly south of the peninsula in about 30 ft of water. Although it is open to the northeast, satisfactory anchorage can still be found here under most summer conditions, and the swell does not reach into this cove.

Continuing north, Cook Channel offers no obstacles to free passage, even for the large freighters that ply this route on their way to the mill at Tahsis, further up the inlet. To the east are a number of inviting islands known as the Spanish Pilot Group, which look as if they would harbour a yacht in any of a number of small coves and bays. However, except for those fronting Bligh Island, none of these offers secure convenient anchorage. The islands are great for exploring by dinghy, however, and reported to be full of cod and red snapper.

6 Marvinas Bay

This indentation in Nootka Island just 4 miles into the sound was often used as an anchorage by early traders in preference to Friendly Cove which was smaller, and subject to the Pacific swells. For modern craft anchorage is not as convenient as at Friendly Cove. Anchor just north of the mouth of the small

The Cook monument on San Rafael Island.

river which flows into the bay or, for even more protection, set your ground tackle directly north of the small islet south of Boston Point. Both anchorages are exposed to the southeast, but under normal summer conditions offer satisfactory respite from the weather. The name is an adaptation of the Indian word "Mawina", which means "a village along the way, or along the channel". It was thus called because it is situated between the great villages located at Yuquot, Tashsis, and Tlupana Arm.

It was from this bay that the American ship *Boston* was captured by Chief Maquinna after a dispute with its captain over the gift of a rifle. When the captain called the chief a liar and several other abusive names, he did not know the full extent of Maquinna's

98

command of the English language. He also underestimated the chief's pride — a mistake he paid for with his life and the lives of all but two of his crew. Maquinna, after carefully arranging to have the ship almost deserted at the time of the attack, took over the ship and systematically massacred the entire crew. When it was discovered that Mr. Jewitt the ship's weapons-maker was still alive, Maquinna spared him, thinking the armourer would be useful to the tribe. Another man, who was later found stowed away on the ship, was spared when Jewitt told Maquinna the man was his father. Jewitt's account (originally written in berry juice) is one of the most important accounts of Nootkan native life ever written. It was published in 1815. He became a close compatriot of Maquinna, and after more than two years living with the natives he was finally set free and taken back to America aboard the brig *Lydia*. By this time, Jewitt and the great chief had become friends and their parting was more difficult than you might have expected from a captive slave. As Jewitt describes the last day in his narrative:

"Grasping both my hands, with much emotion, while tears trickled down his cheeks, he bade me farewell. I could not avoid experiencing a painful sensation on

Sun-bleached totem stares out at visitors to Friendly Cove.

parting with the savage, who had preserved my life and in general treated me with kindness and, considering their ideas and manner, much better than could have been expected."

Boston Point, and Jewitt Cove on nearby Strange Island perpetuate the incident on today's hydrographic charts.

Beyond Marvinas Bay, Kendrick Inlet opens up between Nootka and Strange Islands. Plumper Harbour is about half way along, and though it is sheltered, is much too deep for convenient anchorage. A small logging camp is operated from here. Jewitt Cove, on the east side of Strange Island is also too deep to anchor in conveniently. Kendrick Inlet and

Tahsis Inlet are connected by a tricky, rock-encumbered route called Princesa Channel. The best route through the channel itself is found by hugging the northern shore of Strange Island, and is used by yachtsmen wishing to find shelter from the chop which often builds up in Tahsis Inlet during westerlies.

7 Galiano Bay

Five miles east of the entrance to Tahsis Inlet there are two deep but fairly sheltered anchorages — one on the north side, one on the south (see Inset map). Galiano Bay is a small cove on the south side of Tlupana Inlet with complete shelter from the wind and swells, but only one small shelf where the water is less than 60 ft. Tucking deep inside the bay, with a stern line attached to a tree or rock on shore will provide you with a remote anchorage, far from the reaches of wind, weather, or civilization. The backdrop is a chain of mountains, very few of which are less than 3000 ft high. Anchoring in such deep water might just be worth it if you seek such solitude.

8 Valdes Bay

The same distance from Tahsis Inlet, but on the north side, is a companion cove, exhibiting almost the same characteristics as Galiano Bay — that is, deep water, good shelter, and a magnificent backdrop. These two bays were named in honour of Captains Galiano and Valdes, the Spanish explorers who met George Vancouver off Point Grey on their mutual voyages of discovery in 1792. It was the last of the Spanish expeditions sent to explore this coast, and one of the few published for the world to see. Both Galiano and Valdes, each in separate ships, were later captured by the English during the Battle of Trafalgar, in 1805.

9 Hisnit Inlet

Branching off Tlupana Inlet, wedged between two mountain peaks is a 2-mile-long inlet which characteristically ends in a drying river mouth. Anchorage here in 42 ft over a mud bottom represents a remote reach in an inlet seldom visited by anyone. If this reach is not remote enough, press on another 5 miles up Tlupana Inlet which is so desolate that Brigadier General Alava, the Spanish governor of Nootka, could not understand how this "inhospitable-looking inlet, with its stupendous precipices and gloomy ravines" could ever have been the object of contention between the respective sovereigns of Great Britain and Spain.

10 Tlupana Inlet

The head of the inlet that Alava referred to is reached by curving around Princess Royal Point, opposite the perpendicular cliff walls which reach from tidewater to the heights of Quadra saddle. From these rock walls, marble was quarried to build the British Columbia Legislative buildings. Thus the inlet which heralded the discovery of B.C. also provided the marble blocks which seat the present day government of the province.

Nesook Bay branches to the east, but aside from the beauty of the scenery, offers little to attract the cruising yachtsman. Tlupana Inlet (named after a rich and powerful Nootka chief) leads to two open bays (Moutcha and Head Bays) which again terminate in drying flats. Where natives once caught salmon at the river mouths and dug clams from the mudflats, log dumps now crack the silence. Anchorage is possible here, but the depths (72-84 ft) make them less than desirable. The road from Gold River to Tahsis and Zeballos passes a short distance behind the bays.

11 Muchalat Inlet

In order to get to Muchalat Inlet, where the town of Gold River is located, one again passes through channels bearing the names of figures closely associated with our early history. From the north, Muchalat is reached via Hanna Channel, while the other entrances are King and Williamson Passages. King and Williamson were lieutenants on Cook's *Resolution*. Muchalat Inlet is a long, steep-sided channel offering

Log dumps and booms crowd anchorage in Tlupana Inlet.

very little for the casual visitor. The wind blows unhindered up the inlet for over 10 miles in either direction, a fetch which is sufficient to create a miserable chop for small boats venturing here. There are active logging camps at McCurdy Creek, Houston River, and Mooyah Bay. Near the end of the inlet, before it branches abruptly to the south and terminates in a blind channel, the ancestral home of the Muchallee tribe is located.

99

12   Gold River

A bustling pulp mill is located at the mouth of a large river which has supplied the needs of the people who have lived on its banks for centuries. The natives named the place "Aaminkis", meaning "mouth of a river", while the Spaniards called it "Rio del Oro", though there is no evidence of anyone ever finding gold there. Chief Maquinna, who had his main village at Yuquot (Friendly Cove) still claimed fishing rights on the river, prizing its supply of salmon enough to raid the local tribes at his pleasure, even at the cost of many lives.

Today the main visitors are on cargo vessels which load the tons of pulp products made at the mill. A public float is located there, but the main town is situated 8 miles inland, and no facilities (including fuel) are available for the cruising yachtsman at the float. In a westerly the seas meeting the large ebb of the river can cause the float to bounce uncomfortably. If you can get a ride to the main settlement, you will find a modern town with a post office, banks, supermarket, stores (including a liquor store), and a hotel. Medical services are also available, if necessary, although the nearest hospital is at Campbell River, 60 miles away. Canoeists and kayakers who want to visit historic Nootka often launch their craft here and visit the inlet from its back door. The *Uchuck III* which takes passengers to Friendly Cove and other points of Nootka Sound also leaves from this location.

13   Bligh Island

If the long trip up Muchalat Inlet is not in your cruising plans, a circumnavigation of Nootka Sound can still produce a voyage through history. For example, you can follow the route that Captain Cook did in April of 1778, and circumnavigate Bligh Island, the largest in the sound. Bligh Island was named after the infamous Captain William Bligh, who gained notoriety for a number of his exploits, but is most remembered for being cast off by mutineers from HMS *Bounty*. Long before those events in the South Pacific, Bligh was the master of the *Resolution* on Cook's voyage, bringing the ship safely through the fog and rough weather to our rugged coastline.

Bligh Island is separated from Vancouver Island by Zuciarte Channel, named for a native chief who was no friend of Maquinna and his people, and who occupied a village site on the east side of the channel. On the west side of this channel, the charted remains of the wrecked Dutch freighter *Schiedyk* which sank after running onto a rocky ledge here in 1968 can still be seen. However, the most famous site on Bligh Island lies further down Clerke Peninsula, in the most

Opposite page, top: Sprawling pulp mill spreads across mouth of Gold River on Muchalat Inlet. Public float (far left) affords moorage and limited protection for visitors making their way to Gold River townsite (left) eight miles inland.

unlikely spot imaginable for such a prominent position in history.

14   Resolution Cove

On the southeast corner of Bligh Island is a small cove that the natives called "Kathniaktl", meaning "a place of driftwood". When Captain Cook eased his ships' anchors to the bottom here, several firsts were recorded. On the shores of this small cove, Cook became the first European to set foot on what has become British Columbia. At this same site, B.C.'s largest industry took its first organized leap into the future when a tree was felled to replace *Resolution's* foremast. As Cook's journal relates, "in going a very inconsiderable distance, you may cut sticks of every gradation, from a Main Mast for your ship, to one for your Jolly Boat; and these I suppose as good as are to be procur'd in any part of the world." Because of the fine choice of wood available here for various ship repairs, Cook's planned two-week stay stretched to four weeks.

One of the striking features of this cove is its rather mediocre disposition as an anchorage. Although it is protected from most winds, the water is deep until very close to shore. There was not enough room for

Friendly Cove, Nootka Sound in 1879

Cook's ships to swing, so lines were run ashore to secure them, a practice advisable even today for anyone planning to use this anchorage overnight. Still, there was a small stream to replenish the water supply, and plenty of spruce from which a beer was made that aided considerably in treating many a sailor's maladies. Today the cove, in fact the whole island, is uninhabited and — save for two plaques erected in 1978 to commemorate the bicentennial of Cook's visit — nothing remains to indicate the prominence of this unassuming spot in the history of this coast. The plaques and a small flagpole are situated on a rocky knoll on the north side of the anchorage. The head of the cove has reverted to being "Kathniaktl, the place of driftwood", and the brash call of the Stellar's jay mockingly announces nature's patent disregard for man's events and accomplishments.

15   Ewin Inlet

The long arm of the Clerke Peninsula embraces an inlet that cuts deep into Bligh Island and protects a pretty cove at its inner reaches. Over 2 miles of curving, narrow channel reduce the swells to insignificance and even the westerlies have a hard time making it into the inner part of the inlet. Tuck in behind the small islet located at the entrance to the inner basin, close to shore with a stern line and take repose in this sheltered refuge. From here the high mountains surrounding Nootka Sound can be seen looking down on the now nearly-deserted landscape where once a bustling seaport, and the centre of commerce on the entire northwest coast of America was situated. One can contemplate the historical significance of a place which was brought into such prominence simply because the skies cleared near here one day in March, 1778.

16   Discovery Point

Just inside the sound, on its southern entrance, a cove is formed between Burdwood Point and a point named after HMS *Discovery*, sailing in company with *Resolution* on their epic voyage. The anchorage is subject to westerly swells reaching around the point, but offers excellent protection from easterlies and southwesterlies that might make anchorage a bit rolly in Friendly Cove, 2½ miles across the sound. Keep clear of the shoals and rocks on the south shore of the anchorage, and get as far into the cove as possible to get out of the swells. The holding ground is sand, and there is a small beach at the head of the cove worth exploring. This anchorage is at the base of the infamous Hesquiat Peninsula, the third of the trio of difficult passages on the west coast (Cape Scott and Cape Cook being the other two). From here you can wait for favourable weather before tackling what many consider to be the worst of the three, a peninsula which also entertained significant figures in the history of this remarkable coast.

LOCAL CAUTIONS
- The anchorage at the former settlement of Nootka has a number of submerged pilings and cables. Refer carefully to Chart #3664 when anchoring here.
- The long fetch of Muchalat Inlet can cause choppy, uncomfortable seas when heading against the wind.
- The public float at Gold River can get rough when winds oppose the river flow.

Captain Cook's arrival in Resolution Cove. Painting by John Horton.

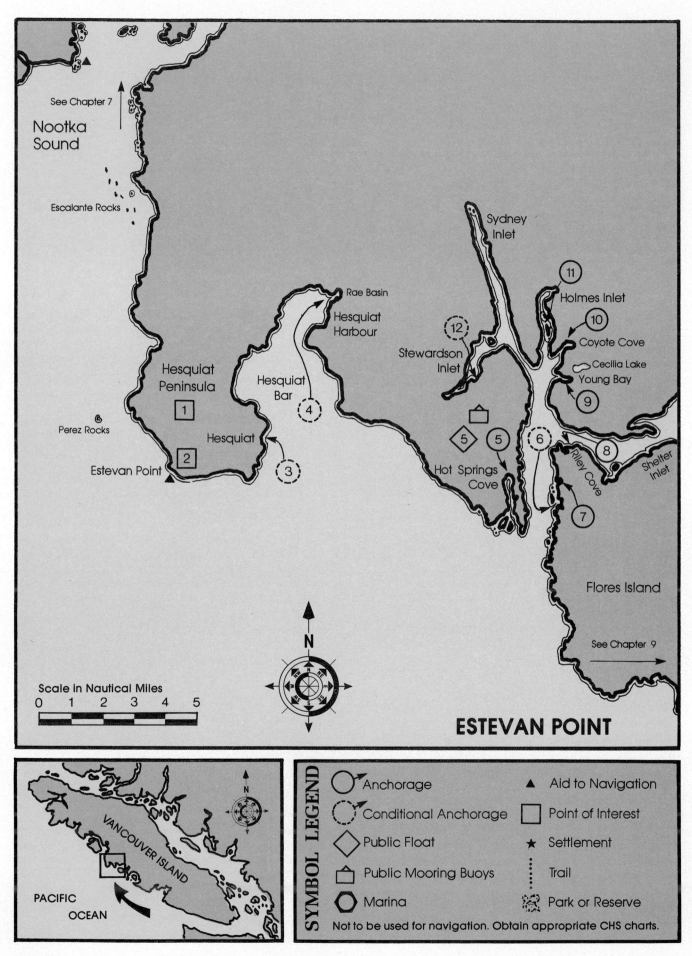

See Chapter 7

Nootka
Sound

Escalante Rocks

Sydney
Inlet

⑪

Holmes Inlet

Rae Basin

Hesquiat
Harbour

⑫

⑩

Stewardson
Inlet

Coyote Cove

Hesquiat
Peninsula

Cecilia Lake
Young Bay

1️⃣

Hesquiat
Bar

④

⑨

Perez Rocks

5️⃣

⑤

⑥

Hesquiat

Hot Springs
Cove

⑧

2️⃣

③

Riley Cove

Shelter
Inlet

Estevan Point

⑦

Flores Island

Scale in Nautical Miles

0 1 2 3 4 5

N

See Chapter 9

ESTEVAN POINT

PACIFIC
OCEAN

VANCOUVER ISLAND

SYMBOL LEGEND

◯→ Anchorage

⬭→ Conditional Anchorage

◇ Public Float

⌂ Public Mooring Buoys

⬡ Marina

▲ Aid to Navigation

☐ Point of Interest

★ Settlement

⋮ Trail

Park or Reserve

Not to be used for navigation. Obtain appropriate CHS charts.

CHAPTER EIGHT

Estevan Point

Hesquiat, Hot Springs Cove, Flores Island

Of the three challenging passages on the west coast of Vancouver Island, many feel that Estevan Point consistently gives the most trouble. Strangely enough, the point on the end of Hesquiat Peninsula which juts out into the Pacific 8 miles from the prevailing shoreline is not referred to as a cape. Still, in all aspects it should be treated as one, with all the respect you would give to Cape Scott or Cape Cook. The reasons for this formidable reputation are related to its topography, its geographical location, and its propensity for being a magnet for sudden squalls. At the same time, with a measure of caution, the hazards can be reduced to a minimum, and there are points of interest in and around the area which deserve exploration and appreciation. What follows is a description of the hazards and sights of the inner-reaches of this intriguing section of the coastline — including a trip to the west coast's famous hot spring pools and waterfall.

1   Hesquiat Peninsula

Although Captain Cook achieved notoriety for landing at Nootka in 1778, he was not the first to sail this coast. Four years before Cook, a Spaniard named Juan Perez (on the ship *Santiago*) was sent on a mission to investigate the Russian intrusion on Spain's sovereign shores in the north. He landed on the shores of Alaska and there is evidence that he also made contact with the local Hesquiat Indians, trading small items. Before he could get ashore, or make sustained contact, a sudden storm hit, and it was all he could do to save his ship from the lee shore, and the jagged rocks off what he called San Lorenzo Bay. Squalls occur sporadically along the outer coast, even during the summer months. When they blow against the tide which ebbs out of large sounds like Nootka, the rolling sea becomes a mixture of wind-blown waves and chop. In relatively shallow water, such as the underwater ledge off Hesquiat Peninsula, the added ground-swell forms a confused, often steep-sided sea that creates havoc for small craft. Even the corvette *Santiago*, the first ship in this area, experienced the difficulties of being off Hesquiat in bad conditions.

In addition to the shelf surrounding the peninsula, several dangerous rocks lie as much as 1½ miles offshore. The most dangerous of these are Escalante Rocks, and Perez Rocks (formerly known as Sunday Rock). The latter are particularly hazardous because they are on the direct route between Nootka Sound and Estevan Point. The peninsula itself (as described on the chart) is "low featureless country", which creates the deception that you are farther from shore than you really are (and therefore closer to the rocks). If the weather is clear, you will notice that Escalante Rocks appear to form a "stairway"; the rocks descend like a series of steps and disappear into the water. It is not known for certain whether these rocks were named for their appearance (escalante being Spanish for "climbing" or "stairway") or after the Franciscan friar Escalante who was in Nootka during the Spanish occupation. After seeing the rocks, it is very easy to support the "stairway" concept, although it is quite possible that both factors may have been involved in the naming by Eliza in 1791. The name for the peninsula originated in the words "Heish-heish-a" which means "to tear asunder with the teeth". Along this coast, eelgrass drifts onto shore in large quantities, especially when the herring spawn. The natives tore the grass with their teeth, to extract the spawn, which they considered a delicacy. They thus became known as "Heish-kwi-ahts", from whence the peninsula and their principal village were named.

2   Estevan Point

Named by Perez on his visit here after Estevan Martinez, his second lieutenant on the *Santiago*, this point made the history books again during World War II. Located 15 miles south of Friendly Cove, this rugged, reef-strewn area (which was named "Breakers Point" by Cook) is marked by the west coast's tallest lighthouse (125 ft). The station gained national attention as the only place in Canada to come under enemy attack, when it was shelled by a Japanese submarine *(I-26)* on June 20, 1942. After the first shells hit the beach in front of the lighthouse, the lightkeeper, Mr. R. M. Lally, doused the light and for about 40 tense minutes, shell after shell (from a 5½-in. gun) whistled past the structure. Several shells (each weighing about 80 lb) landed beyond the radio station, in the vicinity of the Hesquiat Indian village. Fortunately, throughout the entire incident, no casualties and very little damage was recorded. It did, however, bring the reality of the war home to Canadians coast to coast.

When rounding the point, it is a good idea to stay well off to avoid the effect of the groundswell and the unmarked Perez Rocks. If the weather gets bad and the point becomes obscured by rain or fog you can count on the radio beacon to be strong and clear. A radio direction finder (RDF) can reaffirm your position when the light itself is obscured. When the RDF is used in conjunction with other aids (such as depth-sounder and compass) a fix is usually easy to determine, even off the moody Hesquiat Peninsula. The adverse weather conditions here caused Perez to miss being the first to set foot on these shores — an honor bestowed on Cook four years later as a result of the same fickle winds that blow along this coast. Even today when a favourable forecast is made for a passage around the point, the weather can change radically in the three hours or so it takes to get there from Nootka Sound. Be prepared for a rough trip or to turn back if a stiff southwesterly meets you at the point.

3   Hesquiat

Once safely around Estevan Point (a trip that seems to take longer than the distance would dictate), a large harbour opens up on the port side. Just inside the

The West Coast's tallest lighthouse — Estevan Point — was the only place in Canada to come under enemy attack during World War II.

106

peninsula, the bell-tower of an old Catholic Church catches your eye. The church has been an important fixture at this location since Reverend A.J. Brabant established the west coast's first mission here over 100 years ago. After visiting several Indian villages along the coast, the priest chose to establish the mission at Hesquiat primarily because of its central location and the willingness of the natives to learn more about his teachings. With the religious zeal typical of all missionaries in the nineteenth century, Brabant set out to, in his words, "civilize the savages" by showing them what he considered the sinfulness of their heathen practices. He learned the language and wrote accounts of their customs and traditions, giving us a record of native life on the coast during this transitional period of their history. Unfortunately, in his zeal to fulfill his quest, he also ordered the destruction of many totems and other religious artifacts which he considered "ungodly". Still, his diary, collected under the title "Vancouver Island and its Missions" has become an important chronicle of the cultural traditions of the west coast people, the Nootka. It has been republished under several titles, the most recent edited by Charles Lillard, entitled "Mission to Nootka."

The first mission (no longer standing) was built with timbers from the unfortunate barque *Edwin*, which grounded on the peninsula in December 1874 with its load of lumber, at the cost of four lives. Today

Rae Basin is the most secure anchorage in Hesquiat Harbour, but it means crossing a potentially troublesome bar at the entrance.

you can anchor directly off the village in about 20 ft of water, usually in the company of the local native fishboats. There are no public floats or facilities here, but if you choose to dinghy ashore, you will be welcomed by friendly people whose ancestors survived the smallpox epidemic which nearly devastated the entire village in the nineteenth century. Just west of Matlahaw Point on one of the foreshore rocks, there is a petroglyph (rock carving). A trail continues along the shore all the way past Estevan Point to the abandoned native village at Homais Cove. Groups of canoeists and kayakers often camp along the shores of the village, and wild cows — remnants of early farming attempts — still roam the peninsula.

4 Hesquiat Harbour

In order to get into the protected inner waters of Hesquiat Harbour it is necessary to cross over Hesquiat Bar. The shallows stretch right across the mouth of the harbour with kelp-covered rocks and shoals ranging from 12-20 ft below low water. In bad weather it is dangerous to cross the bar; seas can break heavily over it. In moderate conditions, however, this bar serves to break up the swell, making the harbour a more pleasant anchorage than it might otherwise be.

Hesquiat village was site of the first Roman Catholic Mission on the west coast, established during the 1870s.

Because of the depths, anchorage is possible almost anywhere in the bay, although the attractions there (i.e. beaches and caves along the shoreline) suggest that you should anchor as close to shore as draft will allow. The most sheltered part of the harbour is at the head of the bay, in the sheltered nook known as Rae Basin. Here there is protection from winds and waves, but access to and from the basin is subject to crossing the bar, so it must be considered a conditional anchorage.

Archeologists studying the burial caves along the shoreline have determined that a native of this area had a life expectancy of little more than 21 years. The Hesquiat Band has removed all cultural and skeletal items from the caves due to vandalism, so it is now possible to visit the caves without violating their sanctity. Get permission from the band members at Hesquiat before entering them. Remnants of a pathway known as "Smuggler's Trail" may still be seen along the shores of the harbour all the way to Hot Springs Cove.

5   Hot Springs Cove

If nature has made Estevan Point a tough and moody obstacle to easy passage down this coast, then she has balanced her debt by providing a safe harbour a few miles away, with one of her truly rare and remarkable creations — a steady stream of hot water emanating from an inconspicuous hole in the ground and tumbling down over the black rocks straight into the sea. Hot Springs Cove is the west coast cruiser's mecca. For many, it is the highlight of the trip, a reward for those who go down to the sea in yachts and successfully negotiate the outer reaches of our rugged coastline.

The simple fact that the springs provide an endless supply of hot fresh running water is enough to draw sailors, fishermen, loggers, natives, and now even landlubbers who can afford the roundtrip by float plane from Tofino. There is no doubt that the 122°F

water which cascades down into a series of therapeutic pools at 100 gallons per minute is an irresistible drawing-card for anyone with the means of getting there. At high tide, the ocean swells roll into the lower pools, cooling them down for those who prefer their bath more tepid. The sensation of being in one of the hot pools as a great Pacific swell rolls in and temporarily wraps its cold fingers around you is quite unusual. If you like to stew in water a bit hotter, simply take residence in a pool higher up, where the ocean waters cannot reach. For those who like it really hot, make your way over the slippery rocks and stand directly beneath the small waterfall. The heat and the weight of the waters act like a heavenly Jacuzzi, soothing the aches and bumps accumulated on the voyage. The water smells of sulphur, but is clean and fresh, making an ideal stop for cleaning both bodies and clothes. However, since the place has been "discovered", it is difficult to find a time when the pools are not crowded with people of all ages in various states of undress. Twice-daily flights by Pacific Rim Airlines out of Tofino (604-725-3295) directly to the Cove have made it accessible to almost anyone, and the flights are often fully-booked.

Highlight to any west coast expedition is a stop at Hot Springs Cove, here experienced as it should be...

Although it is true that the solitude of the place has been lost, it is interesting to mingle in a relaxed atmosphere with strangers from all walks of life. The springs are part of Maquinna Provincial Park, thanks to the generous donations of land by Ivan Clarke in 1954 enabling the government to assemble the essential parts of the park. Mr. Clarke was a local resident who established the general store in the cove over 50 years ago. The store, school, and post office no longer exist, although the derelict buildings still stand. The ancestral name for the hot spring is "Mok-se-kla-chuk", meaning "smoking water", and there is evidence to suggest that the Indians knew of its therapeutic value centuries ago and used the springs to treat a variety of ailments.

The entry to Hot Springs Cove is straightforward. There are few offlying dangers, and aids to navigation mark both sides of the entrance to the harbour. Stay in the middle of the channel to avoid the few submerged rocks which lie close to shore on either side. The expanded chart (#3643) gives a clear outline of the cove, as well as expanded views of Hayden Passage, Matilda Inlet, and Tofino, making it important for navigating these waters. Large-scale harbour charts are extremely useful everywhere on the coast, but more particularly as we approach Clayoquot Sound, which is fraught with shallows and strong currents.

The two public floats have a total dockage space of over 700 ft but these can still get crammed with fishing and pleasure boats in the summer, necessitating rafting. Garbage can build up at the wharf, collection is infrequent, so be prepared to keep your trash from

Public floats and mooring buoys provide shore-access at Hot Springs Cove. A floating store is sometimes on hand.

110

preciation of the springs. Sunset there is also a spectacular experience.

When leaving Hot Springs Cove towards Tofino, there are two common routes: the inside passage up Sydney and Shelter Inlets, or around the outside of Flores Island.

A rough trail leads from Hot Springs Cove to the bubbling waters about 1½ miles away.

6 Sydney Inlet

The western entrance to the intricate and historically rich Clayoquot Sound is a beautiful, sheltered fjord indented in a number of places by small, private anchorages. When leaving Hot Springs Cove and entering the inlet, be careful as you round Sharp Point: there are two detached rocks, one close off the point, and a more dangerous rock almost ½-mile off the point. Neither of the rocks are marked by aids to navigation. A wind generator powers the fog horn and light on the point. On the east side of the inlet, on Flores Island, the Provincial Parks Branch has set aside about 410 acres as a possible addition to Maquinna Park. Unfortunately the proposed park area does not contain any useable anchorage for yachts, although kayakers and canoeists enjoy the beach and sheltered upland for camping. However, just north of the boundaries of the park are two fine, unnamed anchorages worth visiting.

The first of these refuges is due north of the Indian Reserve (#28) shown on Chart #3648, and sports a fresh stream, an interesting shoreline, and numerous small islets covered with mussels and barnacles. The anchorage is also blessed with a small beach, so any yacht anchoring here could easily enjoy the beach in complete privacy, or languish in the charms of Hot Springs Cove, just 2½ miles away. Anchor in 15 ft over sand in either the northwest or southwest corners of the cove, depending on the shelter desired. The only drawback to the anchorage is its exposure to swells emanating from the south. Though they are dissipated, they can cause the anchorage to roll slightly.

Entrance to Hot Springs Cove is straightforward; there are few offlying dangers.

adding to the piles. The five public mooring buoys just north of the public float are not indicated on the charts. Anchorage is secure throughout the cove (its former name was Refuge Cove) in 15 to 30 ft over mud, so even in a crowd there is always room to set your own groundtackle. On the west side of the harbour a small group of modern houses is cut out of the woods. The Alaskan earthquake in 1964 caused a tsunami (seismic wave) to funnel up the inlet, and many Indians at the head of the cove lost their residences.

The public float is on the east side of the cove, on the Openit Peninsula, where the springs are located. The springs are not located right at the public float area. A 1½ mile walk over a very rough trail maintained by the Ministry of Highways is the required penance for visiting the springs. The trail seems about twice as long on the return trip when, after an hour or so in the hot waters, the muscles in the legs are replaced by something akin to rubber. Still, the walk through the second growth over the rickety boardwalk trail heightens the anticipation and ap-

7 Flores Island

Less than a mile north of the small anchorage on Sydney Inlet is an even smaller nook with just enough space for one yacht to find complete shelter. The chart (#3648) shows a 3 ft rock in the middle of the entrance with a narrow, but clear passage on either side. Contrary to what the chart shows, the deeper channel is actually on the north side of the rock, though both are navigable. Once inside, anchor in the middle of this almost totally landlocked harbour. The holding ground is mud, and the swell that rolls into some of the outer anchorages does not penetrate this cove, making it an ideal refuge in all weather.

Flores Island itself is a very large island (second in size only to Nootka Island) with its central mountains reaching to 3000 ft. While its south and west shores rise only gradually to the peaks, its north and east sides rise abruptly. The shores are impressive because the dense uncut green borders directly with the beaches on the exposed shores of the island. It was named in 1791 by the Spanish Lieutenant Eliza after the Viceroy of Mexico, Don Manuel Flores, who dispatched Martinez to take over Nootka in 1789, sparking the Nootka controversy.

8 Riley Cove

Proceeding north up Sydney Inlet, usually with the winds from behind, will bring you to Starling Point, marking the entrance to Shelter Inlet. Immediately east of the point on the northwest tip of Flores Island is a small, sheltered cove with several interesting ruins to explore. Use your depth sounder to find the 24 ft mud bank deep in the cove before setting your anchor. A stern anchor or line to shore would be useful here. The overhead cable marked on Chart #3648 no longer exists, although the ruins of one of the west coast's 26 fish reduction plants still occupy the shoreline. The cove was named after Reece Riley, a pioneer of Clayoquot Sound who came here from Colorado in 1898 to establish a boat repair shop and marine ways. He was later known for operating a number of launches from the cove taking a variety of prospectors, timber cruisers and mining engineers to the remote inlets around the sound. He got to know the sound better than any other resident, and assisted in opening up the west coast to industry.

9 Young Bay

Three miles further up Sydney Inlet is another protected anchorage, also the site of a pilchard reduction plant at one time. Entry is straightforward with no dangerous hazards to avoid, and anchorage ranges from 54 ft at the centre of the bay, to 30 ft near the shore. Because of the shelter afforded by the multitude of peaks surrounding these inlets, an anchor

---

Opposite: Sydney Inlet and the anchorage across from Hot Springs Cove

Pretty pocket beach on Flores Island is best for kayakers only.

Dense, uncut coastal vegetation abuts the waters edge in Flores Island anchorage.

Riley Cove (above) takes its name from that of an early pioneer who established a marine repair yard and ways on its shores. Young Bay (below) once site of a 1930s era pilchard reduction plant affords access to inland stream and lake suitable for bathing.

dropped in these coves stays right where it is put. Usually there isn't enough wind to even straighten the chain. The islet in the bay still sports the concrete foundations of the wharf serving the reduction plant once located here, though the wooden buildings and wharf have long since disintegrated. A stream flows into the bay from Cecilia Lake, just ¼-mile away, an easy walk. This large freshwater lake is clean and a good place to swim, bathe, or wash clothes. Wildlife abounds in the area; deer, weasels and kingfishers make regular appearances.

10 "Coyote" Cove

In the more remote inlets you often get the impression that you are the first to ever set groundtackle in the soft mud of one of its coves. That impression is reinforced by the immense silence, shattered only occasionally by the haunting cry of an eagle proclaiming his territory. On shore, trees tower silently over the scene, their proud crowns reaching for the distant sun. The tide enters the cove, bringing suspended nutrients for the immobile shellfish clinging in dense patches to the rocks. Small fish dart in and out of the shallows. Wherever you look, nature seems to be proclaiming in capital letters, just one word: LIFE.

When trying to direct others to such places, difficulties arise because some of the best smallcraft anchorages are unnamed, even locally. Such a place is the inlet immediately north, between Young Bay and Holmes Inlet. It is a small indentation in the shoreline leading through a deep, but extremely narrow channel (75 ft wide), to a perfectly land-locked lagoon. The shores are dense with the virgin green that only a Pacific coast rainforest can generate. The bottom is soft mud about 27 ft below the placid calm

The author's Coyote Cove off Sydney Inlet.

of the lagoon which is warm enough to swim in. Since this beautiful cove had no name, I took the liberty of naming it "Coyote Cove", after my own 34 ft sloop. That name will not appear on any chart, but if you want to spend some time in this other-worldly place, far from the ravages of the west coast, then at least you can refer to it by a name.

11 Holmes Inlet

Beyond *Coyote* Cove to the north, a 2-mile inlet cuts even farther into the shoreline of Vancouver Island. There is no convenient anchorage at the head of the inlet unless you can locate the narrow 30 ft shelf near the edge of the shoals in Pretty Girl Cove. However the two islands that appear in the inlet create a nook where a totally secure anchorage can be found. The entrance to the refuge is between the small island labelled "215" and the main part of Vancouver Island. Here a small basin, 24 ft deep is surrounded by the verdant cloak of the quiet forest. The cove gives complete protection in even the wildest west coast weather. A small stream bubbles into the cove, accentuating the vibrant mood of the place. These small sheltered coves are such a change from the exposed outer shores that it's easy to forget where you are. More akin to the shelter of Desolation Sound than to the image of the west coast, it is still a part of the complex landscape mosaic that makes up the west coast. The incoming tide flows past this cove and out through a small channel back into the main part of Holmes Inlet. At high tide, the channel is navigable, even though you can touch the trees on either side as you pass through. Negotiating this tricky channel builds confidence, and creates a scale to measure which channels are wide enough to navigate.

12 Stewardson Inlet

Sydney Inlet continues past Adventure Point, but its precipitous shores offer no shelter or anchorage along its entire 5-mile length. The inlet terminates in a drying shoal that drops off suddenly to depths that make anchoring extremely inconvenient. However, the steep-sided inlet is among the prettiest of the west coast fjords, and a side trip here is sure to provide breathtaking views. The mountains punctuate the skyline in a series of peaks and cones, rising dramatically from the depths of the inlet to heights of more than 2500 ft.

If you want to nestle in the arms of these mountains there is one small nook in Stewardson Inlet (the southwest branch of Sydney Inlet) where, with determination, you could find anchorage. Because of the convolutions of the coastline here and the heights of the peaks, no real wind or sea can build up in the inlets, rendering otherwise marginal anchorages into feasible destinations. You can find a small refuge at the very end of Stewardson Inlet, or on the south side where a small headland contains a cove which is suitable for one boat. Streams cascading down the

The West Coast is rife with such tantalizing areas for exploration as Pretty Girl Cove on Holmes Inlet.

steep slopes have pushed enough sand and gravel into the inlet to create a 12 ft patch in this nook where a yacht could be secured.

Across the inlet, the ruins of a copper mine can just be made out on the shoreline. It is interesting to note that actually fewer people populate the shores of the west coast than there were 50 years ago. Mines have closed, logging camps have moved on, and modern refrigeration methods have reduced the number of packing plants needed to can or keep fish fresh. Throughout the inlets on the west coast are ruins of one doomed enterprise after another, and while some struck it rich, most did not — at least not monetarily. The west coast has a way of making every visitor feel richer for the effort of going there to experience the western wilderness. The contrasts between the rugged shores and these remote inlets adds to the sense of adventure that one feels when visiting the west coast, and are part of the tapestry that makes this area totally unique.

LOCAL CAUTIONS

- Westerly winds opposing large ebb tides out of Nootka Sound can generate steep, choppy seas.
- Perez Rocks, off the Hesquiat Peninsula, are not marked and pose a hazard in poor weather.
- Shoals off Estevan Point can cause large ground swells close to shore. Stand off as far as the 20 fathom line to avoid problems.
- The passage from Friendly Cove to Estevan Point requires plotting on two separate charts. Take careful note of your position when changing charts.
- Hesquiat Bar at the entrance to Hesquiat Harbour can break in heavy weather. Do not attempt to cross it under foul conditions.

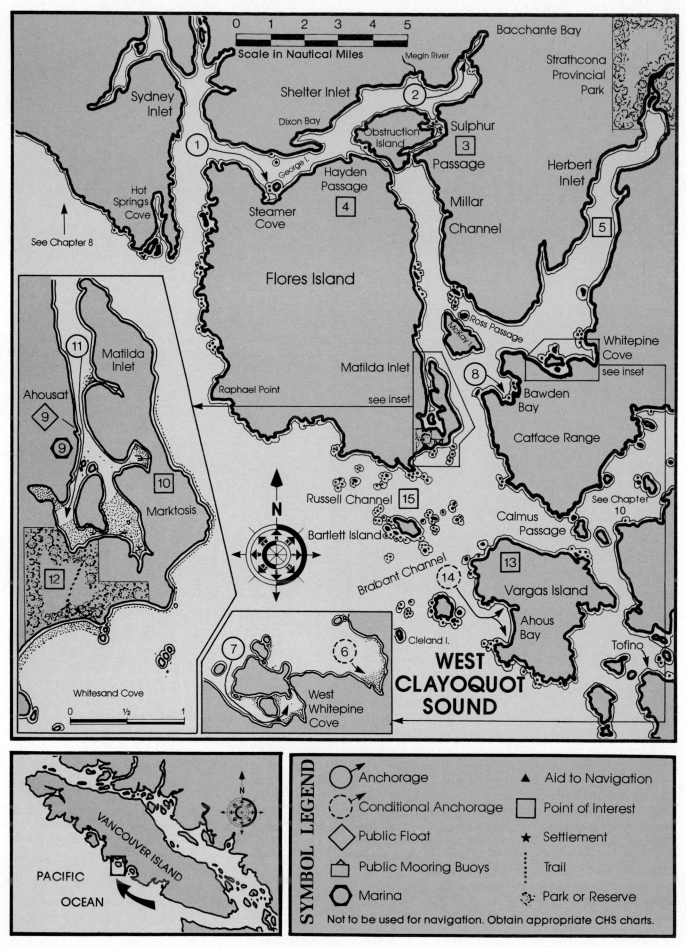

Scale in Nautical Miles
0 1 2 3 4 5

Bacchante Bay

Strathcona
Provincial
Park

Megin River

Shelter Inlet

②

Dixon Bay

①

Sydney
Inlet

Sulphur

③

Obstruction
Island

Passage

Herbert
Inlet

Millar

⑤

Hayden
Passage

④

Channel

George I.

Steamer
Cove

Hot
Springs
Cove

See Chapter 8

Ross Passage

McKay I.

Whitepine
Cove

see inset

⑧

Flores Island

Matilda Inlet

Bawden
Bay

⑪

Matilda
Inlet

see inset

Catface Range

Ahousat

Raphael Point

⑨

⑨

See Chapter
10

⑩

Russell Channel

⑮

Calmus
Passage

Marktosis

N

⑬

Bartlett Island

⑭

Vargas Island

⑫

Brabant Channel

Ahous
Bay

Tofino

⑦

⑥

Cleland I.

WEST
CLAYOQUOT
SOUND

Whitesand Cove

West
Whitepine
Cove

0   ½   1

PACIFIC

OCEAN

VANCOUVER ISLAND

N

SYMBOL LEGEND

◯ Anchorage   ▲ Aid to Navigation

◯ Conditional Anchorage   ☐ Point of Interest

◇ Public Float   ★ Settlement

⬠ Public Mooring Buoys   ⋮ Trail

⬡ Marina   Park or Reserve

Not to be used for navigation. Obtain appropriate CHS charts.

116

CHAPTER NINE

Clayoquot Sound

Steamer Cove, Ahousat, Matilda Cove

Clayoquot Sound, with its myriad channels, inlets and islands is almost as closely associated with the early history of this coast as Nootka. It was the ancestral home of Wickaninnish, chief of the Clayoquots, a powerful tribe because of the wealth of natural resources available in the region they controlled. Captain Charles Barkley (Barkley Sound) named it Wickaninnish's Sound after the great chief, but to their neighbours they were the "Cla-o-quahts", from the root words "clao", meaning "different" and "aht", meaning people or place. According to Indian tradition, the inhabitants were originally quiet and peaceful, but later became quarrelsome and treacherous; hence they became known as the Clayoquots ("different people").

The area controlled by these people was filled with beauty and an abundance of resources unmatched anywhere on the coast. Clayoquot Sound has steep-sided fjords, volcanic cones, sheltered harbours, shifting sandbanks, the best beaches on the coast, several salmon rivers and large shellfish beds. The great whales migrating up the coast gave the Nootka whalers a wealth of food, as well as an opportunity to develop their culture and great power.

Today the bounty of the land remains for those who can get there to enjoy it. However, there are shallow sandbanks to avoid, sweeping currents to negotiate, as well as the notorious fog which can plague the coast at any season. So, unless your means of travel is by canoe, like the original inhabitants, extra caution must be applied when cruising this area. It is unlike any other part of the coast. Clayoquot Sound can be entered from seaward from any one of four separate channels, or via Sydney Inlet, the "back way" behind Flores Island. This northwest entrance will be discussed first.

1 Steamer Cove

When heading north up Sydney Inlet, you will probably have following winds; the prevailing westerlies — whether northwest or southwest — get funnelled by the local topography and blow up the channels. Once behind the 2500 ft peaks of Flores Island, however, the water becomes as calm as a lagoon, and the winds extremely light. This arm of the sound is appropriately called Shelter Inlet. About 2 miles into the inlet, on the south shore, is a small bay with four small islands in its opening. The bay is deep, but if you continue right around to the southwest corner, an ideal small-craft harbour opens up. Steamer Cove is used extensively by local workboats because it is almost always completely sheltered. The inner part of the cove has a mud bottom beneath 30 ft of calm water, but unfortunately the entire area has been recently logged, detracting from the aesthetics of the harbour.

When leaving Steamer Cove, you can pass either side of George Islands, both channels are deep. Two miles further into Shelter Inlet another bay opens up on the Vancouver Island shoreline to the north. However, most of this (Dixon Bay) is over 300 ft deep, and only when you are a few yards from shore is the water

Protection of Flores Island provides calm waters for appropriately named Shelter Inlet.

At the head of Shelter Inlet amid some of the West Coast's highest peaks is the all-weather anchorage of Bacchante Bay.

shallow enough for anchoring. The low-lying land at the head of the cove offers little protection from any winds, so Dixon Bay is not recommended as an anchorage. However, nature has provided a sheltered haven in the area for those who wish the solitude and shelter of these remote fjords, just 5 miles further up the inlet. Along the way you might also try the trout fishing off the Megin River, which is reported to be good, although there is no secure anchorage there.

2 Bacchante Bay

This small bay — actually the head of Shelter Inlet — lies in the shadow of some of the west coast's highest peaks. It has a narrow entrance, and is completely protected from wind-driven seas and ocean swells. A creek flows into the head of the inlet, filling the bay with the mud which gives it such good holding ground. The ancestral Clayoquots regularly fished the stream, adding salmon to their already ample diet. This pretty little bay is now deserted, and lies waiting for the twentieth century adventurer to rediscover its attractions. When negotiating the shallow entrance, keep to the west shore. There is an unmarked submerged rock just east of the middle of the channel at the entrance.

3 Sulphur Passage

From Shelter Inlet there are two passages into Millar Channel enroute to Tofino and the rest of Clayoquot Sound. The easterly route twists in a zigzag around Obstruction Island and is encumbered by rocks. Because of the rocks and shoals throughout the passage, the channel is used mainly by small runabouts with local knowledge. Although the passage is not recommended, it is certainly navigable if one adheres closely to Chart #3448. It is not necessary to expose a yacht to this hazard, however. The main channel, clearly shown on the expanded chart (#3643), lies just 2 miles to the west.

4 Hayden Passage

The main navigable passage between Millar Channel and Shelter Inlet is so important, and used so frequently that it is listed as a secondary current station in the Hydrographic Service tide books. The channel connects two of the west coast's deepest fjords, and currents here can run 4 knots, in both directions. The flood tides meet at the northwest part of Hayden Passage and their meeting point is usually quite visible. When transiting the channel, wait until slack tide before heading through. The submerged rocks are clearly shown on the chart (#3643) but keep an eye on sideways drift as you pass through. The currents can push you off your plotted course and close to the rocks off Obstruction Island. Once clear of the narrows, the waters of Millar Channel again open up, and there is very little tidal influence.

Preceding page: View north over Clayoquot Sound, Blunden Island in foreground.

Opposite page: Rock-choked Sulphur Passage is one of two routes around Obstruction Island. The other is Hayden Passage.

Looking over West Whitepine Cove and Herbert Inlet.

Canadian Coast Guard vessels maintain west coast aids to navigation.

5   Herbert Inlet

Small craft can enter Herbert Inlet by going the long way between Bawden Point and McKay Island or by taking the more intricate Ross Passage. With the exception of Gibson Cove on the east side of the inlet (a marginal anchorage) the extreme depth (on average, over 450 ft) makes anchorage difficult even for the larger coastal freighters. Bedingfield Bay is deep and has foul ground and booms at its head. The head of Herbert Inlet known as Moyeha Bay is a good fishing area, and was once the site of several hundred gold claims. Two mines eventually came into production, but little ore was ever shipped. Moyeha Bay is the only part of Strathcona Park (B.C.'s oldest Provincial Park) that reaches tidewater. It is too deep for practical anchorage and there are no facilities here for campers or yachtsmen.

6   Whitepine Cove

One of the few places within the deep fjords of Clayoquot Sound where the average yacht's anchor can find bottom, is Whitepine Cove, a somewhat open bay which, although picturesque, offers little shelter. Close to shore the water shallows up to an acceptable 42 ft over a gravel bottom. It is open to the west but since the winds don't usually howl in these inlets, anchorage is acceptable here, and you are sure to have the cove to yourself. Take care to avoid Sutlej Rock on the south side of the cove, the only unmarked danger as you enter. If you like a more sheltered anchorage, ideal for small craft, a small un-named cove lies a mile to the west beneath the benevolent slopes of the Catface Range.

7 West Whitepine Cove

Although this ideal sheltered anchorage is un-named, the entrance is immediately west of Whitepine Cove and could be considered part of that cove. There is a great deal of difference between the two anchorages: the western one is completely protected from both winds and waves. If you tuck in behind the islet marked "240" you will find a completely land-locked lagoon with a mud bottom beneath 18 ft of glassy calm water. There is a small beach, and a stream flows into the head of the cove. Don't go in too close to the shore, there are shoals on all sides; stay in the middle of the lagoon for secure moorage. Entry to the lagoon is north of the 60 ft islet on the south part of the entrance, but stay close to the larger islet to avoid the shoals on the south shore. The shoals are shown clearly on Chart #3648.

8 Bawden Bay

Another 2 miles west of Whitepine Cove is a bay with a convoluted shoreline, sprinkled with several small islets. In the southeast corner of this bay is a small nook, clear of dangers, ideal for a small boat to find secure anchorage. The backdrop here is the steep slopes of the multi-coned Catface Range. A good-size stream flows into the little cove, and the trickle of the water echoes throughout the cool quiet of night.

The bay was named after Charles Bawden, R.N., the master of several ships on this coast, and around the world. Bawden Bay was the site of one of the Indian villages which were shelled by the ships *Sutlej* and *Devastation* in retaliation for the attack by the natives on the trading schooner *Kingfisher* at Matilda Inlet, 3 miles to the west.

9 Ahousat

At the southern entrance to Millar Channel — between the McNeil Peninsula and the main part of Flores Island — is one of the most protected harbours in Clayoqout Sound, a thriving Indian village, the west coast's only Provincial Marine Park, natural springs and a public float with a store and marina. The float and store are on the west side of Matilda Inlet, which is best entered using the large scale chart (#3643). The inlet is narrow and a few rocks lie close to shore that can be easily picked out on the expanded chart. A black spar buoy marks the edge of the rock shoal near the narrow part of the inlet.

Ahousat is the ancestral name of the tribe of Clayoquots who resided in this area centuries ago. Although today the main village is on the other side of the inlet, the general store and marina still retain this name. Originally the native "A-hous-ahts" lived on the shores of Vargas Island, facing the open sea, where they were known in their native tongue as "the people living with their backs to the land and the mountains".

There is plenty of docking space; two floats give almost 200 ft of moorage for visitors to the store. Fuel and water are available, and the General Store, like most on the coast, sells everything from fresh produce to fishing gear, although no liquor is available here. Fuel prices here are about the same as Tofino, 14 miles to the southeast, and service just as quick and friendly. There are postal and telephone services, and the marine ways can haul boats up to 44 ft. The store also serves the large Indian village of Marktosis on the east side of the inlet, and small runabouts buzz across the inlet at all hours filling the role of the automobile in this isolated marine community.

Bawden Bay was the site of a retaliatory attack on a nearby native village by Royal Navy ships in last century.

Facilities at Ahousat (foreground) on southeastern shore of Flores Island also serve the Indian village at Marktosis across Matilda Inlet.

Top: *Overview of Matilda Inlet, Clayoquot Sound with Marktosis village pictured at centre. Above: Conditional anchorage at Marktosis village can be found off eastern Flores Island beach in foreground.*

10   Marktosis

One of the biggest entirely native Indian villages on the coast is located in a small cove cut into the west side of the McNeil Peninsula — a cove with a 4½-ft deep entrance which is also narrow and rock-strewn. As the "Sailing Directions" describes it, "no attempt should be made to approach Marktosis from Matilda Inlet unless in possession of local knowledge." The advice should truly be heeded; even the expanded chart indicates the difficulty of entering the anchorage. However, the village itself is interesting and can be visited by dinghy, or by anchoring (temporarily) on the eastern shore of the McNeil Peninsula on the sandbank which forms on the outer shore. Marktosis is a name derived from "Mak-yak-sats", meaning "coffin" or "Mak-yak-witl", meaning "to bury". In ancestral times this site was the burial ground for the now extinct tribe of "out-sos-aht" Indians who once lived on Flores Island. Today you can visit the cemetery where more contemporary gravestones mark the graves of deceased natives. As is the custom, some of the graves are decorated by possessions of the deceased, including a rusty sewing machine, a tricycle,

and a favourite pair of shoes. There is a trail (½ mile of bush, and ½ mile of shoreline) from Marktosis to the springs in Gibson Marine Park. It is crude, and not maintained, but passable.

11   Matilda Inlet

Using the large scale chart you can carefully make your way deeper into the inlet to find complete shelter in an ideal harbour. Keep to the extreme western side of the inlet to avoid the hazards in the fairway, but don't go too far into the inlet, the mud bank at the head of the inlet extends over 1400 ft from the high water mark, and dries completely. When you reach the 15 ft depth (low tide) you're as close as you can get to shore without doing any unplanned dredging or surveying with your keel. The eelgrass bed covering the mudbank, an important link in the food chain of Clayoquot Sound, shelters countless fish and crabs.

The anchorage here is so calm that an anchor rode usually remains vertical throughout the entire stay. Sitting in the calm silence of this refuge is one of the highlights of a west coast trip. Perhaps it is the contrast between the rugged outer shores with the restless swells and the placid calm of the inner fjords with their brooding peaks and penetratingly green panoramas. Hummingbirds buzz curiously about the anchorage and eagle cries become as familiar as the sunset. Alone at anchor here, a yacht could provide the perfect setting for some yet unmade film on the Canadian wilderness.

It is hard to imagine that this was the site of violence when a subchief of the Clayoquots (Cap-Chap by name) attacked the schooner *Kingfisher*, killing its captain and crew in 1864. When the news reached Victoria, ships were dispatched to rout the culprits. Several villages were flattened, 15 natives killed and several prisoners taken for trial, but all were acquitted. Cap-Chap was never found, and lived in a secret hiding place for many years afterwards. Shells fired into the villages from the *Sutlej* and *Devastation* are still found near the villages, and some can be seen in the maritime museum in Victoria.

12   Gibson Marine Park

Once securely anchored in Matilda Inlet, a variety of attractions await you on shore. Perhaps the most famous of these are the sulphur springs at the head of the inlet. Although neither as hot nor as dramatic as the hot springs further up the coast, the warm fresh water is just as welcome. Look for what appears to be the concrete foundation of a small house on the grassy southwest corner of the inlet — this is actually the pool which has been built to contain the tepid waters (77°F) of the spring. It is approximately 8x20 ft square, 4½ ft deep, somewhere between a small swimming pool and a large bathtub. It is used regularly as both by visiting yachtsmen, and locals. Its waters are drinkable at the source, which flows at the rate of 2½ gal per minute.

From this "warm spring" a rough trail leads to one

Soothing man-made bath at head of Matilda Inlet is fed by tepid sulphur spring nearby.

Whitesand Beach in Gibsons Marine Park can be reached over rough trail from Matilda Cove (background).

of the finest beaches on the entire west coast, appropriately named, Whitesand Beach. The trail, marked by surveyor's tape, is about ½-mile long, and covers some pretty swampy ground, so take your boots, not your sneakers or deckshoes. The reward for your trek is an almost perfect sweeping arc of a beach, facing the islands which mark the southern entrances to Clayoquot Sound. There is enough shelter from the offlying shoals and islets to disperse the large crashing waves that ravage other west coast beaches; this semi-private beach has an easy, rolling wave action ideal for swimming and watersports. It is even more enticing because of the fine sand, and the fact that a freshwater bath is available on the way back to the boat. The government made a wise acquisition when they included the beach and springs in the marine park. Aside from the trail between the springs and the beach, there are no other developments in the park, although camping on the beach is a practical en-

deavour. The mile sweep of beach offers everything that is at Long Beach, further down the coast, plus the added attractions of privacy, and a spectacular view across Russell Channel to the wild islands on the seaward side of Clayoquot Sound. By tramping west of Whitesand Cove past Kutcous Point (watch the tides) you can get to the "outside" beaches which are great for exploring.

13 Vargas Island

Once you leave Matilda Inlet and head south towards Tofino, or the archipelago which forms the seaward entrance to Clayoquot Sound, you enter an area where extreme caution is warranted. It is different than any other part of the west coast, with hazards that few yachtsmen are familiar with. Glacial outwash from the last ice age has filled Clayoquot Sound with sand and rubble, creating shallows which pile up between the islands to form extensive submerged sandbanks. Tides swirl between these sandbanks as water rushes in and out of the island's deepest fjords. The first encounter with these sandbars occurs between the Catface Range and the southeast shore of Flores Island, where the water shoals up from 132 ft to 30 ft in less than a mile. Lines of crab traps dot the passages, their marker floats bending in a current that often resembles the flow of a river. Dozens of trap floats lie in the fairways of the channels, so a sharp lookout is needed to avoid wrapping your propeller

California grey whales often congregate off sand-fringed shores of Vargas Island (foreground) at entrance to Clayoquot Sound.

shaft with the lines attached to the traps. It is often very difficult to find a path through the traps without a lot of maneuvering at reduced speed. This short passage is an omen of things to come; traps are peppered throughout Clayoquot Sound all the way from Millar Channel to Tofino Inlet.

The same sand which creates the hazard of the submerged sandbars also covers the shores of the islands of the sound. One of the great cruising areas of the coast is in this maze of sandbars, islands and beaches and a favourite destination is the remarkably flat Vargas Island.

After crossing into Russell Channel you will be in water that rarely exceeds 40 ft for miles in either direction, so in theory you could anchor easily anywhere in this area of the sound, if conditions allow. On your way to Vargas Island, in Brabant Channel you might be able to drop your lunch hook near Bartlett Island to go ashore on a stretch of pure, golden sand completely surrounding the larger of the Whaler Islets. On a sunny day it resembles a South Pacific atoll (without the palm trees, of course).

Thousands of seabirds — including petrels, guillemots, and auklets — cover every bit of habitable rock and shoreline in this area. B.C.'s first ecological

126

reserve (Cleland Island) was established here in 1971 to protect the marine wildlife that makes its home in this area. And the greatest of all the sea creatures, the whales, often make an appearance here, much to the awe of any observer. The sand-fringed shores of Vargas Island are a common rendezvous for the California grey whales which stop on their annual migration to Alaska. A good place to observe these leviathans is Ahous Bay, the 1½-mile-long perfect beach on Vargas Island.

14 Ahous Bay

The ancestral home of the Ahousats was once located near Ahous Point, at the south end of this bay. Today a yacht can anchor as the natives did, "with their backs to the land and the mountains", to watch the sun set over foaming reefs and the open Pacific. Although the bay is somewhat protected by the reefs, and by Blunden and Cleland Islands, the surf can still

Former mission building at Kakawis on western Meares Island burned to the ground in 1983.

crash magnificently on the beach. When the winds are westerly, it may be difficult to land a dinghy, so make your landing in the protection of the rocky headlands at either end of the beach. The anchorage has a sand bottom, ranging in depth from 42 ft near the centre of the bay, to 25 ft nearer shore. Because the anchorage is completely open to the prevailing summer westerlies it should only be considered an anchorage in easterly winds.

If the whales are in the bay, be careful not to venture carelessly in the dinghy for a closer look. Although whales are not known to attack boats, a dinghy could easily be swamped by the giant tail of one of these cetaceans without the beast even knowing it. They can sometimes be seen browsing in beds of kelp, or rubbing themselves on the sand of bays such as this one. They also feed here on the marine worms and fish that make their homes on the bottom (grey whales are the only whales that feed mainly off the ocean floor).

Fortunately for visitors to Vargas Island, there is a recreation reserve on the shores of Ahous Bay extending all the way from Ahous Point to the beaches on the west and north sides of the island. This status reserves the land for the "use, recreation and enjoy-

ment of the public", and is often referred to as a U.R.E.P. Reserve. The report on Ahous Bay recommended that a strip of land around the shore be protected and left as a wilderness beach for public recreational use. After visiting this wild and beautiful place, one can appreciate the wisdom of establishing a reserve here.

15 Russell Channel

If you choose the "outside" route from Hot Springs Cove to Tofino around the south shore of Flores Island, you will have four separate channels to choose from in making your entrance from seaward. The most direct, and clearest of these is Russell Channel, between Flores and Bartlett Islands. Skirting the west coast of Flores Island will treat your eyes to an island with a cloak of untouched green ringed by a necklace of white foam. Flores Island's south shore is a ribbon of sand behind an almost impenetrable barrier of breakers, rocks and reefs. This wild and rugged shore has torn apart many ships since seafarers first came to this coast, and deserves a wide berth, even when the weather is calm. Most of the wrecks (the *Lord Weston*, 1854, *Transport*, 1856, and *Mololo*, 1920) were lost in the vicinity of Raphael Point, on the southwest corner of the island. Boats continue to find themselves in peril off this point, so give it a wide offing. Shoals extend off the south shore for up to a mile, causing the seas to build to large proportions. This barren shore offers little shelter for the cruising yacht and there are no safe anchorages.

In transiting Russell Channel it is safest to find Bartlett Island and head for it. Less than a mile west of this island is Tibbs Islet, which displays a navigation marker which is easy to identify and locate. If you steer close to this islet, you will avoid the offshore hazards of the Garrard Group, and find the deeper waters of the channel. As you pass Bartlett Island and Whitesand Cove, you should be able to pick up the navigation marker on Monks Islet which will lead you into Calmus Passage, where the complicated and tricky access across the shallow bars into the heart of Clayoquot Sound and Tofino begins.

LOCAL CAUTIONS
- There are many shallow sandy areas throughout the channels between the islands. Follow the charts and aids to navigation very carefully in this area.
- Currents sweep through the channels and across the banks in irregular patterns. Be sure to look behind you as you pass near the banks to see if you are being swept sideways into it.
- Crab traps appear in long lines throughout the area. It is often difficult to see all of them, currents often pull the floats beneath the surface. Proceed with caution in Calmus Passage.

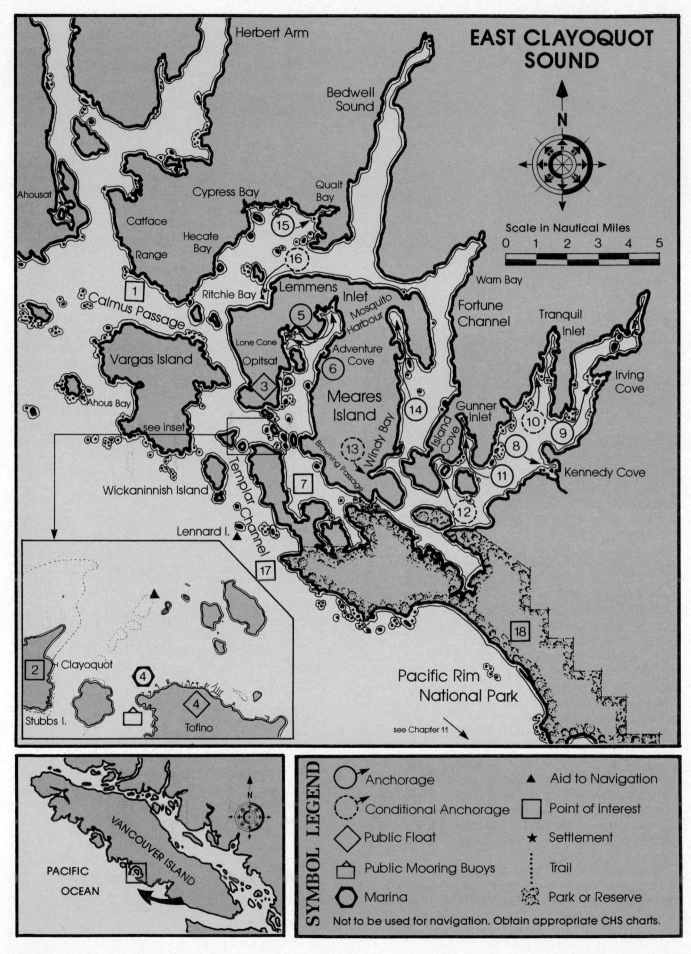

EAST CLAYOQUOT SOUND

Herbert Arm

Bedwell Sound

Ahousat

Cypress Bay

Quait Bay

Catface Range

Hecate Bay

(15)

(16)

Warn Bay

Calmus Passage

Ritchie Bay

Lemmens Inlet

Fortune Channel

Tranquil Inlet

1

Mosquito Harbour

(5)

Lone Cone

Opitsat

Adventure Cove

Irving Cove

Vargas Island

(6)

Meares Island

3

Ahous Bay

Gunner Inlet

(10)

see inset

(14)

Island Cove

(9)

Browning Passage

Windy Bay

(13)

(8)

Wickaninnish Island

Templar Channel

7

(11)

Kennedy Cove

Lennard I. ▲

(12)

17

▲

2

Clayoquot

4

4

Pacific Rim National Park

Stubbs I.

Tofino

18

see Chapter 11

Scale in Nautical Miles
0 1 2 3 4 5

PACIFIC OCEAN

VANCOUVER ISLAND

SYMBOL LEGEND

○→ Anchorage

◌→ Conditional Anchorage

◇ Public Float

⌂ Public Mooring Buoys

⬡ Marina

▲ Aid to Navigation

□ Point of Interest

★ Settlement

⋮ Trail

Park or Reserve

Not to be used for navigation. Obtain appropriate CHS charts.

CHAPTER TEN

Tofino

Clayoquot, Adventure Cove, Pacific Rim Park

In historical significance, Clayoquot Sound is second only to Nootka, and even more exciting as a cruising destination. The American ship *Tonquin* was plundered and destroyed here, and the second ship constructed on this coast was built from trees of the sound. The powerful chief Wickaninnish ruled over this large and diverse area from the village of Opitsat, which thrives even today. The Royal Navy used the sound to tidy and refurbish their ships after rounding Cape Horn so that they would arrive at Esquimalt in Bristol fashion. The scalps of the hapless victims of the 1855 battle with the Kyuquots were displayed on the shores of one island in the sound for years, until missionaries eventually had them removed. The first trading post on the west coast was established here, and since there was no lighthouse in the area, the enterprising storekeeper built his own to steer business to his part of the coast.

Today, Clayoquot Sound, which is the western terminus of the Trans-Canada Highway, supports a large fishing industry and a large national park. A cruiser's paradise, it is *the* undiscovered and unspoiled gem of the west coast.

The thorn in the rosebush is the shifting shallows which — along with currents that run like rivers through them — must be negotiated. Add to this the presence of countless crab traps, local runabouts and workboats and you have an interesting maze to navigate before you can enjoy the rewards of the sound. The first step towards tackling this unusual area is to fully understand the buoyage system, and follow the aids religiously.

1 Calmus Passage

Whether you are heading to Tofino from the protected waters of Millar Channel, or from the seaward entrances of Russell and Brabant Channels, you will have to pass through Calmus Passage. Located between the lofty peaks of the Catface Range and the low greenery of Vargas Island, this channel is the yachtsman's introduction to the navigational challenge created by the currents and shoals that set this area apart from all others on the coast. The problem is not so much the ferocity or turbulence of the currents, it is their unpredictable direction. Aids to navigation — coloured buoys which mark the sandbanks along the way — appear throughout the passage but often their colours are confusing. The reason for the confusion is that the currents flood in and around the islands in various directions, and the simple standby "red right returning" does not apply here. The system for marking channels in coastal areas is as follows:

- When entering a harbour, red markers are kept on the starboard side (red right returning). When leaving a harbour, of course red buoys are then kept on the port side.
- When heading up an inlet (with no harbour), red buoys are again kept to the right.
- When in an open channel, red buoys are kept to your right when proceeding in the direction of the flood tide. This is the basic rule from which the other rules are derived, and with which they are usually consistent.

It is important to understand these rules because in

Tufted puffins share a thoughtful moment atop a rocky seaside ledge on Cleland Island.

this area the tide may flow into a harbour from two different directions, making it difficult to determine which side of a channel marker you should pass. If you know the direction of the flood (as shown on the chart) you should not end up doing any unscheduled channel dredging (i.e. grounding). It is absolutely essential to have the large-scale chart (#3643) when navigating this area; the passages are very narrow, and a small mistake can easily put you out of the channel and onto a sandbar. The waters are so shallow that the chart for this area shows depths in feet. Be careful when switching from one chart to another, or you may be aground on what appears to be the 5-fathom-line.

When heading east through Calmus Passage, the beautiful shape of Lone Cone on Meares Island will dominate the view, as it does throughout the sound. This extinct volcano (2470 ft) can be seen from all points, and besides the ubiquitous crab, could well be considered the symbol of Clayoquot Sound. The memoirs of a resident of the sound, Dorothy Abraham, were collected under the title "Lone Cone", which provides delightful insight into life on the west coast of the Island in the 1920's. An English warbride, she and her husband lived through the transitional times on the west coast, and her reminiscences make for extremely humorous and interesting reading.

Once clear of Calmus Passage, a sharp turn to the south brings you to Maurus Channel and around Elbow Bank. More than a few boats have spent the afternoon on the sands of this shoal, so be sure to swing wide to the east when rounding this area. On the west side of Meares Island is a small cove, on the shores of which was once the site of the Christie Indian Residential School, established in 1899. This Roman Catholic institution, which could accommo-

Preceding page: View north across island-studded Clayoquot Sound, Tofino at centre.

132

date up to 150 boarders, was recently used as a rehabilitation centre for native Indians. Unfortunately the beautiful white buildings burned to the ground in 1983. All that remains is the large wooden cross, and the name on the chart, Kakawis, meaning "many berries".

2   Clayoquot

Once clear of the shoals and into the relatively deeper waters of Father Charles Channel (after Rev. Charles Moser who succeeded A.J. Brabant as missionary on the coast) a low, sand-fringed island appears to the south. Stubbs Island was named after Napoleon Fitz Stubbs, a ship's captain who circumnavigated Vancouver Island in the cutter *Templar* in 1861. The settlement of Clayoquot — now just a hotel and a few buildings — was the first on the west coast. It started as a trading post where one could purchase such items as anchors, chain and other ships' chandlery. Its original proprietor, Captain Pinney, thought that coastal schooners might like to refit in this area, and since there was no lighthouse to guide the ships safely in, he built an iron framework upon

Broad sand beaches and a fine restaurant are shoreside treats at Stubbs Island off Tofino.

which he piled driftwood and set fire to it each night.

The island is unusual in that like an iceberg, two-thirds of it is underwater, but close to the surface, and the shoal area (which dries on a 4-ft tide) extends northward from the island as much as ½ mile from the high tide line. If you want to splurge, there is a fine restaurant at the lodge on the island. If you make dinner reservations and go there in your own boat, be careful of the shoals on either side of Van Nevel Channel, and follow the buoys and beacons to the private dock at Clayoquot. The current runs up to 3 knots in the channel, so docking may be difficult. Get directions from the hotel keepers, before heading over, or take a water taxi from Tofino to be on the safe side.

It was on the sandspit extending from this island

that the heads of the victims of the last great Indian battle fought on this coast with the Kyuquot tribe (1855) were displayed at the end of long poles. Scalps were found as recently as 1926 when the sands of the spit, reshaped by winter storms, gave up their grim trophies (see Chapter 4).

3 Opitsat

The main residential settlement of the Clayoquots, once the residence of chief Wickaninnish, is on the sun-washed southern shores of Meares Island. Today the village on the reserve is a colourful collection of contemporary buildings, where modern fishboats and runabouts come and go in a steady stream. Although the public float has 200 ft of docking space, it is crowded with local fishboats, and very few transient boats tie up there. The approach to the float is

Ancestral home of Maquinna was Opitsat, now a thriving Indian community north of Tofino.

surrounded by shoals off Meares and Stockham Islands, but the edge of the latter bank is marked. The marine ways handles boats up to 40 ft, but is usually busy with workboats. If you are looking for a float to spend a quiet evening, chances are you will not find it here, and there are no other services or facilities. Supplies for the village are purchased in Tofino, a mile to the south.

4 Tofino

To get to Tofino from Heynen or Van Nevel Channels, the easiest way is the buoy-marked channel between the shifting sandbanks off the Deadman Islets, appropriately called Deadman Passage. Take note of the direction of the flood tide, because the shoals dry just a few feet off the channel. This is one place where the "red right returning" rule does not prevail. Also, keep an eye on your track as you pass through (by looking back as well as forward) to make sure that you are not caught in the current, and sideslipping onto the sandbanks. Once inside, head directly for one of the public floats on the shore — there are two small ones (120 and 140 ft of docking space) near the

downtown area and a larger one (over 1000 ft of docking space) used mainly by fishboats, ¼ mile east (see inset map). All are usually crowded. The current runs right through the harbour, sometimes making it difficult to dock, so this should be calculated into your approach.

There is also a seaplane float (and a great deal of air traffic) east of the public floats. These are not available for public moorage. (A small commercial airport also serves this area from a landing area about 10 miles to the southeast.) After securing to the float, a short walk will take you to a busy little village providing all the amenities needed for a cruising yachtsman, and then some. It has a small marine museum full of local artifacts, collected mainly from shipwrecks in the area. Several fine restaurants serve some of the best seafood on the coast; after zigzagging through the maze of crab traps on the way to Tofino, you might want to savour the fruit of your labours by candlelight with your hard-working crew. When people say "Tofino has crabs", they aren't kidding.

There are several good stores where provisions can be purchased, as well as a good hospital, post office, bank, laundromat, liquor store, and a hotel with a lounge and a bar. Several fishing trips, scenic tours, and dive charters operate from the docks near the downtown area. Tofino is the home of one of the two lifeboat stations on the coast (the other is at Bamfield) and the Coast Guard operates a large radio station here. The lifeboats can go out in all weather to perform marine rescues if needed, and many heroic res-

Busy public floats at Tofino provide ready access to the town's host of stores and restaurants.

cues have been carried out in these virtually unsinkable 40-footers.

Although it is possible to anchor in the harbour, the constant traffic and strong currents make it impractical. The four public mooring buoys in the small bay immediately south of Grice Point are seldom used because of their exposed location and distance from the facilities. They are not shown on the charts, but

Tofino lifeboat in 1910. Ten long sweeps was then its only power.

Shallows off Tofino look challenging but careful attention to chart and markers will ease the passage.

are easy to locate just a few hundred feet from the point. Fuel and water are available at two locations on the shore, but again you must watch for the currents when docking, especially near Grice Point. Power into the stream rather than trying to reverse when docking, or you may literally, get "carried away". Limited marine repair facilities are available at both marinas; propane, water, and ice are available at Chevron Marine.

Tofino takes its name from that given to the nearby inlet explored by Galiano and Valdes in 1792. It lies on the tip of the Esowista Peninsula which shelters an almost deserted cruising ground of incredible beauty and historical significance. A tour of Clayoquot Sound from here requires a circumnavigation of Meares Island, the largest in the sound, and the location of one of Canada's National Historic Sites.

5 Lemmens Inlet

Our excursion into history begins in the shelter of Lemmens Inlet (known locally as Disappointment Inlet), 4 miles north of Tofino. After taking Deadman Passage and turning east around Stockham Island, a course due north will carry you between the open arms of Meares Island. At high tide the inlet has a width of more than a mile of water at its mouth — when the tide drops to 4 ft or less, the deep water channel is only a few hundred feet wide, and an extensive drying bank connects the Arakun Islands in the inlet to the east side of Meares Island. The contrast is shocking when you first experience it, and makes you appreciate why the currents in this area are so strong, and thankful for good charts.

At the head of the inlet, and on the west side are sheltered bays, each with a number of coves suitable for anchoring. Except for the one at the extreme end of the inlet, these coves are safe and free of rocks. The bottom is sand and mud, below 24 ft of calm water, and there is shelter from all winds. These anchorages are less than an hour from the bustling port of Tofino, and deserted most of the time. However great these coves are, though, the best and most interesting anchorage is on the eastern shore, where history was made almost 200 years ago.

At high tide the entrance to Lemmens Inlet is almost a mile wide; at low water it narrows to a few hundred feet.

6 Adventure Cove

Just behind Columbia Islet is a landlocked cove with a small stream running into it, the perfect place to spend a summer's day — or the entire winter, as Captain Robert Gray (skipper of the *Columbia*) did in 1792. After trading for furs farther up the coast, Captain Gray decided to stay the winter here, rather than immediately heading to Macao with only a partial load of sea otter pelts. He selected this tiny cove on Meares Island because it is protected, has good holding ground, and because the area was easily defended against attack. Because of the uncertainties of native acceptance of trade ships wintering on this coast, Gray and his men built a stockade they called Fort Defiance on the eastern shores of the cove, where they lived and worked. To keep his men busy, and as a worthwhile enterprise, Gray had a small schooner built out of the cedars on shore, and called it the *Adventure*. Today you can see remnants of the fort, overgrown by two centuries of rainforest vegetation, but marked by survey ribbons, and preserved as a National Historic Site. The ship was built on the beach, and if you look carefully you can see a wide strip where rocks have been cleared to facilitate the launching of *Adventure*. One can imagine the excitement of launching such a craft into the waters of Clayoquot Sound, and putting it into service as a coastal trading vessel. It served Gray for 6 months, until he sold it to the Spanish Captain Quadra at Nootka for 70 choice sea otter skins.

Before leaving Clayoquot, Gray uncovered a plot to overpower the fort and take the *Adventure*. In retalia-

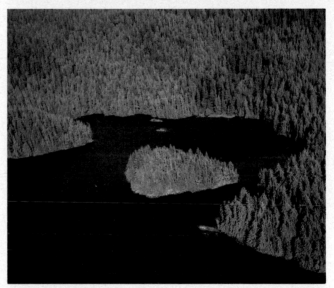

Adventure Cove where American fur trader Robert Gray built the schooner Adventure *during the winter of 1792.*

tion Gray ordered the destruction of Opitsat. As John Boit, fifth mate on the *Columbia* wrote in his journal in 1792,

"I am sorry to be under the necessity of remarking that this day I was *sent* with three boats, all well man'd and arm'd, to destroy the Village of Opitsatah it was a Command I was no ways tenacious off, and am grieved to think Capt. Gray shou'd let his passions go so far. *This* Village was about half a mile in Diameter, and Contained upwards off 200 Houses, generally well built for *Indians*... ev'ry door that you enter'd was in resemblance to an human and Beasts head, the passage being through the mouth, besides which there was much more rude carved work about the dwellings some of which was by no means *innelegant*. This fine Village, the Work of Ages, was in a short time totally destroy'd."

Gray left in *Columbia*, and discovered the great river in Oregon which now bears the name of his ship. The view of Lone Cone and the feeling of excitement felt in this historic site certainly make a visit here worth the effort.

A controversy is presently raging between conservationists and forest product companies who want to carry out extensive logging on Meares Island. Although there are two sides to this controversy, there is no question that logging will adversely affect the appearance of this island, a backdrop that is second to none on this coast, behind Canada's most magnificent national park. Effects on the fish and wildlife should also be considered in the greater context before any move is made to cut the verdant cloak off Meares Island.

7 Browning Passage

In order to circumnavigate Meares Island and get to the seldom visited cruising areas of eastern Clayoquot Sound, the shoal and current-ridden Browning Passage must be negotiated. However, the expanded scale on Chart #3643 makes this task a lot easier. If the current is with you (i.e. flooding), the trip is made quickly and easily. On both sides, shallows provide nesting areas for thousands upon thousands of

Cloudless sky brightens perspective over Tofino and Browning Passage. Long Beach is in the distance.

Good steelhead fishing in Kennedy River draws visitors to the anchorage at Kennedy Cove.

shorebirds, for which the area is famous. After passing through Tsapee Narrows (which runs 4 knots in either direction), the waters open up into the more familiar deeper fjordlike waters of Tofino Inlet. The southern shoreline from the narrows to Grice Bay (including Indian Island) is part of Pacific Rim National Park, and used frequently by canoeists and kayakers seeking protected waters.

8 Kennedy Cove

About 5 miles from Browning Passage, the Kennedy River reaches tidewater and small boats are often seen taking advantage of the opportunity to catch fine steelhead here. For the yachtsman, a small cove offers secure anchorage in a pleasant setting close to the fishing area. The cove is about 15 ft deep, and has a mud bottom, but don't go in too far, a mud bank extends almost half way out into the cove. The logger's axe has been falling on this end of the sound for some time, and much of the virgin timber has been replaced by lighter, deciduous second-growth timber. One advantage is that this green covering will be left to grow for at least another 30 to 40 years, giving you plenty of time to visit the cove before it is cut again. Years ago there was a trail along the river, connecting the lake and its beautiful beaches with Tofino Inlet. Kennedy Lake is the one of the largest on Vancouver Island.

9 Irving Cove

Farther up Tofino Inlet, another cove on the south shore gives protection from the winds and waves that batter the outer shores. Anchorage is in 26 ft behind the small islets that front the entrance to the cove. Entry requires caution, but there is deep water around

the islets, and the shoals are correctly charted. As is the case in most of the sound, this anchorage is usually empty, offering solitude to the yacht venturing into this beautiful area. The rest of Tofino Inlet is too deep to offer convenient anchorage.

10   Tranquil Inlet

When this inlet was named, there were no buzzing chain saws or logging trucks traversing the back shores as there are today. The head of the inlet is now filled with booms, offering only temporary moorage on the logs. A small cove on the west side of the inlet, however, can give you secure anchorage in all except southerly winds. The more protected Rankin Cove, 1½ miles farther south is choked with booms, and unusable as an anchorage at the present time.

11   Gunner Inlet

If your navigation is good, and you don't mind dodging rocks on the way in, Gunner Inlet offers considerable shelter between the high hills of the coast. By favouring the far west side of the inlet the three charted rocks in the fairway can be avoided, and you can make your way into the inner reaches of the inlet where the depths range from 8 to 24 ft. The mud bottom will hold you in solitude; the wind and waves will have great difficulty finding you.

12   Island Cove

If you don't mind a little deeper anchorage, more exposed, but free of dangers, take the north entrance

to Island Cove, just a mile west of the entrance to Gunner Inlet. There is room for more than one boat to swing on an anchor here, so if you plan a rendezvous with other yachts, Island Cove will give you more room than Gunner Inlet. The disadvantage is that it is over 40 ft deep until close to shore, and a lot more rode must be let out for safe anchorage.

13   Windy Bay

Situated between two beautiful peaks on Meares Island, this otherwise ideal anchorage is aptly named. A private little bay with a mud buttom where a creek trickles over a beach into tidewater looks like an ideal place to anchor. However, the head of the bay is not protected by any hills, so the prevailing westerlies blow unhindered across the Esowista Peninsula and between the peaks of Meares Island and into the Bay. If the westerlies are not strong, however, this would make a satisfactory anchorage.

To continue around Meares Island, you must negotiate Dawley Passage, a narrow pass running as much as 3 knots, but free of rocks. It is shown on the expanded chart for Clayoquot Sound (#3643) and leads to Fortune Channel.

14   Mosquito Harbour

After clearing Dawley Passage, the waters again widen to resemble the more familiar channels of the west coast with steep-sided mountains rising above

Mosquito Harbour on Meares Island affords good holding and protection in nearly all conditions.

deep waters. About halfway up Fortune Channel a harbour opens up behind a barrier of small islets. The clearest entrance is the westerly one, keeping the larger islets to starboard as you enter. The shelter here is remarkable for such a large harbour. The inlet is shallow almost from its entrance, making anchorage possible nearly everywhere. Pick a spot behind the Blackberry Islets and your anchor, as it pierces the surface, will send rings of ripples over the calm waters here. Because Meares Island is as yet unlogged, Mosquito Harbour takes on a special colour and mood of tranquillity, making it a pleasant place to visit again and again. The huge cedars at the head of the harbour were used by the natives to fashion their remarkable canoes. The western shores of this waterway was also the site of Sutton's Mill (1907) which exported shingles made here. The Sutton Brothers were the first permanent white settlers of Ucluelet (Chapter 11).

Fortune Channel continues a few miles past this inlet and terminates in a large bay. Warn Bay, however, is deep and open, offering no convenient anchorage. The same can be said about Bedwell Sound, unless you choose to take shelter in one of its nooks, with a stern line ashore. Logging in the sound is extensive, and none of the nooks are recommended as an anchorage. However, just 2 miles past Bedwell Sound is a secluded anchorage with a narrow entrance where a yacht could safely sit out any storm.

15 Quait Bay

The narrow and rocky entrance to Quait Bay should not prevent you from entering it. The channel is deep, and the rocks are accurately shown on the chart (#3649). Inside is a strikingly beautiful, totally protected lagoon that takes you somewhat by surprise. Without a chart one would hardly know it existed, but once inside, a pleasant anchorage suitable in all conditions is there for the taking. There are a number of dangers to avoid in Cypress Bay on the way into Quait Bay (i.e. several unmarked submerged rocks), but these are shown clearly on the chart, and are easy to avoid.

Narrow entrance leads to excellent all-weather anchorage in Quait Bay. Entry is made by going east of islets shown.

Cypress Bay was once used extensively as an Admiralty Anchorage by H.M. ships of the British West Indies station, who after rounding Cape Horn, rendezvoused there to repair and repaint their ships before sailing to Esquimalt harbour. Today, the main

activity in the area is the logging centred in Hecate Bay a few miles to the south. The dock and mooring buoy there are private.

16 Ritchie Bay

As we continue around Meares Island beneath the velvet slopes of Lone Cone, there is one more anchorage where one could spend time peacefully in Clayoquot Sound before heading out into the open waters of the west coast. On the way to Ritchie Bay, beware of Yellow Bank that extends a mile southwest from Saranac Island. It takes on a yellowish colour because the sand reaches within 3 ft of the surface; give it a wide berth entering or leaving Ritchie Bay. The bay itself is shallow enough for convenient anchorage, with a sandy bottom, so it should be considered an excellent spot to drop the ground tackle. However, it is open to westerlies which blow through Calmus Passage right into the bay. This makes a choppy ride when the tide is running, and the wind builds up as it often does in summer afternoons. If the winds are light or from the east, however, the view of Lone Cone from this anchorage is excellent. Take either the northeast or southeast corners — you are sure to have the bay to yourself. After rounding Robert Point, at the southern entrance to the bay, you will have completely rounded Meares Island and will be entering the current-ridden waters of Calmus Passage and Maurus Channel, where the circumnavigation began.

17 Templar Channel

The most common route for leaving Tofino is the intricate, but well-marked Templar Channel to the west of the Esowista Peninsula. It was named after the small cutter owned by Captain Barrett-Lennard, which circumnavigated Vancouver Island in 1861. However, the event which put this area of the coast into such historic prominence occurred 49 years earlier, off Wickaninnish Island.

In 1811 a brash American, Captain Jonathan Thorn, sailing the trade ship *Tonquin* (owned by John Astor) insulted chief Wickaninnish. Thorn's manner exasperated the Indians, and his contempt for the chief became his downfall. He was advised by the supercargo, Alexander McKay, not to continue abusing the natives. McKay, familiar with the pride of the chiefs, had been with Alexander MacKenzie when he crossed Canada by foot, and reached Bella Coola in 1793. His advice went unheeded. One day the *Tonquin* was attacked, the Captain and all but five of the crew were killed. The five survivors managed to clear the ship, and made an escape under darkness in the ship's boat only to be killed later. The next day, while natives swarmed over the apparently abandoned ship, it mysteriously exploded and sank. The explosion covered the surrounding waters with scores of dead or wounded Indians, fragments of canoes, and parts of the ship.

Pacific combers roll ashore near Schooner Cove in Pacific Rim National Park.

It is thought that a badly-wounded crewmember, Mr. Lewis (the ship's clerk) had hidden on board until the ship was filled with Indians. He then ignited the powder magazine rather than be captured and killed by the natives and took the ship and its invaders with him. The *Tonquin* (or what's left of it) still lies on the bottom somewhere between Lennard Island and Wickaninnish Island. (Wickaninnish Island was formerly called Village Island.) Thorn Reef and Tonquin Island in Templar Channel commemorate this event in history. Recent efforts to locate the wreck of the *Tonquin* (and her seven brass cannons) have not located any definitive relics of the ship, though efforts are expected to continue until she has been found. When conditions are settled it is possible to anchor off these islands, but none are recommended for overnight moorage.

Just beyond Wickaninnish Island, the primary lighthouse for Clayoquot Sound is located. The Lennard Island light is on a small offshore island known as Observation Island in the days of the fur trade. The island marks the boundary between the current-ridden shoal areas of Clayoquot Sound, and the deep blue Pacific off Canada's first National Marine Park.

18   Pacific Rim National Park

Once clear of Templar Channel, and back into the rolling swells of the west coast, the long beaches in Pacific Rim Park open up on the port side. One after another of these white beaches scalloped out of the coastline grace the shore. What strikes you from the seaward view, is the fact that it is astoundingly unimpressive. If you didn't know the magnificent beach was just beyond the breakers, you might easily sail right past it without any knowledge of its existence. Because the rhumbline down this part of the coast keeps a boat about 3 miles from the centre of Long Beach (also called Wickaninnish Bay), the low scrubby trees and beached logs are all that can be seen on shore. There, thousands of people in campers and tents splash and run along the white sands, while your yacht remains a mere speck on the shorebound vacationer's western horizon. This unit of the park has no facilities for yachtsmen, except for the rolling waters which often rush you on your way down the coast on a sleighride of white foam.

LOCAL CAUTIONS
- Unpredictable and strong currents run over the submerged sandbanks in Clayoquot Sound. Pay close attention when making passages here during times of high tidal flow.
- Depths in the Tofino area are measured in feet while other charts in Clayoquot Sound are measured in fathoms and metres. Take note of the scale when changing from chart to chart.
- Crab traps abound throughout the sound, with a line and float marking them on the surface. Proceed slowly and cautiously through the trap areas to avoid wrapping your propeller with the lines.

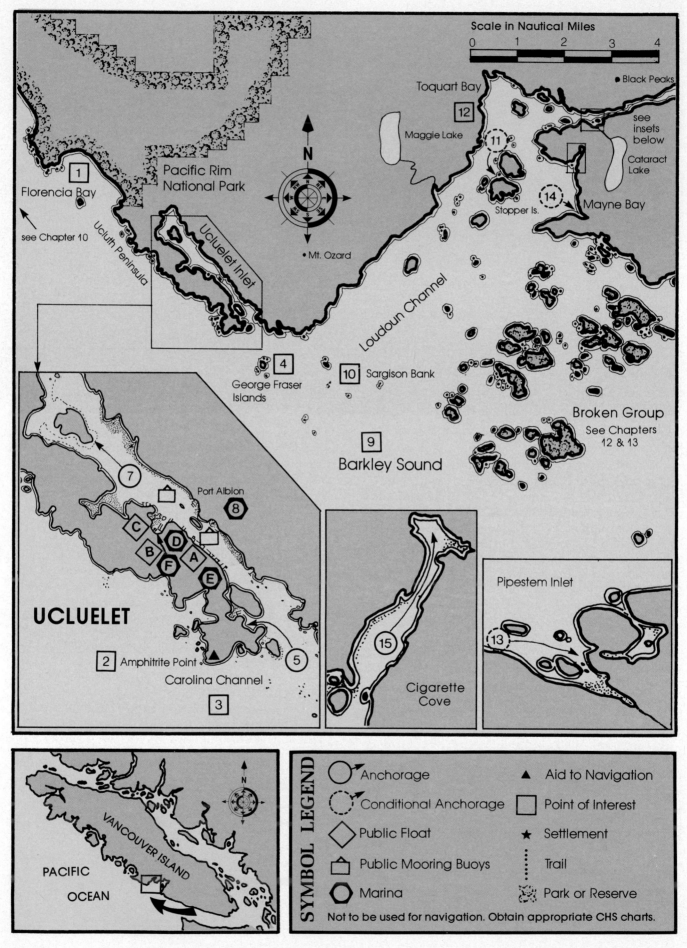

Scale in Nautical Miles
0 1 2 3 4

• Black Peaks

Toquart Bay

[12]

Maggie Lake

see insets below

Cataract Lake

Pacific Rim National Park

N

(11)

(14) Mayne Bay

Stopper Is.

1 Florencia Bay

see Chapter 10

Ucluth Peninsula

Ucluelet Inlet

• Mt. Ozard

Loudoun Channel

4
George Fraser Islands

10 Sargison Bank

Broken Group
See Chapters 12 & 13

9
Barkley Sound

7

Port Albion

8

C

B D A

F E

UCLUELET

2 Amphitrite Point

5

Carolina Channel

3

15

Cigarette Cove

Pipestem Inlet

13

PACIFIC OCEAN

VANCOUVER ISLAND

N

SYMBOL LEGEND

⟳ Anchorage	▲ Aid to Navigation
⟳ Conditional Anchorage	▢ Point of Interest
◇ Public Float	★ Settlement
⌂ Public Mooring Buoys	⋮ Trail
⬡ Marina	░ Park or Reserve

Not to be used for navigation. Obtain appropriate CHS charts.

140

CHAPTER ELEVEN

Ucluelet

Amphitrite Point, Spring Cove, Barkley Sound

When the Pacific High becomes established, and the summer westerlies blow with predictable regularity, sailing along the west coast can be one of the greatest yachting experiences. Winds on this part of the coast, usually light in the morning, rise gradually to about 20 knots by late afternoon, and drop suddenly at dusk to near zero — perfect conditions for getting to, and spending the night in your chosen anchorage. Under way, the sun shines on foam-crested waves out over the deep blue Pacific as mile after mile rolls away beneath your hull: dream passages. This experience is what we go to the west coast for — this is why we always go back. Barkley Sound is the prime reward for any yachtsman who ventures beyond Juan de Fuca and Johnstone Straits. When conditions allow us to enjoy the raw nature of its beauty, the west coast has no equal. Barkley Sound can truly be a paradise.

But nature is not always so benevolent, and sends storms or fog to plague the sound, making it a dangerous place for the uninitiated. Between these two extremes, the cautious mariner tests both his skill and his capacity to appreciate the rugged beauty of the coast. Barkley Sound is the world in microcosm for the sea-going venture: surf-lashed rocks, quiet coves, sandy beaches, shipwrecks, deserted villages, and glassy calm lagoons waiting to be explored. Our Barkley Sound exploration will begin at the northwesterly entrance. Several coves and bays will be explored, and historic sites revealed in an effort to bring B.C.'s new boating frontier closer to home.

1 Florencia Bay

After rolling past Long Beach (Wickaninnish Bay) on the southward journey from Clayoquot Sound, another sweeping beach appears between two rocky headlands — this is *Florencia*, or "Wreck" Bay. As is the case in much of the coastline in this vicinity, the bay was named after the hapless ship that met her doom on these unforgiving shores. The 200-ton brig *Florencia* out of Peru with a load of lumber foundered off of Cape Flattery in December 1860, and drifted into Nootka Sound, where she anchored safely. While being towed to Victoria for repairs, her towboat, the gunboat *Forward* (Forward Inlet) developed engine trouble and had to cast her tow adrift. This time, however, the *Florencia* lost the battle with the seas, and wrecked in the bay that now bears her name. The bays on this part of the coast do not afford any shelter or anchorage; to find protection, continue on to a point behind the Ucluth Peninsula 5 miles further down the coast.

2 Amphitrite Point

The tip of the Ucluth Peninsula is one of the most rugged parts of a very rugged coastline, and situated here is one of the most important light stations on the coast. A Coast Guard radio station occupies the same site, and many lives have been saved because of this modern facility and the men and women who operate it. Named after H.M. frigate *Amphitrite*, 1064 tons, which once sported 42 guns and was on this coast in

Coast Guard and Vessel Traffic Management stations spread across rocky headland on Amphitrite Point.

the mid-nineteenth century, the light has directed people away from the hazards of this part of the coast since 1905, and now forms an important part of the west coast Vessel Traffic Management Service. The prominent white dome atop 2200-ft Mt. Ozzard provides the station with radar coverage of all vessels within a 60 mile radius. Amphitrite was the mythological wife of Poseidon, and as such was goddess of the seas. The name is appropriate here, because fishboats caught in winter storms in this area have often called on her divine intervention to help them make it safely into the harbour.

3   Carolina Channel

According to the "Sailing Directions," Carolina Channel (close southeast of Amphitrite Point) "is the channel most frequently used by vessels of light draft approaching Ucluelet from seaward in calm weather; in bad weather, when a long swell rolls in from seaward, several rocks and shoals with less than 10 m (33ft) over them in the fairway make it dangerous." For the average cruising boat, the shoals are so deep that there is no real danger of hitting them, although the sea can pile up over the shoals. In normal conditions, this is the channel to take, because buoys

clearly mark the passage. Take the red whistle buoy (Y42) to starboard and the green bell buoy (Y43) to port. The biggest hazard in this area is Jenny Reef, which is unmarked, except for the breakers that constantly comb its back. The new chart for Barkley Sound (#3671) and the expanded scale chart (#3646 — Plans in Barkley Sound) mark the passage a lot more clearly than the older ones which were cluttered with soundings. Be careful, however: both of these charts use the metric scale, and soundings are in metres, rather than fathoms or feet. When you switch from chart to chart, take careful note of the scale used.

There are two other ways to enter Ucluelet harbour — Alpha Passage and Felice Channel. The former is unmarked, and wedged between Jenny Reefs and the George Fraser Islands, a mass of submerged and above-water rocks and islets, all unmarked. Felice Channel, 2 miles to the south of Carolina Channel, is safe and clear of hazards but is an unnecessary detour under normal circumstances.

4   George Fraser Islands

This group of rocks, reefs and islets (only two of which are wooded) was named after an early Scots settler who had gained fame as a horticulturalist. He grew azaleas, rhododendrons and his native heather; his efforts were greatly appreciated by visitors who were surprised to see such exotic and colourful plants in this remote area. Although there is no safe anchorage around the islands, on a calm day a motorized tender could be beached on the lee shore, where the

Spray flies as the author's Coyote beats to weather off the West Coast.

Preceding page: View north over Ucluelet Inlet, Amphitrite Point and town of Ucluelet centre left.

144

visitor might find wild onions growing, or see wild goats which are said to roam the islands.

5 Spring Cove

Just inside the Ucluelet harbour limit is a perfectly protected cove which offers everything you want in an anchorage, plus one thing you won't find anywhere else in the Ucluelet area — a bit of privacy. This cove is the centre of operations for the B.C. Packers fish plant, and the floats in the cove belong to that company, but it is still one of the quieter parts of the harbour. The rocks and shoals (which used to be hazards on the way in) have all been marked, and navigation into the cove, especially with the harbour chart (#3646) is quite straightforward. The cove is shallow, and anchorage can be in as little as 8 ft of water in much of the cove. Spring Cove was named for Captain Charles Spring who operated a trading post

Surfers' paradise and popular recreation area at Long Beach north of Ucluelet.

there in the 1870's. In 1910 one of the two west coast life boats was stationed here, but it was moved to Tofino 3 years later where it was needed more often.

6 Ucluelet

This great harbour is the main supply centre for cruising yachts visiting Barkley Sound, and because buoys and spars mark all the dangers, entry is straightforward. For many, the only difficult thing about Ucluelet is its pronunciation (try "you-cloo-let"). The name is derived from a local tribe, the Yuclutl-ahts — "the-people-with-the-safe-landing-place." Although this harbour is indeed a safe place to land (a canoe or small boat) the name actually refers to another site, north of Long Beach where the natives

145

once lived. There are three public floats, about ¼-mile apart, each with advantages and disadvantages (see inset map). The first one (A) on the port side as you enter is known as "52 steps," (there are actually 53) which is 450 ft long and usually has space because many people prefer to avoid the long haul up the hill from whence it is named. **Note:** an uncharted rock lies about 10 ft from the southern end of the float — care is needed to avoid it if you wish to tie up to the end of the float. It is clearly visible a few feet below the surface at low tide. Try to get a berth on the inside of the float — wash from harbour traffic can be annoying and uncomfortable.

The second public wharf (B), with two floats attached to the inner side offer 150 ft of public moorage, is closer to town, but often noisy and crowded. The third set of floats (C), another ¼ mile north are primarily for fishboats. They are beyond Lyche Island and behind the small peninsula at the northern end of town. Use caution near Lyche Island: the shoal extends a long way from the western shore. The fishboat fleet in Ucluelet is large — 400 or more make their home there (the other main industry is logging). Other harbour services for the yachtsman include three marinas (D, E, F, one with docking space) and two machine shops in town. Electronic repairs can also be carried out in town. Because Ucluelet connects to the east coast of the island via a paved road,

Ucluelet is home port for the west coast fishing fleet, of which 400 boats regularly take wharfage in the friendly coastal community.

parts can be delivered to a disabled yacht relatively easily. In addition, Alberni Marine Transportation Company operates a regular ship schedule from Port Alberni to Ucluelet (thrice weekly in summer) carrying freight, and up to 100 passengers, with scheduled and unscheduled stops along the way in Barkley Sound. For schedules and fares call (604) 723-8313. Ucluelet offers the most complete range of services and facilities for yachtsmen on the west coast.

Ashore is a pleasant town of 1700 fulltime residents whose town motto is "enjoy yourself". The locals make that easy to do, with a variety of entertainment and culinary services available. There are hotels, motels, pubs, lounges, grocery stores, laundromats, banks and hardware stores. There is also a post office, library, and liquor store, as well as tourist-oriented shops and services.

Among the best is the floating hotel, the *Canadian Princess*, a former survey vessel which, although permanently moored to shore, is fully operable and perfectly restored. Formerly the *William J. Stewart*, this 235 ft ship helped to chart this coastline for 46 years before being retired and converted to its present

146

function. Besides accommodation, the *Princess* offers mini cruises in and around the waters of Barkley Sound, from its 43 ft auxiliary cruisers. Activities include sightseeing excursions, fishing, whale-watching, and diving. Several other charter companies also operate out of Ucluelet — see the tourist bureau or the *Pacific Yachting* "Yacht Services Directory" (published each October) for more information.

One of the other exciting tours available to yachtsmen (this one free) is a visit to the Coast Guard light station at Amphitrite Point. The manicured lawns and the viewpoint overlooking the jagged coast are good vantage points from which to observe the marine traffic negotiating the reefs off the point. A Recreation Reserve of 21 acres preserves a significant portion of shoreline and beach area near the station.

It is also worthwile to make a sidetrip to the Pacific Rim National Park information centre located about 8 miles up the road from Ucluelet. Here you will find all

Ucluelet public boat basin is also home for the 235-ft Canadian Princess (centre) floating hotel and restaurant.

sorts of information regarding the 3 units of the park — Long Beach, the Broken Group (in Barkley Sound), and the west coast trail, farther down the coast. You can get free maps, showing walking trails of ½- to 45 miles long and information on nature interpretation programs, and campsites in the park. Or, play tourist and simply head to Wickaninnish Bay and marvel at the majesty of the always incredible Long Beach. The view here provides an interesting contrast for the yachtsman who has just made a passage and viewed the shoreline from the other side of the breakers.

The brand new Wickaninnish Centre, reconstructed from the popular Wickaninnish Inn, offers visitors an interesting look at the natural history of the park area in magnificent surroundings. The centre itself is a marvel, and well worth the shoreside expedition. For more information, contact Pacific Rim National Park, Box 280, Ucluelet, B.C. V0R 3A0 (726-4212).

7 Ucluelet Inlet

Although you can anchor safely almost anywhere in the inlet beyond the fishboat basin, it is of little interest for the yachtsman as there are no facilities or services. Most of the remaining waters are covered with booms which are constantly on the move. There are two public mooring buoys just south of Lyche Island which are seldom used; if you want to get out of "downtown" Ucluelet, but remain close to shore, these can offer a handy alternative. They are not shown on the chart, or listed in the "Sailing Directions". Four more were placed on the south side of the island, north of the boat harbour, in 1984.

8 Port Albion

This small settlement on the eastern shore of the inlet just past Lyche Island is the site of a disused herring processing plant. Today only a small settlement with a store and small marina — selling fuel and water — remains. If you need supplies or fuel, or just want to visit, you can tie to the private float at the small settlement and go ashore; Port Albion has no public float. Since the reduction plant closed down the site gets few visitors, but the deserted buildings are interesting to explore.

9 Barkley Sound

This beautiful sound is not like any other on the B.C. coast on either side of the Island. About 20 miles wide, 10 to 15 miles long, it is sprinkled with hundreds of islands, islets and rocks. These islands are arranged more or less in rows, with wide channels separating them. The outer coast of many of the islands have shorelines of shattered rock, the result of defiantly facing the open Pacific over the years. On the leeward side of the rocks and the twisted shorepines (deformed because of the ferocities of the winter storms), the waters are remarkably calm, and anchorage can be found in dozens of nooks and coves. It is a land of sea caves, surge channels, tidepools, kelp beds, birds and other marine life. You could anchor in a different spot every night, and rarely see another yacht. Many islands have a special character to them because they are in Pacific Rim National Park, and will be kept free of development in perpetuity.

The sound was discovered in 1787 by Captain Charles William Barkley of the English trading ship *Imperial Eagle* (ex-*Loudoun*) sailing under Austrian colours (to avoid paying a licence fee to the East India Company, who placed trade restrictions on this coast for British ships). Being 400 tons and fully rigged, Barkley's ship was one of the largest to visit the coast up to that time. His trip was even more remarkable, because he was only 26 years of age, and brought with him his 17-year-old wife (née Frances Hornby Trevor), the first European woman to visit this coast. Until then, ships had been sailed to these shores by men alone, much to the puzzlement of the Indians who thought that the "mamathni," the white men, had no women. Mrs. Barkley kept a diary of the voyage and collected her notes under the title "Reminiscences", which is now in the Provincial Archives in Victoria. Beth Hill, a noted B.C. author, has collected other letters and articles and published an excellent account of British Columbia's "first lady." It is appropriately titled "The Remarkable World of Frances Barkley: 1769-1845".

Barkley had been trading in Nootka Sound earlier that year when he picked up John Mackay, who had been left there (at his own request) by Captain Hanna the previous year (see Chapter 1). Because of his familiarity with native customs and language, Mackay helped Barkley immensely in trade transactions both in Nootka Sound, and later here as well. After leaving Nootka Sound, Barkley sailed southeast where he discovered and named Wickaninnish (now Clayoquot) and Barkley Sounds. (The Indian name for the sound was Nitinat.) Besides his name for the sound, Imperial Eagle Channel, Loudoun Channel, Trevor Channel, and Cape Beale (Barkley's purser) all take their names from Captain Barkley's visit here in 1787. He also re-discovered (and named) the Strait of Juan de Fuca which had not been seen by any other

Sunset provides glowing backdrop for boats moored at Ucluelet. Three public floats provide access to the town's extensive services and attractions.

trader or explorer (even Cook, who was looking for it) since that famous pilot had first described it almost 200 years earlier.

10   Sargison Bank

As you leave Ucluelet and begin your exploration of Barkley Sound, it is important to keep a very accurate account of your position. The insidious fog which plagues the sound in summer months can roll in, unannounced and unwelcome, eliminating all landmarks from view in very short order. Although

distances in the sound are not great, they can seem that way when you're navigating reefs on your way to a safe anchorage, and one by one your landmarks disappear behind a grey veil.

One of the great attractions of the area is also invisible, except by depth sounder. Sargison Bank, a shoal area in Loudoun Channel 4 miles east of Ucluelet, is such a good place to catch fish that people often light their barbecues *before* they go fishing! Jig for cod while anchored on the bank, or troll over it on your way to the islands in the sound. For the most part, the bank is from 12 to 30 ft deep, and presents no hazard to navigation. One rock, however, less than a mile east of Chrow Island, is unmarked, and dangerous. Although

West Coast fishing troller waits out fog off Ucluelet.

shown on the chart, is is not easy to locate; give it a wide berth when transiting the channel.

When proceeding northeast in Loudoun Channel there is no preferred course; most of the smaller channels are deep and wide. Note the rocks between Curwen and Bryant Islands and Warner Rock, south of St. Ines Island. The water gets calmer as you proceed into the inlet, so these may not show up as breakers as they do on the outer part of the coast.

11   Stopper Islands

Although the bulk of the islands in Barkley Sound lie in rows, a few in the northern corner of the sound do not fall into the main groups. As such, the group that includes the Stopper Islands are seldom visited, and survive today as pristine as they were in Captain Barkley's day. To see a rare stretch of native west coast vegetation that hasn't been touched by axe or chainsaw, go ashore for a visit. Anchorage here is marginal, at best; if not for its location far up the sound — where swells are tame and wind-whipped seas almost fully dispersed — there would be little chance for moorage here. Anchor between the islands where the water shallows up to 30 ft, or in the little channel between

the largest Stopper Island and Larkins Island to the west. In either case, run a stern line to shore, and don't put it away when you leave. Stern lines and stern anchors are extremely valuable in Barkley Sound, and open up a variety of smaller anchorages.

Toquart Bay serves as the area's primary launching site for small boats visiting Barkley Sound.

12 Toquart Bay

This bay takes its name from the To-quaht tribe (a branch of Nootka) who resided at the mouth of the small rivers which flow into the bay. These lands have been occupied by entrepreneurs since Captain Spring (Spring Cove) established a trading post there in 1860. Other developments have included a cannery (abandoned in 1940), a mine and a wharf, from which thousands of tons of crushed iron concentrate were shipped to Japan. In addition to the spectacular west coast scenery with which you will be quite familiar by the time you reach Toquart Bay, ruins of the distinctively cone-shaped shed and conveyor system are one of the main attractions of the area. Today the bay serves as the primary launch site for the hundreds of small boats which visit Barkley Sound each year. On a summer day the shores are lined with vehicles and campers, launching and retrieving boats, or just enjoying the scenery. Because of the sheltered waters and easy access, Barkley Sound — unlike many other west coast areas — can be enjoyed by the cartopper as easily as the luxury yachts. A few simple campsites in the area are well used in the summer months. There is no convenient anchorage in the bay, but the sheltered waters allow exploration by dinghy. If you go ½-mile upstream in the Toquart River you will find a beautiful waterfall.

Note: One significant detail of the bay is that the same ore body that provided the iron which was shipped out also contains the ore magnetite (Maggie Lake and River are thought to take their names from this fact). Compasses will not read accurately here, so beware of magnetic anomalies, especially when re-

150

Best anchorage in Pipestem Inlet is behind small islands (centre).

lying on a compass course in fog. This is not mentioned on the chart (#3671).

13   Pipestem Inlet

This long, narrow inlet (which resembles a gorge in places) is wedged between mountain peaks that rise abruptly to over 3000 feet. Barkley Sound does not have the great number of fjords of Nootka or Kyuquot Sound, but what it lacks in quantity, it makes up in quality. This inlet should definitely be on the itinerary of any Barkley Sound explorer. About two-thirds of the way along this inlet, on the north side, a graceful waterfall tumbles into tidewater from its source in the Black Peaks. Near the end of the inlet, the channel narrows to less than 200 ft while the pristine shoreline reaches for the sky. The head of the inlet has no convenient anchorage, but close to the entrance (behind a group of small islets) good shelter and holding ground provide a nearly ideal spot to savour the inlet: no crowds, no ocean swell, a series of small streams to explore (see inset map). The largest stream leads up to Cataract Lake, interesting to explore but a tough walk. The anchorage is open slightly to northwest winds which, when light, do not reach all the way into the inlet; when they do, the funnelling effect caused by the steep peaks makes anchoring here somewhat rough. If a strong front is moving onto the coast, choose an alternative overnight anchorage. The local name for this site is Cataract Cove.

14   Mayne Bay

This large open bay, directly south of the entrance to Pipestem Inlet, is named after Lieutenant Richard Mayne, R.N., who assisted with the survey of this coast on both the *Plumper* and the *Hecate* in 1861-1862. This interesting character was later employed surveying the Strait of Magellan at the tip of South America. Today the Canadian Navy uses this bay on occasion in its exercises; the large orange mooring buoy there is for their use (see chart #3671). From here you can look back towards Toquart Bay with the

magnificent sawtoothed MacKenzie Range as a backdrop. Even in summer the snow tips the peaks in iridescent white, exaggerated by the deep amethyst hues of the range. The profile of the closer mountains resembles a sleeping warrior. Attempts to photograph this profile are futile, the nuance of shadow and valley are too subtle for the camera to capture.

There is one conditional anchorage in the extreme southeasterly portion of the bay, where the water shallows up to 30 ft and less. The nook is completely

Mayne Bay and entrance to Cigarette Cove.

open to the west, but is free of swells, and would provide good protection from all other quarters.

15   Cigarette Cove

This tiny inlet is not named on the chart, but is located in the extreme northeast corner of Mayne Bay. The chart shows a small, perfectly land-locked lagoon. Two narrow openings prevent all waves and swells from entering its inner reaches. It is sheltered and calm, with a minimum low-water draft of 6 ft in the channel. The 12 ft depth over a mud bottom makes it an ideal spot for yachtsmen to find solitude, but alas the tiny inlet has been "discovered," and a small floating community (complete with float plane) occupies its shores. Still, if a storm is brewing on the outside, its wicked winds won't reach you here; and there's always room for more in the community.   ⚓

LOCAL CAUTIONS
- Charts for Barkley Sound use different scales (feet, fathoms, metres). Take note of the scale on the chart you're using.
- There is an uncharted rock 10 ft south of the end of the public float known as '52 steps', (A) on the inset map. Take note of this if mooring to the south end of the float.
- There are magnetic anomalies in the area of Toquart Bay: use caution when using a compass in this area, especially in foggy conditions.

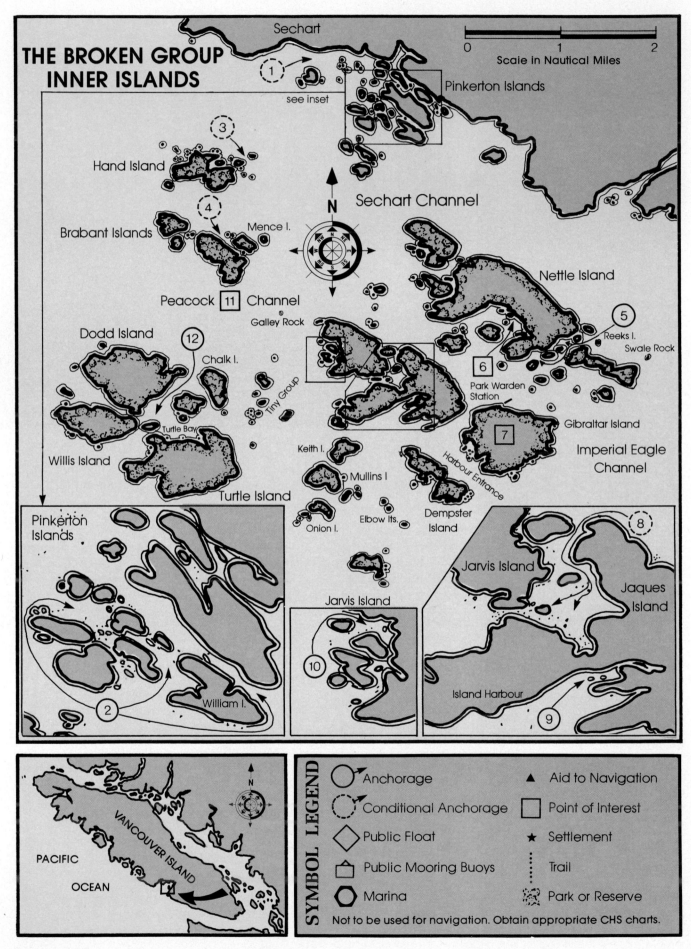

CHAPTER TWELVE

THE BROKEN GROUP
INNER ISLANDS

Sechart

see inset

Pinkerton Islands

Hand Island

Brabant Islands

Mence I.

Sechart Channel

N

Peacock [11] Channel

Galley Rock

Nettle Island

Dodd Island

Chalk I.

Reeks I.

Swale Rock

Tiny Group

Park Warden
Station

Gibraltar Island

Turtle Bay

Keith I.

Imperial Eagle
Channel

Willis Island

Mullins I

Harbour Entrance

Turtle Island

Elbow Its.

Onion I.

Dempster
Island

Pinkerton
Islands

Jarvis Island

Jaques
Island

Jarvis Island

Island Harbour

William I.

SYMBOL LEGEND

⭕ Anchorage   ▲ Aid to Navigation

⭕ Conditional Anchorage   ☐ Point of Interest

◇ Public Float   ★ Settlement

☐ Public Mooring Buoys   ⋮ Trail

⬡ Marina   Park or Reserve

Not to be used for navigation. Obtain appropriate CHS charts.

Scale in Nautical Miles

0   1   2

VANCOUVER ISLAND

PACIFIC

OCEAN

N

152

The Broken Group
— Inner Islands

Sechart, Pinkertons, Turtle Bay, Nettle Island

The Broken Group is a scattered collection of drowned mountains, including over a hundred rocky outcroppings of various sizes, most in the central unit of Pacific Rim National Park. There is little or no development on the islands; one of the main objectives here is to allow access to the untouched west coast habitats without destroying the delicate natural balances that exist. As more and more people gain access to this previously undisturbed area, this becomes the major ongoing challenge for park planners and naturalists. Primitive facilities for small boats (canoes and kayaks) are provided on some of the islands, but there are no major developments for transient yachtsmen. Therefore, do not expect mooring buoys, docks, rubbish removal, or other services. Instead, be prepared to rely on your own resources in a multitude of wilderness anchorages which are close together and each worthy of exploration for as long as your intinerary allows.

Anchorages are generally more protected the farther you get into the sound. Here the winds are greatly reduced, and the inner reaches are hardly affected by the swell that literally explodes on the outer islands, only a few miles to the west. So, depending upon the conditions, and your desire for shelter or excitement, the Broken Group offers something for everyone. The best chart for exploring the area is #3638 (Broken Group) or new Chart #3670.

The group is such a complex maze of islets and channels that anchorage would be possible around almost any of the islands if the conditions were calm.

However, weather changes quickly on the coast, and since most of the area is unlit, a move at night is very dangerous. The anchorages covered here are the recommended locations where safe moorage can be found, subject to the various conditions listed.

1 Sechart

Immediately east of the Pinkerton Islands (which are not in the Park) is one of the ancient summer camps of Alberni's Tseshaht Indians. The site was later developed as a mining site (1892), a whaling station (1905), and a pilchard-reduction plant (the 1930's). For all of these developments, the shallow mud-bottomed area just west of the Pinkertons, off Equis Beach, served as the prime anchorage. Although fairly sheltered, it is open to westerlies. The gently sloping beach behind Canoe Islet served the natives as a landing place, and later served as the site where hundreds of whales were hauled out and rendered into oil and fertilizer. Whalers became so efficient that whales were virtually unseen on this part of the coast for many years, and the station closed down. Not much remains of the old station buildings, but the sheltered beach is a pleasant and private place to spend some time while exploring the ruins for relics of its past occupants. About 2 miles east of the anchorage the old cannery ruins can be seen decaying year by year. The "conspicuous tower" shown on chart #3638 has long since crumbled away, but the cannery ruins are still easy to locate on the shore.

2   Pinkerton Islands

When people in the Broken Group say they are going to "visit the Pinkertons", it does not mean that they have relatives in the area. Instead, they are heading for an archipelago in miniature which provides some of the most cosy and protected anchorages in Barkley Sound. Anchoring here requires judicious navigation because the channels that join the islands and form the anchorages are small and narrow. Most will accommodate only one boat and require a stern line or stern anchor, but the quiet beauty of these intimate yacht havens makes them worth the extra effort.

The Pinkertons are not part of the Pacific Rim National Park, but nevertheless possess the same pristine qualities. The islands were named after James H. Pinkerton who homesteaded here in 1891, and of whom little is known. Secure anchorage is available in three separate locations (see inset map). The westerly anchorage requires passage between two charted rocks, but is especially good in southeasterly weather. The middle anchorage is free of any adjacent dangers, provided you have made it safely past the two rocks to the south of Williams Island. The most easterly of the three anchorages can be entered safely from the east

The Pinkertons, named after an early homesteader, afford quiet anchorage and ready access to some superb fishing.

end of Williams Island. Anchor in the middle of the small channel (24 ft) where the only water movement you experience will be the pull of the tide by our celestial companions.

From any of these anchorages many enjoyable hours can be spent exploring tide pools, beachcombing, or collecting dinner. The waters around here offer some of the best fishing in the entire sound. **Note:** Before you fish B.C. waters, you need a tidal

Preceding page: View north over Broken Group in Barkley Sound; Turrett Island in foreground, Turtle, Dodd and Willis islands behind.

water sports fishing licence from the Government of Canada, Fisheries and Oceans Branch. They are available at boat chandleries, marine stores, fuel stations, and general stores throughout British Columbia. Because the area is so sheltered, the insects that are joyously absent from the rest of the sound collect here in good numbers. Keep the repellent handy.

3   Hand Island

This pretty island, with its three sandy beaches, is the closest island in the Park to the boat launch site at Toquart Bay, and so receives a great number of small-boat visitors. A small campsite (one of only seven on the islands) has been established here by Parks Canada, so the beaches are often occupied by canoes and kayaks. This should not deter yachtsmen

Sandy beaches and a small campsite are attractions on Hand Island. Anchor near small islets centre left.

(especially families) from visiting the island, because the protected beaches here are a rarity anywhere in the sound, and the grassy fields make a good recreation area. There is no preferred area on the northeast shore to set an anchor, as long as you avoid the one submerged rock shown in the centre of the bay on the north side of the island. The leeward (northeast) side of Hand Island ranges in depth from 12-30 ft, depending how close to shore you choose to set your ground tackle. Only winds which blow from the northerly quadrant can reach you here, but northwesterlies are common when yachts are likely to be there (i.e., summer) so this anchorage must be considered conditional. The island was named for Henry Hand, a lieutenant aboard the vessel *Hecate* which surveyed this coast in 1861. The grassy field on the island was the site of a small summer trading post at the turn of the century.

4   Brabant Islands

Immediately south of Hand Island is a group of five small islands named to honour the Roman Catholic missionary who served on this coast for over 30 years

Some of the best, most sheltered anchorages in the inner islands are found off Nettle Island.

(see Chapter 8). Like most others in the Broken Group, these islands have never been inhabited or developed to any measurable extent. If you want to find repose in a purely natural setting, the small channel between the largest island and Mence Island can offer it to you. Find the 21 ft shoal area tucked well inside the smaller islets west of Mence Island (taking care to avoid the one detached submerged rock shown there) and run a stern line to shore. Although the 3-ft-deep channel blocks most of the swell from rolling in, southeasterlies can blow through the gap, making this anchorage less than ideal. Anchor here in settled weather; you will have no problems, and privacy as well. From here you can explore the extensive middens on Mence Island.

5 Nettle Island

Two of the most beautiful and completely protected anchorages of the inner islands are located on the southeasterly shores of Nettle Island. The safest approach is via Sechart Channel from the north. While you're in the area, try trolling for salmon off Swale Rock where Sechart and Imperial Eagle Channels meet. This area has long been a reliable dinner spot for the angler who takes the time to troll a lure.

To enter the Nettle Island anchorages, take the centre of the channel between Nettle and Reeks Island. Once past the narrowest part of the channel, a small cove will open up on the starboard side, flanked by a rocky islet on the south side, and a sandy beach on the north. Pick your spot almost anywhere in the cove, taking care to avoid the drying rock close to the 10 ft-high rock, closer to the southern entrance. There is room enough for a couple of boats to swing freely

Shelter from westerly winds can be found in the Brabant Islands, off Peacock Channel.

Inviting waters of Nettle Island off Sechart Channel provide safe swinging room for two or three boats.

without stern lines in 8-18 ft of calm water. The shore on the north side has an extensive midden, and this area is part of the Sechart Indian Reserve. The grassy bottom once supported a large population of crabs, but in recent years the number and size of these west coast delicacies has definitely decreased. (When crabbing, return all undersized crabs, as specified in the fisheries regulations, so the numbers can regenerate to their former status. If possible, learn to tell males from females, and return the females, which are fewer in number, and allow them to continue hatching their brood.)

If you find that the first cove on the island is occupied, press on a few hundred feet to an equally well-protected cove on the starboard side. There are two submerged rocks in the cove, both clearly shown on Chart 3670, and easy to avoid. Whether the wind is northwest or southwest (the only directions which can bring a strong blow in this part of the sound) you will be completely protected from waves and swell in either of these two refuges. The sun shining on the surrounding islets, especially near dusk, sets the colours off in hues that you won't find anywhere else, and since these precious places are within the bounds of the park, they will grow even more beautiful with time.

6   Park Warden Station

The working station for the wardens who patrol the Broken Islands is located on a floathouse on the south side of Nettle Island. On the way there, take note that there is a rock in the centre of the channel between Nettle and Jaques Islands. (As you travel about the Broken Group you will inevitably find a rock right in the middle of your channel, especially if the channel is narrow. The rocks, clearly shown on the charts, are usually covered with kelp in summer months. After you have been in the group awhile, you will refine your ability to read charts, and these hazards will become less and less imposing.) The park wardens regularly patrol the islands in high speed inflatable boats, enforcing regulations regarding camping, fishing and fires. They also provide helpful information regarding the history, natural history and locations of points of interest in the park. In addition, they are responsible for park safety, and keep tabs on every boat in the park area. They are a helpful source of information regarding such things as red tide, and shellfish closures, so if you see the wardens, and have any questions, don't hesitate to ask them. Even if they are away from the station, pertinent regulations will be posted there. Yachtsmen are asked not to moor to the float house.

Most of the remainder of small islands immediately adjacent to Nettle Island are interesting to explore by dinghy, but offer little opportunity for convenient anchorage, and for one reason or another are seldom used. In an area blessed with so many fine, safe and close anchorages it is not really necessary to choose a marginal one, or one that jeopardizes your boat in any

way. In the sheltered waters of these "inner" islands, a motorized dinghy, rowboat, or even a small sailing skiff will take you to some very interesting spots, while your larger boat rides gently at anchor in one of the safer harbours of the sound.

Detached floats off popular Gibraltar Island serve as terminus for campers arriving on the passenger/freight boat the Lady Rose.

7   Gibraltar Island

Named by Captain Richards in 1861 because it is reported to resemble the famous rock at the entrance to the Mediterranean, Gibraltar Island is now one of the park's main camping areas. Two unattached floats serve as landing platforms for unloading canoes and kayaks, primarily from the passenger and freight boat the *Lady Rose*. Three times a week during the summer months, this versatile little ship makes return trips from Port Alberni to Ucluelet, and stops at Gibraltar Island to unload adventurers in small boats who wish to examine the sound, but don't wish to make the open water passages to get there. For information on fares and schedules call: 723-8313.

Gibraltar Island is interesting to explore by dinghy. Its southern shores are riddled with sea caves, and there is a very large and interesting saltwater lagoon (entry is on the western shore) which dries completely at low water.

8   Jaques-Jarvis Lagoon

The largest lagoon in the Broken Group — and by far the most sheltered anchorage in the sound — also has the trickiest entrance (see inset map). After avoiding the submerged rocks in the middle of the unnamed channel between Jaques and Nettle islands, look for the gap between Jaques and Jarvis islands; this leads to an inner lagoon which has several in-

teresting attractions. The channel leading to this entry, however, is only 3 ft deep at low water. This is not really a problem, because the tides on the west coast are normally high enough twice a day to allow access to the lagoon. However, other factors also come into play here, making access trickier than it might otherwise be. First, safe entry requires an S-turn in order to avoid shoals on opposite sides of the entry. Second, the eel grass and debris in the water renders it murky, so the bottom cannot always be seen clearly. So why bother going in? There are a number of reasons: the lagoon is flat calm, completely land-locked

A watch forward eases passage through the Pinkerton Islands.

and, because of the restricted circulation, the waters here are the warmest in the sound. Silence pervades the lagoon and a stone fishtrap, centuries old, can be seen on the shore. Here's how to enter: time your entry (and exit) for the last hour or so of a rising tide, which should give you plenty of water, and if you happen to go aground, the extra rise in tide will help you get off. Proceed slowly, and favour the right-hand shore as you enter to avoid the shoal extending west from Jaques Island.

Once inside the first part of the lagoon, keep the islet in the centre of the lagoon to starboard, and turn your bow east. From here on in, favour the left (Jaques Island) side of the lagoon; there are a number of detached, submerged rocks immediately east of the islet (marked '70' on Chart 3638 and '21' on Chart 3670). These can usually be seen a few feet below the surface, and are all close to the small islet. Once clear of these rocks, you're in. Anchor in the centre of the lagoon using your depth sounder to keep you from straying onto the shoal area on the lagoon's outer edges. Your anchor will be from 14-17 ft below the calm surface of the lagoon, resting in soft mud. It's so calm here that your anchor rode will probably remain vertical all night. In other parts of the world this lagoon would be called a perfect "hurricane hole". The anchorage is considered conditional only be-

159

cause the access is restricted by tide height. The stone weirs used by the natives to trap fish are located on the lagoon's western shore. Fish swam over the rocks at high tide, and were trapped as the tide ebbed away. Nobody knows for sure how old the weir is, but it is thought that the rock latticework is several hundred years old.

9 Island Harbour

On the south shore of Jaques Island is an open area listed in the "Sailing Directions" as being suitable for "small vessels", but the small freighters that once anchored here regularly no longer call. The main harbour is too deep as a convenient anchorage for pleasure craft, but the northern side of the harbour (Jaques Island) offers secure small-craft shelter. No matter which of the four routes you take into the harbour, there is a rock mid-channel. All of these are shown clearly on the chart, but only one, Eussen Rock — between Gibraltar and Dempster Island — is named.

The recommended anchorage is the cove on the southwest part of Jaques Island, closest to the lagoon. There is a good mud bottom and right up in the

One of the most accommodating anchorages in the Broken Group is Turtle Bay between Dodd, Turtle and Willis islands.

northern part of the cove the water is only 15 ft deep. The cove immediately east of this one is used extensively by canoes and kayaks because a park shelter (cabin) is situated at the head of this cove. This area is ideal for small open boats because it is so sheltered, and consequently makes an excellent anchorage. From here you can explore the local islets by dinghy.

Keith Island is a private Indian Reserve, where the fishing station of the Secharts is located. You can take Harbour Entrance to where the best sea caves in all of Barkley Sound are located, on the south shores of nearby Dempster (formerly Protection) Island. When the swell is not rolling too high, you can take a dinghy right into some of these caves. Others have blowholes which make an eerie sound as spray flies out of a hole in the roof of the caves, when the tide is at the right height. From here you can safely explore Mullins Island and the beaches on Onion Island. Try fishing off the Elbow Islets, or try to identify some of the more than 230 species of birds which make their home in the islands. In the fall, mushrooms can be gathered to add a treat to your meals — chanterelles are abundant, and easy to identify. These islands offer so much for the adventurer who goes to the effort of getting there. Because there is no other way to get to them, or around them, they virtually belong to yachtsmen. Their history is steeped in boats, from the first dugout canoes to modern power-cruisers with every imaginable luxury. The coves have looked the same to both cultures, and thanks to their park status, will remain in their wild state. Go ashore, these are your islands. "No trespassing" signs are conspicuous by their absence. This is what makes the Broken Group a true yachtsman's paradise.

10   Jarvis Island

After carefully making your way westward out of Island Harbour, take the channel between the Tiny Group and Jaques Island until you are near the western end of Jarvis Island. Tucked in behind the three islets off its western shores is a secluded anchorage, suitable for one boat to anchor in complete protection (see inset map). If you want privacy in an anchorage, it's easy to get by occupying a choice spot which only has room for one boat. A great deal of these anchorages exist in the Broken Group, but this is one of the best.

It would be impossible to point out all of the dangers in this island group; submerged and partly-submerged rocks are everywhere, but for the most part these are clearly shown on the charts. However, one rock in particular seems to cause people concern because it is detached, several hundred feet from any island, and near midway in an otherwise clear channel. This mini-menace is known as Galley Rock, in Peacock Channel, between Jarvis Island and the Brabant Islands. It dries when the tide reaches the 5 ft level, so watch for it.

11   Peacock Channel

Entering the inner islands of the Broken Group from Loudoun Channel is most easily done through Peacock Channel, between Dodd Island and the Brabant Islands. The channel is deep, wide and free of dangers. Once a yacht turns eastward into the lee of Dodd Island, the swells and winds abate, cruising becomes even more pleasant. From Peacock Channel, safe passage can be made to the Pinkerton's, Nettle Island, or the Jaques Island lagoon. It was named by Captain Richards while surveying the sound in 1861, but he gave no particulars as to why the name was chosen.

12   Turtle Bay

Perhaps the most frequently used all-weather anchorage in the inner islands of the Broken Group is the relatively large harbour formed behind Dodd, Willis, and Turtle islands, known locally as Turtle Bay. Entry is most easily made between Dodd and Chalk islands, from Peacock Channel. With room for several boats, the anchorage, in many respects, is similar to Silva Bay (on Gabriola, in the Gulf Islands) except that it is completely undeveloped. Anchorage can be found in depths ranging from 24-33 ft over a mud bottom. Strong westerlies can reach into the bay via the gaps on either side of Willis Island, and the tide can run quite strongly through the channels, but no waves of any significance build up, and one could weather almost any storm here. The small group of islands offer typically good exploration with uncut shores, and fine beaches such as the one on Willis Island. However, one of the former attractions of Turtle Bay is no longer there.

"Salal Joe", as he was called (his real name being Joe Wilkowski), was the hermit-baron of the Broken Group who added further colour to the mysterious tapestry of his past by disappearing in 1980. He is believed to have drowned somewhere in the group of rocks, reefs and islands that he made his kingdom for over 25 years. He got his nickname in his early years when he collected salal branches as evergreen decorations to be sold back in the frozen east during winter months. When other entrepreneurs also got into the business, there was not enough left of the market for this old man in this remote place, so Joe turned to beachcombing and odd jobs. When the park was established on these islands the officials did not want to evict the old squatter, with his dishevelled old floating shack in Turtle Bay, so they employed him in casual maintenance work. He built a garden on top of the midden on Dodd Island, and jealously guarded it against both two and four-legged poachers. He tried raising chickens, but one day the eagles apparently got the whole brood. His tiny efforts to domesticate the islands were dwarfed by the wilderness which formed the backdrop to his little home in the Broken Group. His skiff was found washed up on a beach one day, and old Salal Joe has not been seen since. Paradoxically, salal bushes are again taking over the garden that he so vigorously protected.

The remainder of the Broken Group south and west of Turtle Bay are more exposed to the waves and the swells of the outer coast. While no clear demarcation line notes where the "outer" islands begin, the outer shores of the remaining islands are pounded a lot harder and more frequently by the mighty Pacific, and require an added measure of caution and preparation in order to explore them in safety. Next, we will cover these outer islands, and the anchorages and attractions hidden among their wild exposed shores.   ✸

LOCAL CAUTIONS
• Galley Rock in Peacock Channel is often difficult to locate. Use caution when navigating this area.

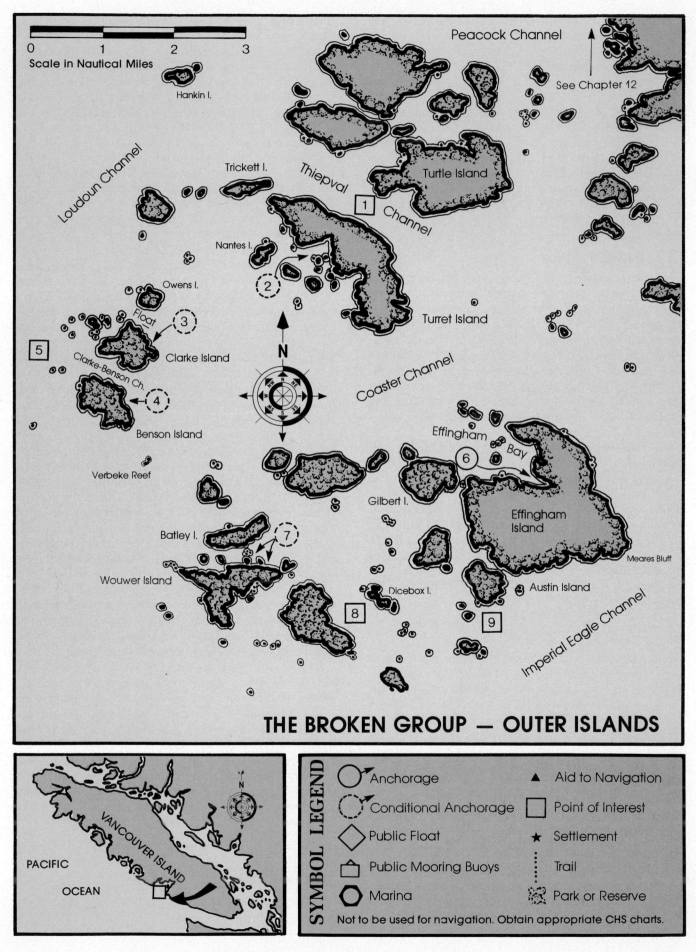

Peacock Channel

See Chapter 12

Hankin I.

Scale in Nautical Miles
0 1 2 3

Turtle Island

Loudoun Channel

Trickett I.

Thiepval Channel

□1

Nantes I.

Owens I.

Float

○2

○3

Turret Island

Clarke Island

□5

Clarke-Benson Ch.

○4

N

Benson Island

Coaster Channel

Verbeke Reef

Effingham Bay

○6

Effingham Island

Gilbert I.

Meares Bluff

Batley I.

○7

Austin Island

Wouwer Island

Dicebox I.

□8

□9

Imperial Eagle Channel

THE BROKEN GROUP — OUTER ISLANDS

N

PACIFIC

OCEAN

VANCOUVER ISLAND

SYMBOL LEGEND

○→ Anchorage	▲ Aid to Navigation
◌→ Conditional Anchorage	□ Point of Interest
◇ Public Float	★ Settlement
⬓ Public Mooring Buoys	⋮ Trail
⬡ Marina	Park or Reserve

Not to be used for navigation. Obtain appropriate CHS charts.

CHAPTER THIRTEEN

The Broken Group — Outer Islands

Turret Island, Clarke Island, Effingham Bay

The outer islands of the Broken Group are among the most exposed and wild islands on the west coast, though they can be explored safely by a cruising yacht. Waves lash the outer shores, and their relentless pounding has created a natural breakwater for the other islands of the sound. Eagles fill the sky, sea lions dot the shores. Tide pools abound with life, providing a natural classroom, accessible to the yachtsman from a limited number of safe anchorages.

But like sirens luring the adventurer for a closer look at the jagged rocks projecting menacingly through the Pacific foam, there are dangers in the seduction. A quick look at any shipwreck map of the coast reveals just how unforgiving this shoreline can be if a navigation error is made, or nature unleashes a tempest in this area. Even when the weather is settled, there are dangers: currents run along the coast and between the islands; the ocean swell rolls relentlessly into the sound; and winds blow hard enough to distort the trees into grotesque shapes, with their spindly branches trailing to leeward. Then there is the silent danger that multiplies all the other dangers tenfold: the insidious fog that plagues the outer coast during summer months.

It's not that Barkley Sound is inherently more dangerous than any other part of the west coast, but more yachtsmen are finding their way to this area — often as their first offshore adventure — and may be unprepared for the sudden changes in conditions the west coast is famous for. On the other hand, Barkley Sound is an excellent proving ground for a well-found yacht handled by a responsible crew in search of a challenge.

Because the area is particularly close to the ominous grey bank which usually hovers just offshore like some velvet sword of Damocles, fog can be a problem in these outer islands. Without notice, the bank (which may extend along the whole outer coast) can drift in and blanket every island, rock and reef in a matter of minutes. If you are more than a mile from a safe anchorage when it blows in, you may spend a few anxious hours listening for breakers and searching for any temporary refuge. Because of this potential hazard, it is important to always know your precise position, and the location of the nearest safe shelter. Here are a few pointers to remember about west coast fog:

- It tends to fill in the channels, while it may be clear over the land areas;
- It can move in or out quickly even in the apparent absence of wind;
- It can be foggy and windy at the same time;
- It generally stays offshore in the morning (making it a good time to move around) but blows in when the westerly picks up, later in the day;
- It usually burns off by mid-afternoon.

Because the fog is more of a late summer phenomenon, west coast cruises are usually planned for June and July rather than August (locally known as "Fogust") or September. Fog statistics and data for several points on the west coast (including Pachena and Tofino) are contained as an appendix in the

"Sailing Directions", along with precipitation figures and hours of sunshine for each month of the year. These statistical averages are essential in planning a west coast voyage, and should be consulted to determine the best time to go.

1. Thiepval Channel

Entering the Broken Group from Loudoun Channel between Turret and Turtle islands can be a hazardous experience. It certainly was for the 130 ft mine-sweeper, HMCS *Thiepval*, when in 1930 she struck a rock in the centre of the channel and sank on the spot. The crew was rescued by her sistership HMCS *Armentieres*.

The six submerged and two exposed rocks in the channel are not marked, but correctly charted and offer no specific danger. Until you have been in the Broken Group for a while, and are familiar with the chart and the local conditions, I suggest you take either Peacock Channel, Coaster Channel, or even the narrow gap between Clarke and Benson Islands to enter the Broken Group. The wreck of the *Thiepval* is an interesting one to dive on, but be sure to time your dive for slack tide. Although there are no specific currents shown in the channel, the tide does rip through there, making the dive even more difficult and dangerous. The wreck is shown on Chart #3638 and the new metric charts (#3671 and 3670). Remember to watch the scale when changing from chart to chart.

2. Turret Island

Whether the winds are from the southwest or the northwest, the wind and waves will roll into the seaward sides of the outer islands. This reduces the number of good all-weather anchorages considerably, because westerlies are the prevailing summer winds on this coast. When the weather is steady, however, the wind usually dies down in the evening, allowing overnight anchorage in bays and coves that may be tenuous in the afternoon. Still, some of the most exciting exploring and beachcombing will be found on these outer islands, and the temptation to visit them is difficult to resist. The anchorages on Turret Island are in this category. If the Pacific swell rolling in from Coaster Channel is not running too high, you can anchor in the cove on the southeast side of Turret Island, or tuck in behind the small islets near the south central part of the island east of Nantes Island for a bit more shelter. Make certain that your anchor is well set before leaving the boat: the holding ground consists of patches of bare rock mixed with mud, and an anchor may skip over the bottom for a long time before it grabs securely.

Once secured, there are a number of interesting side-trips. Besides the beaches on Turret Island, the nearby group of islets — known collectively as Trickett Island — are literally joined by sand at low tide, an unusual phenomenon on our coast. Beachcombing here is among the best in the sound; treasures from around the Pacific Rim wash up on these shores. If you are going to come across a glass ball (still used by Japanese fishermen as net floats) in Barkley Sound, it is likely to be here. Each tide change can bring new treasures. In addition, caves on the leeward sides of the islands penetrate deeply into their granite faces, so take a flashlight and explore their fern-covered roofs. It is very easy to spend an entire day snooping around on this island group.

3. Clarke Island

Situated on the westerly edge of the outer Broken Group are two very similar islands, each about 40 acres in size, which are a very popular destination for

A soft blanket of moss creeps across the roof of a park cabin on Clarke Island. Park facilities also include a small detached float and camping area.

small open boats. The park has provided a cabin for shelter, a camping area, and a small detached float for unloading and launching. The islands, however, offer a good deal of interesting shoreside excursions as well. The shores consist of an interesting array of beaches and driftwood, and the rocks are covered with the rich sea life that thrives on our exposed outer coast. Clarke Island clearly demonstrates the contrast between the inner and outer shores of the sound. The leeward (eastern) side of the island has a beach where waves quietly lap against the salal which grows right to the edge of the high-tide mark. The exposed western shores, battered by waves year after year, support thick clumps of wave-resistant kelp, mussels and barnacles. You can clearly see the natural zoning that occurs by walking around the water's edge at Clarke Island, or you could take one of the two trails which traverse the dense forest. The more westerly trail leads to a pretty gravel beach facing into the channel between Clarke and Benson Islands. The other trail leads to a natural water source.

Preceding page: The jagged, exposed outer islands of the Broken Group provide a natural breakwater for islands in their lee.

Snug pocket beaches and clean green water bring adventuresome visitors to remote beaches in the Broken Group.

Top: Anchorage off Clarke Island should only be considered a day stop except in very stable weather when there is no threat of wind from the southeast. Above: Subtle tones of brown and grey tint a quiet beach on Clarke Island.

Binoculars are a handy navigational aid when negotiating the intricate passages of the west coast.

The anchorage is somewhat marginal. Choose a spot close to the beach on the northeast side of the island, where the sand bottom will hold your anchor securely, or tie to the float if you do not plan to stay overnight. Approaching from the east, watch for two charted submerged rocks (which are also in a protected area where the swell doesn't usually break, and therefore doesn't indicate their location). The anchorage is completely open to the southeast, so in stormy weather, this spot would not offer any protection. Strong westerlies can also push waves over the

reefs and islets facing Clarke and Owens islands, and sometimes cause the anchorage to roll. If the weather is settled — that is, calm at night with winds rising throughout the day and falling off again towards sunset — this anchorage would be suitable; if a westerly is approaching the coast, you can expect strong winds the first day, and a move out of this anchorage is advisable. If these are the conditions that prevail, an interesting anchorage exists just ½ mile to the south on Benson Island.

4. Benson Island

If necessity is the mother of invention, then she is also the mother of discovery. A look at the chart of anchorage surrounded by a striking array of jagged pinnacles and the twisted forms of Sitka spruce.

This unlikely refuge is just off the gravel beach on the east side of Benson Island between the rocky headland on the northeast side, and the kelp-covered reef on the south side of the tiny cove. Here the strongest westerlies can blow with all their fury while a yacht rides comfortably on the edge of the tempest, as if in the eye of a hurricane. The swell rolls past, over Verbeke Reef and down Coaster Channel to pound against the outer shores of islands further in the sound. Here, a westerly or northwesterly can actually curl around the island and blow a yacht toward shore, a phenomenon known as "backwinding."

More reasons than just safe anchoring can entice a visitor to Benson Island. As isolated and rugged as it is, part of the island was cleared in 1893 and a small hotel was built, complete with an orchard and garden. The hotel was operated as late as 1922 by the widow of John Benson, an old time sealing captain after whom the island was named.

Today there is a park campsite on the island, and a few crude trails lead from the beach to the exposed outer shores. Look for remnants of the hotel and or-

From 1893 until 1922 the isolated shores of Benson Island (above) supported a small hotel and orchard. The island was named after the hotel's owner.

Benson Island reveals offlying reefs, islets and rocks projecting inhospitably from the shoreline — not an area where one would expect sheltered anchorage. During an any-port-in-a-storm situation — where nature suddenly and completely envelops the unbelieving yachtsman in the soft grey muffler of fog in this treacherous area — a small nook on the eastern side of the island can take on a welcome appearance, and the yachtsman can find safe shelter in the midst of the very rocks he was trying to avoid. With an anchor set, a stern line is taken ashore to a convenient tree (which keeps the stern of the yacht from drifting onto the hazardous rocks). No sooner is the yacht secured than, as if in reward, the sun will often pierce the grey mat around the island to reveal a safe and protected

chard, or spend the day watching waves riding up the outer shores of the island. The anchorage is safe in north and westerly winds, but southeasterlies make staying in the little cove undesirable. If a southeasterly is imminent, move to the all-weather anchorage on Effingham Island.

5. Clarke-Benson Channel

The narrow channel between Clarke and Benson Islands is often used by yachts travelling from Ucluelet to Bamfield, or through the Broken Group. At first glance, this route looks fraught with hazards, but a closer look shows that the majority of dangers between Ucluelet and Coaster Channel are above water and easy to locate. From Ucluelet, a common route is to go north of Chrow Islands, south of Alley Rock, and straight through the Clarke-Benson Channel. Although narrow, its saving grace is that it is straight, free from rocks, and lit by a small green beacon on its easterly end, making it easy to locate. Once through the channel, the swells abate considerably, and the crew of your yacht can choose the next island destination from the clear and wide breadths of Coaster Channel.

6. Effingham Bay

The only secure, all-weather anchorage in the outer islands of the Broken Group, is in the sheltered northwest corner of Effingham Island, the largest in the whole group. There is anchorage throughout the bay (which is indicated as an Admiralty anchorage on Chart #3638) but the most sheltered spot is located in

The best all-weather anchorage in the Outer Islands is in Effingham Bay, a large, sheltered haven on the northwest corner of Effingham Island.

the easterly part of the bay, tucked right in close to shore. The swells do not reach into this bay, and the wind has little effect on the anchorage.

The bay has been a protected shelter for boats since its first visitor, Captain Charles Barkley, anchored here in his ship *Imperial Eagle* in 1787. As Frances Barkley (young wife of the Captain and the first white woman to visit this coast) describes the scene in her diary: "We anchored in a snug harbour in the island, of which my husband made a plan as far as his knowledge of it would permit. The anchorage was near a large village, and therefore we named the island Village Island." Barkley and his crew, along with John Mackay (who had been picked up in Nootka after spending a year living with the natives) carried out a considerable amount of trade with the

Indians, many of whom had never before seen a white man though traders and explorers had been visiting the more northern part of the coast for over nine years. Barkley traded for sea otter skins for about a month before heading eastward, re-discovering (and naming) Juan de Fuca Strait, and on to Macao where his cargo was sold.

Unfortunately for Captain Barkley, it was discovered that his ship had been built and outfitted in England, even though it was re-named and sailing under Austrian colours. This obvious evasion of monopoly taxes forced the owners to sell the ship, and Barkley lost his commission. In the transfer of the ship his extensive log was also lost. It is thought that this log came into the hands of Captain John Meares and assisted him immensely in his later trading endeavours on this coast. Meares followed Barkley's route, and arrived in the sound a year later aboard his

Velvet green fronds of maidenhair fern hang like decorations from the ceiling of a seacave on the eastern shore of Effingham Island.

ship, *Felice Adventurer*. In his journal "Voyages" he describes Effingham Bay as being "sufficiently capacious to contain an hundred sail of ships, and so fortunately sheltered as to secure them from any storm. The anchorage is also good, being of soft mud, and the watering place perfectly convenient." It was Meares who changed the name from Village Island to honour the Earl of Effingham, the Deputy Earl Marshall of England.

Not only did Meares enjoy the anchorage, but the beauty of Barkley Sound as well. He describes it in his journal this way: "It was now the height of summer; the weather warm and pleasant, and we very sensibly enjoyed the benign influence of the season. Not a single patch of snow was visible on the summits of the lofty mountains which surround the sound. We could not, therefore, but derive a most refreshing satisfaction from our temporary repose in this calm and charming situation." The 305 ft bluff on the easterly tip of Effingham Island which overlooked the Indian village is named to honour this former Royal Navy Commander.

Anchorage for visitors to Wouwer Island (once called Storm Island) can be found between the two small islets at centre of picture.

One of the main attractions at Wouwer Island is the resident herd of sea lions which lounge atop offlying rocks and islets.

Today you can anchor in this same bay and trek overland to the old village site on the eastern shore of the island. Unlike most of the rest of Barkley Sound, you are not likely to have the anchorage to yourself. Many yachts use this bay as a base from which to explore the outer islands. Effingham Bay has Barkley Sound's most spectacular sunsets, so take your camera ashore. If you tuck right inside the inner reaches of the bay, take a stern line to shore to allow more room for fellow yachtsmen to anchor close to the stream where the beginning of the trail can be seen.

After traversing the trail (a 20-minute hike through the cool green forest) the wisdom of choosing this site for a great Indian village is obvious. It has a sheltered, peaceful countenance and offers a safe place to land a canoe. The reserve is private and nothing should be taken or moved from the site. There is a small, temporary yacht anchorage off the village site, in about 24 ft, but this bay is seldom used except by fishboats in foggy weather or as a temporary stop in settled conditions. It is completely open to all easterly winds. If you want to visit, the safest place to moor is still Effingham Bay.

Besides the midden (refuse from centuries of shell-fish diets) and a few scattered remnants of long-houses, there is little left of the village except the priceless view. There are a number of sea caves on the shore southeast of the village site. One of these caves penetrates the island for over 100 ft, with maidenhair fern hanging like green velvet decorations from the roof. Take a flashlight to get the full beauty of the colours. Access is available along the shore only during low tide; and as the tide rises, the headlands can cut off access to and from the caves, so don't get caught by a rising tide. One cave near Meares Bluff is accessible only from seaward and has been pierced all the way through by countless Pacific waves, a situation which results in strange noises emanating from

its depths as the swells roll in. Fishing is good throughout this area, so troll a line or try jigging. The rugged and exciting outer islands can be easily explored from the safety of the overnight base at Effingham Bay. A campsite for small boats has been established on nearby Gilbert Island, and on a summer day, dozens of canoes and kayaks can be seen pulled up on the beach on the north side of the island.

7. Wouwer Island

Nowhere in the Broken Group is the ruggedness of the outer coast more visible than at Wouwer Island. Once known as Storm Island, Wouwer, on the extreme southwesterly edge of the group, is the first island to suffer the pounding of the open ocean. The swell meets this rocky barrier with a dramatic fury. The islets and rocks off the coast of this island are also the domain of eagles and a large rookery of sea lions. These fierce blubbery beasts rule their territory with great authority. If a small boat of inquisitive visitors gets too close, they take to the sea and defend their rocky kingdom as any territorial animal would. By using a telephoto lens from the shore of Wouwer Island you can get good pictures without endangering yourself or disturbing these social animals. With increasing numbers of people visiting these islands, there is a risk of driving the sea lions farther and farther away from areas where they might be observed. They are one of the great attractions of the park, and if left undisturbed they may grow again in numbers and begin to appear elsewhere on the west coast where they can be enjoyed. Park wardens patrol this area regularly to ensure that the animals are not bothered by careless visitors.

The safest anchorage for Wouwer Island is in 30 ft, tucked inside the northeast shore behind two small islets that almost link it to Batley Island. There is just

Looking south from Austin Island.

In March, 1972 the freighter Vanlene *ran up on rocks south of Austin Island. Though its cargo was later recovered, the ship ultimately slipped beneath the waters of Barkley Sound.*

enough room here for one or two boats and because of the attractions of the island the best anchorage is often occupied. In this case there is another limited anchorage immediately to the east of the preferred cove. Watch for the kelp covered rocks. If conditions permit, you can anchor anywhere in the bay formed by Wouwer and Batley Islands, but make sure your ground tackle is firmly set; much of the holding ground is kelp-covered rock, and difficult to set an anchor into. Westerly swells can break over the islets protecting the western shore at high tide, and easterlies blow right into the anchorage. Under reasonable westerly conditions, however, a yacht could safely overnight here with an extra line holding the stern from swinging onto the shore at the change of tide.

8. Dicebox Island

The remainder of the outer islands in the Broken Group provide little in the way of secure anchorage, but offer a wealth of interesting areas to explore by dinghy or small boat. Tiny Dicebox Island, for example, has two interesting caves near the southwest portion of the island, one accessible only by boat, while the other can be explored at low tide. The latter cave has the beginnings of stalactites slowly forming from the ceiling like discoloured icicles. Tide pools, full of creatures left by the receding waters — sea anemones, barnacles, crabs and whelks — provide hours of entertainment and education. The pools are like miniature colour television sets showing continuous nature programs. As the water heats up on a summer day the cold-blooded animals liven up into a frenzy of activity. The next high tide will bring a new store of cooler, nutrient-laden water for the tiny residents of the pools, and the scene repeats itself as the tide recedes.

Recent archaeological studies of Barkley Sound have revealed that this tiny island had nine longhouses during the peak of its summer occupation, and that the whole of Barkley Sound may have had as many as 8000-9000 residents at one time. The Ohiat tribe, a division of the Nootka linguistic family, was a powerful group, but no leader like Wickaninnish or Maquinna ever emerged to lead them into the pages of history with such notoriety.

9. Austin Island

On a rainy March 14, 1972 the Captain of the 8500-ton freighter *Vanlene* radioed that his gyrocompass was not working and he was unsure of his position. He had come across the Pacific from Japan with a load of compact automobiles, and estimated that he was 60 miles west of Cape Flattery. Within moments of the radio call, the *Vanlene* struck a rock just south of Austin Island with such force that it rode half way over the pointed rock, and became impaled by it. Miraculously, the crew escaped injury and were rescued the next day, but the *Vanlene* could not be saved. Efforts by sea-going tugs could not move the ship, and after much of its cargo of automobiles was airlifted off by helicopter, the ship was left to rust. Successive winter storms broke her in two, and then, in final surrender the bow slipped unnoticed one day into 20 fathoms of Barkley Sound water.

Such is the history of shipwrecks on this coast. By missing the entrance to Juan de Fuca Strait, ships have been piling their wooden and steel carcasses on the shores of this sound for over a century. Today the *Vanlene* is marked only by a shipwreck symbol on the chart near Austin Island and is visible only to passing fish and enterprising scuba divers. Much of the superstructure is still visible, and provides a popular dive site for experienced divers who get there in small private boats, or from charters operated from Bamfield or Ucluelet.

The outer islands of the group possess all the attractions that make them desirable destinations:

wrecks, historical sites, caves to explore, and wildlife in abundance. Because these islands are all in Pacific Rim National Park, the same benefits and rules of other parks apply here: feel free to go ashore anywhere that is safe, but be careful about fires, and camp only in designated sites; take your garbage with you when you leave, and do not disturb the wildlife. The Broken Group of islands appear as wild today as they did when Captain Barkley first sailed into the sound almost 200 years ago. If we "take only pictures, and leave only footprints," then future adventurers can view the scene with the same sense of marvel, and respect for the forces that create such beauty.

Like a spotlight, the last rays of a setting sun shine on Batley Island in the Broken Group — Barkley Sound's Outer Islands.

LOCAL CAUTIONS
- Sudden influx of fog into the channels, move in early morning.
- Poor holding ground (kelp over rock) in many anchorages.
- Charts in this area use different scales. Be sure you check the unit of measure being used on each chart.

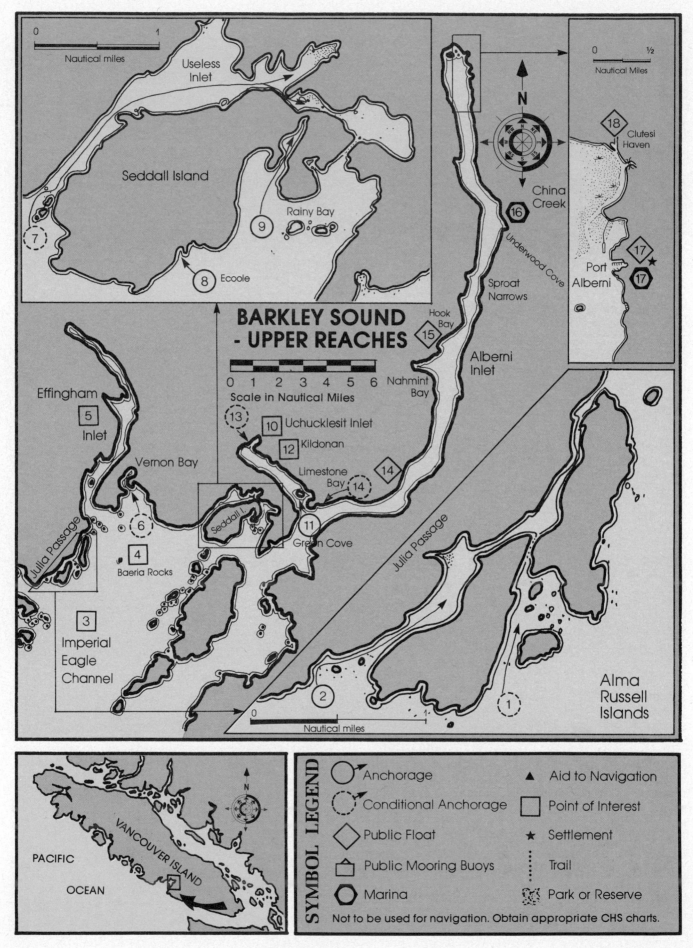

**BARKLEY SOUND
- UPPER REACHES**

Scale in Nautical Miles
0 1 2 3 4 5 6

Useless Inlet

Seddall Island

Rainy Bay

⑨

⑦

⑧ Ecoole

Effingham Inlet

5

Vernon Bay

⑥

4

Baeria Rocks

Julia Passage

3

Imperial Eagle Channel

⑬

10 Uchucklesit Inlet

12 Kildonan

Seddall I.

Limestone Bay

⑭ 14

⑪

Green Cove

Hook Bay ⬦15

Nahmint Bay

Alberni Inlet

Sproat Narrows

Underwood Cove

⑯

China Creek

N

Clutesi Haven ⬦18

17

Port Alberni

17

Julia Passage

② ①

Alma Russell Islands

0 Nautical miles ½

0 Nautical miles 1

0 Nautical miles 1

PACIFIC OCEAN

VANCOUVER ISLAND

N

SYMBOL LEGEND

◯➤ Anchorage

◌➤ Conditional Anchorage

◇ Public Float

⌂ Public Mooring Buoys

⬡ Marina

▲ Aid to Navigation

☐ Point of Interest

★ Settlement

⋮ Trail

Park or Reserve

Not to be used for navigation. Obtain appropriate CHS charts.

174

CHAPTER FOURTEEN

Upper Reaches of Barkley Sound

Alma Russell Islands, Useless Inlet, Port Alberni

The upper reaches of Barkley Sound are well known to local anglers and yachtsmen who frequent the area from their home base at Port Alberni, but less familiar to west coast cruisers who spend most of their cruising time in the Broken Group. As boats begin frequenting Barkley Sound, some of the fringe areas of this remarkable area will become more and more important. At the same time, a greater number of smaller boats are being launched at the head of Alberni Inlet and visiting the sound through its "back door." For these yachtsmen, the upper reaches will be their introduction to the majesty of Captain Barkley's great discovery.

1 Alma Russell Islands

On the south side of these islands (named for the late assistant archivist and president of the B.C. Historical Association) is a little harbour which is protected from the swell by the offlying islands of the Broken Group. Like sentries, two submerged rocks guard the narrow entrance between the highest of the islands and the smallest, Robinson Island. These must be avoided, but there is deep water between them. The small bay formed by the islands is ideal for one or two boats to swing freely in a truly remarkable setting, far from the reach of all but the worst southwesterlies. From here you have easy access to the great sportsfishing area around Swale Rock in Sechart Channel, and yet are far enough from the Broken Group to find solitude in the shelter of the 30ft-deep lagoon here.

2 Julia Passage

If you're looking for an interesting challenge at either end of a placid, fully-sheltered channel, then Julia Passage will certainly oblige. On the west entrance are a collection of 14 rocks and reefs of different sizes (but all of equal hardness) which are strategically located far enough apart to entice entry, yet close enough together to ensure a good flow of adrenaline when passing through them. The northeast entrance (known locally as Canoe Pass) is only about 25ft wide and laced above with spindly branches that reach out to claw your mast as you pass. Between these two entrances is an interesting protected channel which varies in width from about 30 ft to 300 yards and is shallow enough for convenient anchorage throughout. About a dozen floathomes have been moored in the most sheltered spots close to shore, most of them occupied only during the summer and on weekends. If you can't resist the lure of such a sheltered place, here's some advice on how to avoid getting caught between the proverbial "rock and a hard place." For the westerly entrance, keep very close to the western (Vancouver Island) shoreline all the way until well inside the passage. Don't try to go between the rocks — the chart is not thoroughly accurate in marking the location of the reefs. Go just before high tide, proceed cautiously and employ whatever good-luck charms you have to get you through such situations.

The northeast entrance is extremely narrow, but if you go at high slack, there is no real trick to making

the passage. The current goes through this cut at a fair rate, so try to arrive when the tide is slack, or slightly against you so you can maintain steerage. Don't get overconfident, this passage is notorious for causing sudden, unscheduled stops.

3   Imperial Eagle Channel

The widest of the three main channels in the sound takes its name from Barkley's *Imperial Eagle*, at 400 tons one of the largest sailing ships ever to visit the west coast. This channel is relatively clear of dangers, and often provides exhilarating sailing. A passage between the Broken and the Deer Group of islands is almost always made on a reach. As the "Sailing Directions" warn: "During south or southwest gales there is a heavy sea in this channel." Even in west or northwest winds, the swells are more pronounced in this channel than they are in Loudoun and Trevor channels. However, this increased motion does not usually cause major problems for the well-found yacht, expecially in the summer months when conditions are seldom extreme.

4   Baeria Rocks

This group of barren islets, lying near the centre of the northern part of Imperial Eagle Channel, take the full force of the swell rolling in from the open Pacific. They appear so inhospitable, that one would expect them to be devoid of life — such is not the case. The rocks are covered with various species of cormorants, guillemots and gulls, which were the reason they were formerly called the Bird Islands. This group of rocks is a common destination for scuba divers who go there to view the abundant varieties of subtidal life which live on and around the rocks. Good observations are almost guaranteed. The rocks above and below the water are now protected as a Provincial Ecological Reserve (#24), but expect no convenient anchorage except under calm conditions. The islands can be visited by motorized tender from the security of nearby anchorages, or by dive-charter boats originating in Ucluelet or Bamfield. As in all Ecological Reserves, no plant or animal life can be removed from the islands, and every effort should be made not to disturb the wildlife. The islets were named for *Baeria coronaria*, a yellow trailing annual which is extremely rare north of California and is found only here and on Triangle Island (also an Ecological Reserve) west of Cape Scott in B.C.

5   Effingham Inlet

Although Barkley Sound is not renowned for its long, steep-sided fjords, Effingham Inlet provides a respectable example for the interested visitor. As is the case in most west coast fjords, it is extremely deep,

Starfish and urchins brighten the bottom of a tide pool in Barkley Sound.

long and terminates in a drying mudflat. There is little opportunity to anchor in this 8-mile-inlet unless you tuck in close to shore, and let out plenty of rode — most coves in this inlet are very deep right up to shore, and drop off sharply to abysmal depths. The attractions of this fjord are the mountain peaks that rise to over 4000 ft on each side of an often narrow, twisting channel. When winds are strong they can funnel to wicked velocities in these ravines, although the normal condition is light and variable winds requiring motoring. If you wish to anchor among the peaks of Barkley Sound, Effingham is not the best — try the cove in Pipestem Inlet, a few miles to the west (see Chapter 11).

6   Vernon Bay

At the extreme northern part of Imperial Eagle Channel, where the waves hit the shore with ferocity, is an open bay which shows the evidence of centuries of pounding. Beyond this untenable bay — through a curved, restricted opening — is a large cove which, for the most part, is far too deep for convenient anchorage. However, on the southeast part of this cove, beneath the cliffs, enough outwash has accumulated from the nearby river that a small sandy patch 33 ft deep provides a shallow area where one can shelter from wind and wave. Although the anchorage is suitable for all weather, the entrance could be dangerous if the sea was running high in this area (as in strong southwesterly blows) so this condition limits its overall utility.

7   Useless Inlet

When Captain Richards named this beautiful waterway in 1861, he certainly was not thinking of the modern-day auxiliary yacht in search of new and exciting destinations. Useless Inlet was presumably named because its entrance is narrow, and requires making an S-turn to avoid the rocks in mid-channel, making it useless as a harbour for larger ships. However, this mis-named inlet has found favour among yachtsmen who have ventured to this spot to make their own determination of its usefulness. The entry does require caution — first hug the western (Vancouver Island) shoreline until abeam of the small islet in the entrance on the port side. The kelp-covered reef

Preceding page: The head of Alberni Inlet, with Port Alberni centre, and the strait of Georgia, across Vancouver Island, in the background.

178

Top and above: Still waters reflect an overcast sky in Useless Inlet, so named because of the waterways inaccessibility to larger ships in the last century. Latter-day yachts have considerably less trouble.

extending westward from Seddall Island should now be beside and slightly behind you. Waves may break over it, but this should not cause you problems, unless conditions are extreme. Turn east for about 20-30 ft and then complete the S-turn by heading straight up the inlet. The reef will now be behind you, breaking up the swell. There are no further major hazards in the entire inlet.

Inside is another world. Eagles peer down from lofty perches in trees that cling to the cliff sides along both shores. Weasels peer out from behind the huckleberry bushes with large inquisitive eyes, and scurry along the rocks. The inlet opens up into a smooth lagoon with a variety of anchorages, each with a view of the 3000 ft Mt. Aveline. For the most interesting and secure anchorage head all the way into the southeast corner of the inlet near the entrance to Fatty Basin. If you have the large-scale chart (#3646, Plans in Barkley Sound) you will find this area covered in good detail. Be aware that this chart is metric, and depths are in metres, rather than fathoms and feet. You will see that the anchorage has a mud bottom ranging from 14-40 ft depending on where you choose to drop the hook. You should also notice that currents in the narrow channels (which are not navigable) leading to Fatty Basin run up to 4 knots in either direction. The closer you are to this channel, the more effect the current will have on your anchorage.

Clearcut hillsides surround anchorage in Useless Inlet. A narrow dinghy-passage at head of inlet leads to Fatty Basin (background).

Derelict old buildings are all that remain of once-prosperous fish-curing operation at Ecoole on Seddall Island.

There are signs throughout the inlet put up by the Fisheries Research Board that the basin is an experimental area, and no trapping or dragging is allowed here. These signs (and the few concrete foundations of the old hatchery pens) are all that's left of a failed experiment to raise Atlantic lobsters on the west coast. This area, considered an excellent location for such an experiment now supports a growing population of crabs, small fish and, unfortunately, no-see-ums and mosquitoes.

If you are adventurous, you can take a dinghy into Fatty Basin via the narrow channel that connects the two bodies of water. The period of slack water is very short, so don't let the current trap you inside the basin — the 4 knot measure indicated on the chart is not an overestimation. No particulars are available to explain Captain Richards' choice of the name for Fatty Basin.

Although few anchorages on the coast are as sheltered as this one, heavy swells in Imperial Eagle Channel could make entry into Useless Inlet dangerous. Under these conditions the anchorage could not be recommended.

8 Ecoole

On the south shore of Seddall Island is a small cove, just big enough for one boat to find easy anchorage, in front of the deserted trading post at Ecoole. A newly-charted rock dries at a 2 ft tide immediately east of the point of land which forms the eastern shore of the cove, so watch for it. Ecoole is an Indian word that means "the site of an old village," an appropriate name, because there has been settlement here for centuries. Its first white settler was mentioned in 1895 when Melvin Swartout, the sailing missionary, dropped anchor in this "snug little cove" on his way to visit the Ohiats in their winter encampment at Sarita. Here he met a hermit who lived there year-round, and operated a small store, trading with the natives. The ruins one sees today were completed in 1920 when as many as 20 people inhabited the site which consisted of a post office, general store, fish-curing operation and school. The site was abandoned about 1940, and since then relic-seekers have combed the ruins for souvenirs such as old bottles.

9 Rainy Bay

A mile to the northeast of Ecoole is a very protected cove separated from Useless Inlet by a thin neck of land. The anchorage is in a picturesque setting, but extensive logging has defaced the view of the backshore of the bay. As logging moves on to other areas, these coves will again take on the green cloak they have been stripped of and the primitive majesty of Barkley Sound will again prevail. Anchor far inside the cove in about 25 ft where no waves or weather will reach. The flood tide in Junction Passage fronting the bay runs east as much as 1 knot.

180

10 Uchucklesit Inlet

The name for this inlet is derived from "How-chuck-les-aht", meaning "the people who live by a spring situated at the end of a deep inlet." At one time, an entire "boom town" was planned on its southern shores by a land development company established in Victoria. A grandiose town plan — drawn up to attract investors — described the wealth of mineral resources which were practically lying on the ground waiting to be picked up by potential residents. Not much ever came of the scheme, and by 1900 (despite a flurry of mineral claims), the town was forgotten, and no ore of any consequence was ever taken out.

Today the inlet is known for having one of the world's highest annual rainfall measurements (over 300 in.), for its extensive log-booms, and as being the location of the abandoned cannery at Kildonan, the first on this coast, on the north side of the inlet. The rum-running four-masted schooner *Malahat* also ended her days beached on the shores of Uchucklesit Inlet after being swamped off Cape Beale in 1944.

Green Cove (right) at entrance to Uchucklesit Inlet makes a convenient stopping point for yachts travelling between Port Alberni and Barkley Sound.

Uchucklesit Inlet is noted for its abundant rainfall, often more than 300 inches a year. Photo shows private floats near Daller Point.

11 Green Cove

Just inside the entrance to Uchucklesit Inlet is a small, protected cove which once had four gold and silver claims on it. Despite great effort and expectation, none of these claims panned out. Today log booms and tugs are the mainstay of economic activity in the area, and the anchorage (reached by Chaputs Passage) is usually deserted. Watch for the 10 ft drying rock on the north side of the passage. Although the cove is not as scenic as most in the sound, it is a convenient layover spot for small craft making the long trek down Alberni Inlet to Barkley Sound. Even given this advantage there are better anchorages at Limestone Bay, in Alberni Inlet or in Snug Cove, further west. Green Cove usually remains unoccupied except in a southwesterly when Limestone Bay becomes uncomfortable.

12 Kildonan

Small amounts of fish were processed at the cannery built midway up Uchucklesit Inlet in 1903. The cannery was sold in 1910 to other interests who named it Kildonan after their hometown in Scotland. Later, a cold-storage and reduction plant were added to the cannery and Kildonan became a thriving enterprise. By 1960 the entire operation was closed down, the buildings levelled and burned. Such is the history of many small coastal communities — over the period of half a century, the barren site became home to as many as 300 people before changes in technology and economics reduced the viability of the operation, and the town died. Today Kildonan consists of a few families who run the post office and come out to meet the freight boat, *Lady Rose*, when she calls on her tri-weekly summer run to Ucluelet.

13 Snug Basin

Near the head of Uchucklesit Inlet, a narrow channel leads to a cove which Captain Richards determined was protected enough to apply the name of Snug Basin. Far from the crowds of Port Alberni and the weather of the sound and the inlet, this quiet green cove deserves its name. The placid waters of this lagoon provide good shelter for boats going between Port Alberni and Barkley Sound, and is usually warm enough for swimming. With its mud bottom, anchorage would be ideal except for the fact that the average depth in the lagoon is almost 60 ft right up to the shore. At 5:1 scope this means over 300 ft of rode is needed for safe anchorage. However, because the lagoon is so calm, and uncrowded, 3:1 might be

181

adequate here. The almost landlocked shores remain as wild as they were centuries ago and the area's reputation for being very wet is faithfully maintained by the rainmakers which rise abruptly from the shores of the inlet. You can take a dinghy a good distance up the stream that flows out of Henderson Lake into snug Basin. It has a chasm-like appearance and was once the site of a fish hatchery.

Snug Basin off Uchucklesit Inlet provides sheltered, albeit deep, anchorage for boats passing to and from Port Alberni.

14 Limestone Bay

Just outside Uchucklesit Inlet is a small cove frequently used as an anchorage by boats seeking shelter from the winds that blow down the channel. Protected by Limestone Islet, this picturesque little bay nestled into the southern slopes of Hecate Mountain (3200 ft) deserves consideration as a destination rather than just a stopover point. The Port Alberni Harbour Commission has moored a float in the bay with 150 ft of docking space for the convenience of yachtsmen. North of Limestone Islet there is an old mine to explore — at low tide you can go in as much as 500 ft. Take a flashlight and explore this failed enterprise. On summer weekends the bay can get crowded with runabouts lingering in the areas for the big salmon that are frequently caught in the nearby waters. In a southwesterly blow the bay can get choppy and untenable. In this case, head for Green Cove, around the corner, or try Snug Basin 3½ miles to the northwest. Small private marinas are also being established in this area to cater to the needs of the sportsfisherman. There is a marina already at Haggards Cove between Chubb Point and Uchucklesit Inlet.

15 Alberni Inlet

Named during Spanish explorations of the area by Eliza in 1791 after Don Pedro Alberni, his commanding officer, this inlet, over 20 miles long, practically bisects Vancouver Island. (The distance between Port Alberni and Qualicum Beach on Vancouver Island's eastern shore is a mere 12 miles.) Although the shores are steep-sided and offer little opportunity for anchorage, there are some interesting sights along the way. In places, the inlet narrows to less than ¼ mile, accentuating the steepness of the shores.

However, despite its beauty, Alberni Inlet is not considered to be a yachtsman's paradise. This long inlet runs east for about 4 miles before curving due north near its head. Even in 1791 when the *Santa Saturnina* investigated the "Boca de Carrasco" (Barkley Sound), the captain said he could not explore this inlet, "on account of contrary winds and continual rain." The winter of 1861 was so cold that this inlet actually froze over from Pocohontas Point to Port Alberni, a distance of over 18 miles. Fortunately this has not occurred since.

Above: Low clouds hang over hills along Alberni Inlet. Right: The author's Coyote anchored with ground tackle fore and aft.

One of the most popular marinas for Port Alberni boatmen is located at China Creek, several miles down the Inlet.

Currents run up to 1½ knots at the narrowest part and this flow of water can be greatly increased by the winds which funnel regularly up or down the inlet. When the wind opposes the tide, a miserable chop can build, making conditions uncomfortable for the great number of small craft which regularly ply the channel. Although runabouts greatly outnumber all other craft on these waters, the traffic of large freighters to and from Port Alberni is not insignificant, averaging almost one per day. The lower reaches of the inlet offer few attractions other than scenery.

About half way up the inlet is Nahmint Bay — known for its Tyee salmon — which opens up on the west side. This bay offers little shelter, and is too deep for convenient anchorage. However, the Harbour Commission for Port Alberni has moored a float in a small cove known as Hook Bay just north of here. It provides a point mid-way along the long inlet where one can get shelter, especially from a southerly wind. It is just 2½ miles from Sproat Narrows where the Franklin River has pushed a sand and gravel bar far into the inlet, reducing its width to less than ¼ mile. Here, an ebb tide can run up to 1½ knots, a current which is also greatly affected by the prevailing wind. On the west side, just beyond the narrows (which, like the rest of the inlet, has a number of aids to navigation) fish holding pens can be seen moored close to

shore. These pens are often covered by galvanized sheds and rafted together. Avoid creating a wash near these pens, as they are vulnerable to damage. There are more in Underwood Cove, 2 miles further up the inlet, and elsewhere near the mouth of Alberni Inlet. These mariculture projects are proving to be very profitable for the entrepreneurs who started them a few years ago. The young salmon reared here are shipped to buyers around the world.

16 China Creek

Probably the most popular marina for sportsfishermen living in Port Alberni and fishing in Barkley Sound is the one tucked behind the breakwater at China Creek; this location cuts over 5 miles off the long trip down Alberni Inlet. The marina provides fuel, showers and washrooms, is well maintained and borders on China Creek Provincial Park where there are campgrounds. It is connected by road to Port Alberni and many residents keep their boats here. The marina has about 4800 ft of dock space, and is under the jurisdiction of the Port Alberni Harbour Commission. Casual moorage is permitted when space is available. The Provincial Park at China Creek

184

provides no direct services for the yachtsman except for a small concession and commissary. Two miles north of the marina, beneath the steep slopes of Mt. Hankin, is the most constricted part of Alberni Inlet, Stamp Narrows. Here the width is less than 800 ft and a tidal current of 1 knot can be experienced, along with a funnelling of the local winds. The narrows were named for Captain Edward Stamp who established a sawmill at the head of this inlet in 1860. The mill was built 3 miles beyond the narrows where today the largest settlement reaching tidewater on the west coast of Vancouver Island is situated.

17 Port Alberni

This bustling mill town of over 23,000 people with its giant smoking chimneys has all the services of a small city including everything for the yachtsman. The inset on the new metric chart (#3672) is essential for safe navigation in the harbour. It has a large scale, and shows the location of most harbour services. Port Alberni and its companion city, Alberni, are modern towns based primarily on the export of timber products. Loading docks and log booms dominate the shoreline and freighters often anchor in the harbour. You will find a variety of stores and shops — including liquor stores and chandleries — a complete hospital, several laundromats, a post office and several hotels. There is no convenient anchorage for small craft in the harbour, but two large marinas have public floats.

Port Alberni, situated at the end of this long inlet was heavily damaged in 1964 by tsunamis (tidal waves) following the severe earthquake in Alaska. The "Sailing Directions" describe the event: "Waves arrived at intervals of about 90 minutes, and the largest may have had a height from trough to crest of 26 ft. Its maximum height reached more than 7 ft above the highest tide levels and flooded over dikes into the city. Lowest troughs, though not visible in the darkness may have run out to more than 7 ft below lowest normal tides." Although tsunamis are extremely rare, the "Sailing Directions" still warn of the danger in this area.

For the yachtsman, facilities for hull, machinery and electronic repairs are within close proximity of the main public wharf. There is also a marine ways which is capable of handling vessels up to 130 ft in length, making it one of the largest on the coast. All major fuel companies have outlets in the harbour, and Hunters Marina with fuel and water is located near Polly Point. There are several marine chandleries in town all within walking distance of the public floats. The fisherman's harbour is located near the large sawmill in town at the foot of Argyle Street and has 3500 ft of public moorage space. In summer when the large fishing fleet is not in town, there is usually plenty of space for visiting yachtsmen. The marina is immediately adjacent to a large sawmill where there is often a lot of marine activity.

Public floats in Port Alberni lie adjacent to the timber products which are the mainstay of this island town.

A man-made breakwater protects boats at Clutesi Haven from traffic travelling along the Somass River near Port Alberni.

In addition, summer of 1984 marked the opening of the nearby Alberni Harbour Quay, a 3-acre platform of reclaimed land right in the centre of the harbour's industries. It houses a tailgate market, a seafood market, picnic areas, and a small public boatyard. There are also restaurants, boutiques, and companies chartering everything from row-boats to float planes to get sports fishermen to the fabulous salmon fishing areas throughout the Inlet.

The development is integrated into the industrial heart of Port Alberni, and from the dock and tower you can view freighters loading, float planes landing, and the large fishing fleet as it moves in and out of the harbour. The harbourmaster is also located here as are the town's fireboat, the RCMP patrol boat, and a federal fisheries patrol vessel. With its modern architecture and its interface with the local industry, Alberni Harbour Quay promises to be an attraction worth seeing while in Port Alberni.

If quieter moorage is preferred, refer to the inset of chart #3672 and travel a mile up the lower reaches of the Somass River (which flows into the head of the

Opposite: Port Alberni at head of Alberni Inlet provides all needed facilities, including marine ways, chandleries and electronics repair services.

Inlet) to the large and modern marina at Clutesi Haven. If you have a sailboat, and the mast is over 100 ft (a rather significant spar) you will have to watch the overhead cable along the way. At any rate, keep close to the eastern shore, and follow the buoys shown on the chart to avoid the drying bank that fills the head of the Inlet. If your boat has significant draft (over 6 ft) you will need the assistance of the tide to get you over the shallows in the river.

18   Clutesi Haven

This marina, operated by the Harbour Commission offers almost 5000 ft of moorage space, ice, washrooms and showers as well as water and fuel supplies. It's a bit further away from the huge mills this town is built around, and is considerably quieter than the downtown floats. Perhaps more significantly, there is a public boat launch for entry into Barkley Sound's "back door." There is no mast tower here for small sailboats, but once the boat is in the water the derrick at the fisherman's harbour in town can be used to raise the spar. An increasing number of small boat operators are launching here (also at Ucluelet, Toquart Bay and Bamfield) and returning to Georgia Strait or Puget Sound via Juan de Fuca Strait. This avoids the long trip west against the prevailing summer winds and swells that roll down that waterway, yet still allows small boats to visit Barkley Sound. Others launch here, cruise the sound, and return to Port Alberni for the haul back. Clutesi Marina (5104 River Road, Port Alberni, 723-8022) is the closest access point to Barkley Sound from the east coast of the island. For an up-to-date list of companies that can haul and launch pleasure boats check the yellow pages under the heading Boat Hauling, or refer to the "Yacht Services Directory" published by *Pacific Yachting* each October.

Whether you launch a boat here or simply want to explore the upper reaches of the inlet, be sure to take along your sportfishing licence and your favourite lure. Large salmon are common in the upper reaches of Barkley Sound and there are enough yacht havens in this area offering a variety of attractions to give you good reason for making the effort to visit this lesser-travelled part of Barkley Sound.

LOCAL CAUTIONS
- Tidal currents in Julia Passage, Sproat Narrows, Stamp Narrows.
- Choppy seas in Alberni Inlet when wind opposes the tide.
- Shallow river bars north of Port Alberni Public Floats.
- Overhead cable between Clutesi Haven Marina and Port Alberni has clearance of approximately 100 ft.

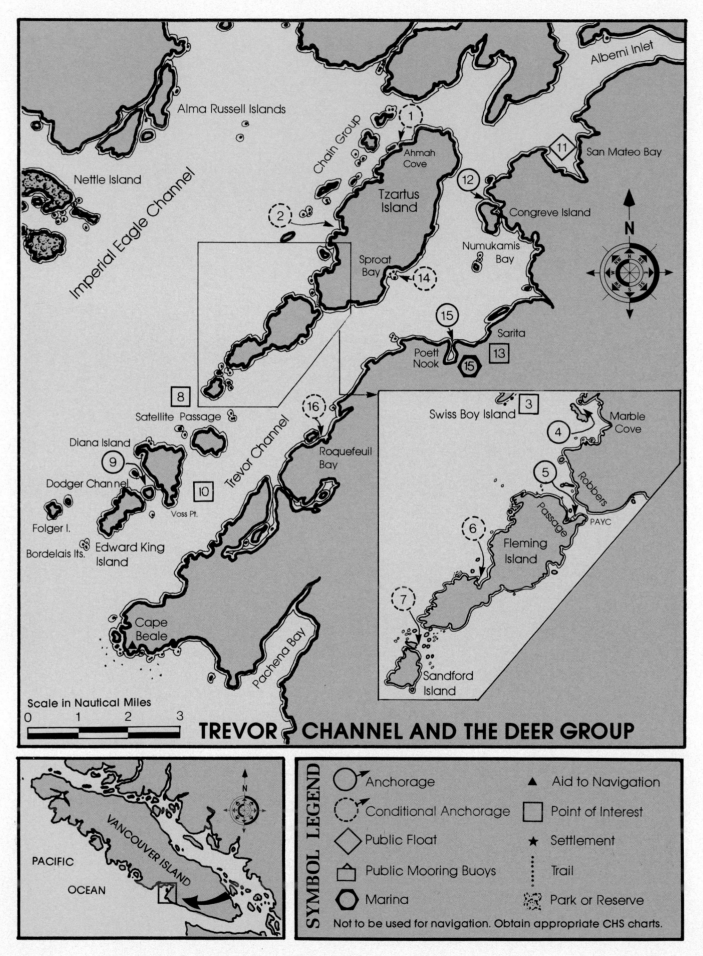

Alberni Inlet

Alma Russell Islands

Chain Group

① Ahmah Cove

⑪ San Mateo Bay

Nettle Island

⑫

Tzartus Island

Congreve Island

②

Numukamis Bay

N

Sproat Bay

⑭

⑮ Sarita

Poett Nook

⑬

⑮

Satellite Passage

⑧

⑯

Roquefeuil Bay

Swiss Boy Island ③

Marble Cove

④

Diana Island

⑨

⑤

Robbers

Dodger Channel

⑩

Trevor Channel

PAYC

Folger I.

Voss Pt.

⑥

Passage

Fleming Island

Bordelais Its.

Edward King Island

⑦

Cape Beale

Pachena Bay

Sandford Island

Scale in Nautical Miles

0   1   2   3

TREVOR CHANNEL AND THE DEER GROUP

VANCOUVER ISLAND

PACIFIC

OCEAN

N

SYMBOL LEGEND

⊙→ Anchorage

▲ Aid to Navigation

⊙→ Conditional Anchorage

☐ Point of Interest

◇ Public Float

★ Settlement

⬠ Public Mooring Buoys

⋮ Trail

⬡ Marina

Park or Reserve

Not to be used for navigation. Obtain appropriate CHS charts.

CHAPTER FIFTEEN

Deer Group & Eastern Shores Barkley Sound

Ahmah Cove, Swiss Boy Island, Dodger Channel

The chain of islands occupying the eastern part of Barkley Sound is not in Pacific Rim National Park and is less frequently visited than the Broken Group. Similarly, the coves and bays of Barkley Sound's eastern shoreline are largely overlooked by the cruising yachtsman. This usually means that the anchorages, though in every way as beautiful and interesting as their neighbours, are more likely to be unoccupied. They lie in a long row between Imperial Eagle and Trevor Channels, with only one major pass (Satellite Passage) between them. As is the case in the Broken Group, the anchorages farther in the sound are more sheltered than those nearer the open Pacific, and exhibit corresponding differences in the natural characteristics of their shores. This, then, may serve as an introduction to this area, even for the yachtsman who has already been to Barkley Sound before.

1 Ahmah Cove

One of the cosiest coves in Barkley Sound is located in the furthest backwaters of the inlet tucked between Tzartus Island (the sound's biggest) and Ahmah Island (one of its smallest). Ahmah is a Nootka word meaning "large grey diver," a probable reference to the grey whales that frequent west coast shores between February and June. Besides being narrow, the cove's restricted entrance carries only about 3 ft of water at the lowest tide. However, unless the tide is nearly at its lowest levels, there should usually be enough depth for your boat. If you didn't know the little cove was there, you might easily miss it, many

have. The mud bottom would hold you in the wildest winds, and no waves of any consequence could reach you here. There are two floating cabins in the bay, where refugees from the populated areas escape on summer weekends. The entrance to the anchorage is guarded by a large submerged reef directly north of the east tip of Ahmah Island, but this hazard is marked on the chart (#3671) and is easy to see.

Beyond Ahmah Island, still in the protection of the scattered collection of islands known as the Chain Group, is Holford Bay. Although the bay looks as if it would offer good shelter from southerly winds, swells wrap around the islands and roll right into the bay. Since it is also open to the west, anchorage here is not recommended. Nor is passage recommended southwest through the Geer Islets (part of the Chain Group) unless you have a taste for adventure and a sharp eye for the rocks that lie scattered about the passage just below the surface. A safer route is to go outside the Chain Group in order to further explore the rest of the islands in the Deer Group.

2 Tzartus Cove

On the west side of Tzartus Island just ½ mile north of Marble Cove is an unnamed cove which offers a good deal of shelter from southeasterlies. Although similar to Holford Bay, a mile to the north, its alignment to the prevailing swells is slightly different, and a quieter anchorage is the result. For lack of any other name, the title Tzartus Cove has been applied. Tzartus

is a Nootka word meaning "the place of the seasonal or intermittent waterfall," although locals still call the island by its original name, Copper Island. A great number of mining claims were placed on the island, which is still thought to hold a good deal of mineral resources.

3   Swiss Boy Island

Just west of the cove lie a variety of tiny islets which are ideal to explore by dinghy. Tide pools and kelp beds abound and eagles crown nearly every tree watching for the errant fish that might become their dinner. One of the largest of these islands is named Swiss Boy, after an incident involving the ship of that name. It seems that the Ohiat Indians of Barkley Sound had accepted the British influence on this coast and considered themselves allies of "King George's Men." When the American brig *Swiss Boy* bound for San Francisco with a load of lumber sprang a leak, the captain pulled into Barkley Sound and beached the boat near this spot to make repairs. The Ohiats, seeing that this foreign ship had ventured into "King George's" waters boarded the brig and took the crew prisoner, thinking it to be a fair prize. They stripped the ship of rigging and valuables but allowed their captives to leave on a schooner which happened by several days later.

When the captain and crew reached Victoria they recounted this "act of piracy" to Governor Douglas himself, demanding restitution. The governor offered to repair the ship and punish the offending natives, but the captain said that the brig had been vandalized beyond repair. The sailors were then sent back to San Francisco at the Colony's expense and the gunboat H.M.S. *Satellite* sent to investigate. After checking the *Swiss Boy* it was discovered that she was rotten and should never have been sent to sea in the first place, and the leak she had sprung was basically irreparable. The sub-chief who was being held in the case was then released, and the "act of piracy" was soon relegated to the status of a "misunderstanding" by King George's new-found allies. The incident was first reported in the February 1859 issues of the *Victoria Gazette*. A year later, William Eddy Banfield, the sound's first white settler, reported to Governor Douglas that the *Swiss Boy* had parted her chain, and lay "on a sandy beach, much grown over with barnacles — both hull and cargo." It's doubtful if any remnants of the ship have survived over a century of winter storms in this exposed area.

4   Marble Cove

A mile to the east of Swiss Boy Island is a beautiful protected bay flanked by marble cliffs which are in all probability the source of its name. A small island (Fry Island) protects the anchorage from westerlies that

Left: View across Whittlestone Point and Trevor Channel to the Deer Group in eastern Barkley Sound.

Floats and cabin at Fleming Island are used as an outstation by members of the Port Alberni Yacht Club.

might otherwise roll into the bay. On the shore of Fry Island the wreck of a steel barge is slowly dissolving and staining the rocks around it with rust. Marble Bay itself is quite striking and one of the best anchorages in the Deer Group.

Beaches, cliffs, and rocky spires surround the bay which offers something special for the adventurous visitor — caves. After finding an appropriate spot to anchor (either the northwest or southeast corners of the cove, depending on the prevailing conditions) take your tender and a flashlight for a visit to one of the many caverns that front the bay. One of these is especially exciting to explore because the waves have penetrated all the way through the islet, forming a natural tunnel through which one can row all the way when swells are not running high. These caves are not dead caverns, but rather a microenvironment unto themselves where life competes for space as vigorously as it does in any other biological setting. A strong flashlight will reveal brilliant colours normally masked by the darkness. Marble Cove has enough attractions that a day could easily be lost exploring its unique features.

5   Robbers Passage

Between Tzartus and Fleming Islands a narrow passage with islets at the entrances guards a landlocked cove that has no equal in the Deer Group. It takes its name from Robber Island, the former name of Fleming Island. (Many locals refer to Fleming as Robber Island.) At first glance, the western entrance to the passage seems to be encumbered by rocks — but close examination reveals that most of these are above water and easy to locate unless visibility is unduly obscured. Once inside, the passage becomes virtually a lagoon with sheltered anchorage for a half-dozen boats. The Port Alberni Yacht Club recognized its beauty and purchased 7 acres of land on Fleming Island as the base for an outstation. On this ideal location they have also built a small floating cabin that serves as a meeting place, providing 300 ft of docking space for their members. They have a beach

and picnic area, with limited power and water also available. Whenever there is room, casual visitors can tie up by paying a nominal daily fee for use of the facilities. If nobody is occupying the floats there is an "honour box" to facilitate payment. The little floating cabin (as well as the rest of the site) is clean and bright, with an ambience which makes you feel welcome. You can anchor in the passage without bothering the club members, but they are so friendly and courteous you will soon be tempted to accept their welcome. The easterly exit into Trevor Channel is partially blocked by two reefs, but a black beacon marks the dangerous submerged one, and if you proceed cautiously, the narrow gap south of the beacon can be negotiated by most yachts.

If you want to contact the yacht club, its address is Box 37, Port Alberni, British Columbia V9Y 7M6.

6   Fleming Island

On the western shore of Fleming Island is a small bight protected by a submerged reef that acts as an invisible breakwater until the tide drops to 8 ft or less. This reef, which extends halfway into the bay and its alignment to the prevailing swells gives the bight a good deal of protection, and this otherwise marginal bay becomes satisfactory anchorage in all but strong northerly winds. If you want an isolated anchorage surrounded by untouched wilderness, this rugged island will give it to you. It is particularly good in southwesterly winds which usually herald a few days of gloomy weather.

7   Sandford Island

There is no clear passage between Sandford and Fleming Islands as over a dozen tiny islets and rocks nearly join them. For the adventurous yachtsman there is a big enough space between the exposed rocks for one boat to anchor. The underwater rocks and reefs make an ideal environment to explore and scuba divers are often seen in the channels among nearby Ross Islets. The anchorage is more protected than it appears on the chart, and lends an air of ruggedness that only the west coast can offer. Carefully enter between Fleming Island and the 40 ft islet (marked "12" on the metric charts) and anchor in the 26 ft spot off Sanford Island. Run a stern line to shore according to the prevailing conditions for extra security.

8   Satellite Passage

This passage, the largest in the Deer Group, was named for the *Satellite*, a gunboat which plied this coast between 1857-1860 and presumably used this channel frequently. It lies between Sandford and Helby Islands with the small, rocky Wizard Islet near mid-channel on the eastern side. Between Wizard Islet and Helby Island is an area known as Entrance Anchorage. Although mentioned as a ship anchorage, it is seldom used, and offers little attraction to the passing yachtsman.

Clear skies and ruffled waters brighten passage across Imperial Eagle Channel in Barkley Sound.

Helby Island, one of the few privately-owned islands in Barkley Sound, is being subjected to residential development. However, the island is being developed in such a way that the housing should have relatively little impact on its overall appearance. The houses (mostly owned by faculty and staff at the Marine Biological Station in Bamfield) are serviced from a common dock and "ring road." Setbacks ensure that the majority of the dwellings will not be visible from seaward. The float on Helby Island's northwest side belongs to the development, and thus is private.

Mackenzie Anchorage, between Helby and Diana Islands is similarly ill-endowed as a destination or point of interest for the yachtsman. Although seldom used, it provides emergency anchorage for small (and large) craft, especially in a southwesterly, so it's good to know it's there. In southwesterlies you could tuck in behind Diana Island's northeast shore in 25 ft, where the island will block the wind and waves to a great extent, or move a mile to the west, where the most westerly all-weather anchorage in the Deer Group is located.

9 Dodger Channel

Between Diana Island and Edward King Island is a body of water which is technically called a channel, though it is commonly used as an anchorage. The channel takes its name from the fact that Captain Pamphlett of the schooner *Meg Merilees* considered it to be "a fine place to dodge (the weather) in." Captain Richards thus called it "Dodgers Cove," and the Hydrographic Service changed it to Dodger Channel to reflect its true geographic nature.

There are two anchorages in the channel, one just north of Haines Island (which occupies the south side of the channel) and the other on the southeast side of the same island near the private float. You can choose the most protected spot depending on whether the winds are from the northwest or southwest. Either spot provides shelter from the swells in 8-15 ft of water, but strong winds can reach inside the channel. One attraction of this anchorage is that its exposure to the open Pacific gives it a rugged milieu (including surge channels, tide pools and caves) similar to the outer islands of the Broken Group. One of the largest summer villages of the Ohiats was located here.

Diana Island was named after the 87-ton steam schooner *Diana*, built in 1860 and operated by the Alberni Saw Mill as a multi-purpose steamship. She was affectionately referred to as "the largest small steamer, or the smallest large steamer" that ever plied the waters of the sound. Voss Point, the southernmost point on the island, honours Captain Voss, who spent some time here before heading out on his famous

voyage around the world in the Indian dugout canoe *Tillicum* in 1902. This world-famous boat is now on display at the Maritime Museum in Victoria. Kirby Point, on the northwest corner of Diana Island is renowned as a fishing spot, and several local skiffs can be seen on any day pulling in sizable catches off the point.

Edward King Island (not King Edward as it is sometimes called erroneously) was actually named for Captain Edward King who founded the *New Westminster Times* and the *Victoria Gazette* and who died accidently here in 1861 while on a deer hunting expedition. Folger Island, the most westerly of the Deer Group, was named by Captain Barkley himself after the first officer of the *Imperial Eagle* in 1787.

10 Trevor Channel

This channel, the easternmost of the three main channels in Barkley Sound, is without a doubt the most heavily used of the three. Pleasure craft must often give way to the large freighters heading to or from Port Alberni, or dodge the patchwork of fishnets strung out behind the sound's large gillnet fleet.

Dodger Channel between Diana and Edward King islands was named by a 19th century navigator who considered it to be a fine place in which to dodge the weather.

When the season is at its peak it is difficult to find a navigable waterway between the maze of nets that criss-cross the channel, and fishermen do not take kindly to yachts that cut or foul their nets. In order to locate the semi-submerged nets, look for the large (usually orange) buoy that marks the end of the net. The net itself is attached to the fishboat, and stretches out between the buoy and the boat. Often the small white floats that indicate the top of the net cannot be seen until you're right on top of them when it may be too late to swerve to miss them. The safest course is to head directly toward each fishboat so you can more easily identify on which side the net is strung. One must navigate slowly and carefully when the fleet is fishing in the channel to avoid confrontation with these "farmers of the sea." The 12-mile-long channel was named after Frances Barkley, wife of Captain Barkley, and the first European woman to visit this coast — her maiden name was Trevor.

194

11 San Mateo Bay

This beautiful bay, located just inside of Alberni Inlet, past the north end of Trevor Channel, rates as one of the most beautiful in the sound. The waters are usually very calm and the shore is graced with a grassy knoll that invites a visit. The bay is so attractive it is being considered by the Provincial Parks Branch as a boating destination and possible camping area — much like the popular marine parks in the Gulf Islands and Desolation Sound. Large, graceful eagles often circle overhead, and Indian paintbrush colours the rocky knolls on the western side of the bay. Because the bay is too deep for convenient anchorage (much of it over 300 ft deep right up to the rocky shore) the Port Alberni Harbour Commission, which controls these waters has placed a public float close to the northwest corner where yachts are invited to moor. The float is not connected to shore, but it is in protected water and is a very easy dinghy ride to shore, which is Provincial Forest land and therefore in public (crown) ownership.

In 1918 there was a cannery and fishpacking plant in the bay, but when the pilchards no longer showed themselves in these waters, the plant closed down. There are fishpens in the southern part of the bay, where this form of mariculture is finding success in the clear waters of Barkley Sound.

12 Congreve Island

Congreve Island, just off the eastern shore of the sound, shelters two coves where secure anchorage can be found amid the backdrop of the green coastal forest. The long narrow cove north of the island is sheltered from all wind and waves, so a yacht could ride out the worst storm here in blissful solitude. A similar, but slightly less sheltered anchorage can be found tucked between Vancouver Island and the eastern shore of Congreve Island. This anchorage is a good spot to launch a dinghy. A quiet lagoon cuts into the island and in the thick forest Spanish moss hangs over the lagoon, hiding a number of birds and other wildlife.

13 Sarita

At the south end of Numukamis Bay is the small logging camp of Sarita, virtually the only remains of a large settlement that once dominated these shores. The substantial Sarita River flows into the bay, flanked by one of the largest Indian Reserves in the sound. This site was the winter camp of Barkley Sound's large Ohiat Indian population. In 1877, the second Roman Catholic mission built on this coast (the first being at Hesquiat) was erected at the ancient village site of Numukamis, on the north side of the Sarita River. This mission was operated by Father Nicolaye until abandoned sometime after 1886. The buildings have since crumbled away to nothing. Mining and logging companies followed the mission. Today little remains of the logging camp at Sarita that

was once home to over 250 workers. The backshore has been extensively logged, and the bay is open to all winds, and not a desirable place to find anchorage.

14 Sproat Bay

Opposite Sarita, on the eastern shore of Tzartus Island, is a bight which is partially protected from winds by a nearby bluff, and from waves by small islets in the bay. Although relatively secure, the anchorage is fairly open, without the famous coziness of other Barkley Sound anchorages. When a southwesterly blows up Trevor Channel the bay certainly affords good protection, but with the wealth of nearby yacht havens, anchorage here is not as desirable as it might otherwise be.

A mile further north behind Clifton Point lies a tiny cove where one boat could dodge a westerly. The cove was operated as a small trading post in the 1850's by Spring and Company, who operated several other stores in the sound. Northeast winds blow right into the cove, and a large private float and residence occupy the site of the former trading post.

Poett Nook Marina off Trevor Channel is often used by Port Alberni boatmen who base their boats here when exploring Barkley Sound.

15 Poett Nook

Notched into the Vancouver Island shoreline, and reached via a narrow channel, is a completely sheltered lagoon with a most interesting name. The cove offers protection from all wind and waves and would get top marks as a cruising destination except for the fact it has been "discovered." Small boat owners, many of them from the Alberni area, keep their runabouts at the Poett Nook Marina on the east shore, and use it as its home base while in Barkley Sound. The cove is connected by logging roads to the Alberni area, and many boat operators keep their craft here, preferring the rough gravel roads to the chop in Alberni Inlet. Still, the cove is picturesque with a flower-covered meadow on the south side. Here you

can anchor in total shelter in 15-30ft over a mud bottom. The creek that flows into the cove was once a favourite native salmon fishing stream.

The cove takes its name from a Dr. Poett who was not a literary artist, but rather a physician from San Francisco who held many of the copper claims on nearby Tzartus (then Copper) Island.

16 Roquefeuil Bay

Three miles southwest of Poett Nook is a bight in the shoreline which was once known as Kelp Bay. In the southwest corner of the bay (behind Dixon Island) is an anchorage used occasionally by boat operators trying to escape the westerlies that blow up Trevor Channel. One of the attractions of the anchorage is the abundance of underwater marine life which inhabits the bay. Scuba divers can often be seen swimming amongst the kelp beds or along the shoreline. The bay seems to shelter more than its fair share of fish and other wildlife. When entering the bay be sure to note the rock north of Dixon Island; it dries at a 9ft tide and has felt the bump of a few keels in its time.

The bay was not named because it is full of rocks, but for the French commander Camille de Roquefeuil who arrived in the sound in 1817 many years after the British and the Spanish had established their influence on the coast. Roquefeuil had come on a trading venture to establish markets for France on this coast aboard the 200-ton ship *Bordelais*. The *Bordelais* stayed about 2 weeks, a brief interlude on a trip around the world which took over 2 years. Bordelais Islets near the entrance to Barkley Sound were named for the ship. Captain Roquefeuil wrote a book of his adventures in which he described Barkley Sound in detail, including interesting anecdotes on the life of the natives here. Before he left, the Indians entreated him to return the following year, but he had no intention to return on a trading venture to an area "which the sea otters had long since forsaken." By 1817 the mammals had been nearly annihilated in this sound. Today sea otters and other sea mammals are making a comeback on the coast, thanks to the ban on hunting, and in part to the efforts of scientists based in research stations on the west coast. One of these stations is located in Bamfield, about a mile from Roquefeuil Bay, perched on a headland overlooking the wild natural study area provided by Barkley Sound. 🐚

LOCAL CAUTIONS
- Fog is common throughout this area in summer months and may blow in quickly from the west.
- Gillnet fishboats are frequently in Trevor Channel. Learn how to locate the nets and manoeuvre around them.

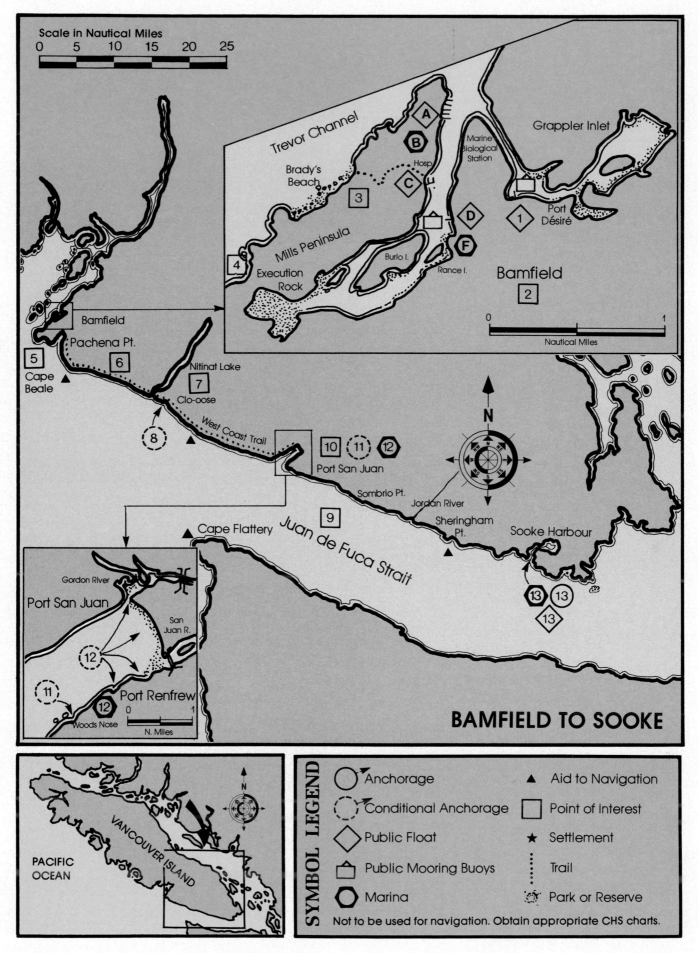

Scale in Nautical Miles
0   5   10   15   20   25

Trevor Channel

A
B
Brady's Beach
Hosp.
C
3
Mills Peninsula
4
Execution Rock
Burlo I.
Rance I.
D
F
Marine Biological Station

Grappler Inlet

Port Désiré
1

Bamfield
2

0   1
Nautical Miles

Bamfield
Pachena Pt.
5
Cape Beale
6
Nitinat Lake
7
Clo-oose
West Coast Trail
8

10   11   12
Port San Juan
Sombrio Pt.
Jordan River
Sheringham Pt.
Sooke Harbour

N

9

Cape Flattery
Juan de Fuca Strait

13   13
13

Gordon River
Port San Juan
San Juan R.
12
11
12
Port Renfrew
Woods Nose
0   1
N. Miles

BAMFIELD TO SOOKE

PACIFIC OCEAN
VANCOUVER ISLAND
N

SYMBOL LEGEND

○→ Anchorage
⬭→ Conditional Anchorage
◇ Public Float
⌂ Public Mooring Buoys
⬡ Marina

▲ Aid to Navigation
☐ Point of Interest
★ Settlement
⋯ Trail
Park or Reserve

Not to be used for navigation. Obtain appropriate CHS charts.

198

CHAPTER SIXTEEN

Bamfield to Sooke

Cape Beale, Clo-oose, Port San Juan

The stretch of coastline between Bamfield and Sooke is the longest uninterrupted passage on Vancouver Island's west coast, and there are only three marginallly conditional anchorages between the two ports. Juan de Fuca Strait, a waterway with a chequered reputation, is often the yachtman's first taste of the open, rolling sea off the west coast. The strait is a fickle and demanding waterway, to be sure, but it should be seen as more of a gateway to a beautiful cruising experience, rather than a giant obstacle to overcome. With good preparation and timing the passage should offer little difficulty, and the rewards more than make up for the effort.

Victoria is closer to Barkley Sound than it is to Desolation Sound, and as yachtsmen get more experienced and search for new cruising areas, this wild and beautiful area will surely host more and more visitors in the years to come. The strait itself, and the Vancouver Island shoreline occupy some very interesting pages in the history of the northwest coast. The following describes the attractions of the area, as well as tips on turning the barrier into a gateway, beginning in one of Barkley Sound's most sheltered refuges.

1 Port Désiré

In 1817 when Camille de Roquefeuil first entered Barkley Sound, he tried anchoring in the mouth of what is now Bamfield Inlet, but discovered that the waters were too deep. As he maneuvered for a better anchorage a sudden wind caught his ship, the *Bordelais*, and almost drove it onto the shore. To escape,

his crew cut the cable and abandoned their main anchor. They then took their ship up the smaller of the two inlets and set their spare anchor in the shelter of a near-perfect cove. He named it Port Désiré. Although they later dragged the bottom for the lost anchor, they abandoned the search after 5 days of effort, so it's probably still down there.

The anchorage de Roquefeuil found is midway on a waterway known today as Grappler Inlet. It is completely sheltered from all weather and the mud bottom will hold a boat snug in any weather. A public float offers 150 ft of dock space and there are three public mooring buoys and a small-boat ramp. The road from here is the "back door" to Bamfield, and goes ultimately to Port Alberni. The unpaved logging roads are subject to time restrictions for private vehicles. Beyond Port Désiré, Grappler Inlet is too shallow for yachts, but it makes an interesting area to explore by dinghy. The area is yet untamed and the occasional bear or cougar can still be seen here. The large scale chart (#3646 Plans in Barkley Sound) shows Port Désiré and Bamfield Inlet in good detail.

2 Bamfield

Named for the area's first white resident, William Eddy Banfield (the "m" in the name today is the result of an original misspelling by the Post Office), this town and inlet played an important historic role when chosen as the terminus for the trans-Pacific telegraph cable. It was chosen because the area has little outside electrical interference, a suitable bottom

A public float, buoys and small launching ramp are attributes of sheltered anchorage in Port Désiré, Grappler Inlet.

Still waters create mirrored images at Port Désiré.

terrain, and little risk of the cable being snagged by a ship's anchor. The cable was a marvel of technology in 1902 as it stretched all the way to Australia, its longest link being the 4000-mile stretch from Bamfield to Fanning Island in a system that encircled the globe, improving world communications immensely in the South Pacific. The cable station was a major link until later replaced by wireless (radio) and telephone cables. The cable station was officially closed down in 1959 and today the conspicuous building on the eastern shore of the inlet houses the marine biological station operated by the Western Canadian University Marine Biological Society. This post-secondary outstation reaps the benefits of an excellent location, with ready access to the west coast's most biologically productive sound. Many excellent scholars have benefitted from the learning opportunities offered at this institution.

For the yachtsman, Bamfield provides a variety of services and facilities. Although the town is smaller than Ucluelet, 16 miles to the west, its primary role as a fishing village ensures that a full range of yachting services are available. There is an excellent machine shop, two marinas on the eastern shore, two waterfront stores and a Red Cross first aid station.

There are no banks here, and fuel must be paid for by cash or Imperial Oil credit card. The freight/passenger ship *Lady Rose*, which can carry 100 passengers, calls here from Port Alberni four times per week in summer, and three times per week in winter, discharging people and goods on both the eastern and western public floats as required. For fares and schedules contact the Alberni Marine Transportation Company (604-723-8313). The return trip down Alberni Inlet takes 8 hours, and is by far the

best mode of transport to Bamfield if making a rendezvous with a boat.

A Coast Guard station is situated midway along the western shore and recognizable as a big white building with a red roof. One of the west coast's two lifeboats are stationed here (the other is at Tofino).

There are three public floats (see inset map). The first is on the starboard side as you enter, has 160 ft of float space close to one of the stores. The second about halfway into the inlet also on the west side has over 1000 ft of dock space, which is often filled to capacity with fishboats. Neither of these floats are connected to the road system, so all traffic on this side of the inlet is by boat or on foot. A pleasant boardwalk connects the houses on this side of the village. The public floats on the east side of the inlet provide over 850 ft of float space, much of it also occupied by the large fishing fleet based here. The dock is connected directly through the road system to Alberni. The marina just south of the public dock has the only year-round fuel supplies in the inlet.

Just opposite the eastern public float (just north of Burlo Island) are two public mooring buoys (not shown on Chart 3671) which are often occupied by fishboats. While there is an absence of good anchorage in the central part of the harbour, go south and east of Burlo Island, ½ mile beyond the public wharf where a quiet, pretty and protected anchorage lends a sense of remoteness that makes the distance from settlement seem much farther. Access to the channel is controlled by an overhead cable with a minimum height of 56 ft, so you should know the height of your mast and the state of the tide before entering if you have a spar near this height. Other minor hazards in the channel include currents, kelp, and a shallow area between Burlo and Rance Islands (15 ft). Once clear of these hazards, an unoccupied lagoon greets the eye, and a convenient mud-bottomed anchorage is yours for the taking. The contrast between the main harbour with outboards buzzing back and forth across the inlet, and this placid, wild area is quite astounding.

Preceding page: Looking south over Bamfield and Grappler Inlets: Pachena Bay in background.

202

Freighters and fishboats pass Aguilar Point near Bamfield.

One of the west coast's two lifeboat stations is located at Bamfield (above); the other is in Tofino.

Protected from winds and waves, this "in-town" anchorage provides the peace and serenity of a more remote anchorage.

Parts of both shores (excluding the Indian Reserve) have been set aside as a Provincial Recreation Reserve, and public access is invited. A trail from Bamfield runs along the shore and carries on all the way to the lighthouse at Cape Beale. Another traverses Mills Peninsula and emerges on Trevor Channel near Execution Rock (get permission to cross the Indian land here, as it is in the Indian Reserve).

Although the water areas of Bamfield are limited, the town is blessed with some of the best walks and hikes on the west coast. The eastern shore provides access to the West Coast Trail Unit of the Pacific Rim National Park which begins near Pachena Bay, 3 miles to the southeast. (More on the West Coast Trail later.) The west side (on Mills Peninsula) has over ½ mile of boardwalks which connect the quaint houses, the Red Cross First Aid Station (located between the two public floats) and the Coast Guard and lifeboat station. Trail signs point direction much as road signs indicate roads in areas where automobiles are the primary mode of transportation. The most popular walk is understandably the one to Brady's Beach on the west side of Mills Peninsula.

3 Brady's Beach

One of the most photographed places in all Barkley Sound is the alternating stretch of sand and rock pinnacles at Brady's Beach. The path to this amazing spot begins behind the small hospital flying the Red Cross flag, and crosses over Mills Peninsula via a pleasant trail which takes about 20 minutes to walk. The beach is actually a series of small sandy strips scalloped between the defiant rocky headlands that project into Trevor Channel. On these offlying headlands, Sitka spruce and shore pine have twisted into tortured shapes as mute testimony to the winds that howl across these shores in winter. In the rocks, anemones, blennies, crabs and whelks occupy the tide pools and consequently the interest of the inquiring onlooker. Surf rolls in constantly, grinding the beaches into finer and finer particles, and kelp piles up on the shores with floating treasures caught

The site of an ancient Indian village, Execution Rock, lies just east of Whittlestone Point (foreground) on Trevor Channel.

in its brown fingers. You need go no farther than this beach to see the quintessential battle between the forces that make the west coast the unique biogeographical treasure it is. When you've made it this far, you've already been initiated to the charms of the west coast wilderness. Continuing the walk across the rocks and beaches to the southwest will expand your experience even further to include an area which was rich in history long before Captain Barkley's sails first appeared on the western horizon.

4 Execution Rock

Near the centre of the Indian reserve, just east of Whittlestone Point, is the site of an ancient village the Ohiats called *"Keeshan,"* which is better known as Execution Rock. This conspicuous spire of granite (clearly visible as you pass by on Trevor Channel) was the final fortress for a large village situated in the woods behind the rock. Remnants of several ancient longhouses (most now crumbled to the ground) can still be seen among the bracken and salal. The large dwellings housed several families, and were a source of amazement to the Europeans who first observed them. According to Captain John Meares, who investigated longhouses in this region and described them in "Voyages":

> "The logs that supported the roof were of a size which would render the mast of a first-rate man-of-war diminutive on a comparison with them; indeed our curiosity as well as our astonishment was on its utmost stretch, when we considered the strength which must be necessary to raise these enormous beams to their present elevation; and how such strength could be found by a

people wholly unacquainted with mechanic powers. The door by which we entered this extraordinary building was the mouth of one of these huge images, which, large as it may be supposed, was not disproportionate to the other features of this monstrous visage.

> "The entrance to the longhouse was a small oval doorway cut through the base of a large totem pole which compelled those entering to bend in order to pass through it; this prevented more than one person entering at a time and placed an enemy at an obvious disadvantage. Inside the entrance was a tier or gallery of some five or six feet in width which formed the uppermost of several similar platforms rising one above the other from the ground floor and running all round the house. A stairway led down from this upper platform to the ground floor."

These were the type of longhouses found at Keeshan during Meares' voyage in 1788. At Keeshan, if a fierce battle ensued, the natives had a final defensive position atop Execution Rock. According to R. Bruce Scott in his book "Barkley Sound" a legend says that the chief built a house on the rock over a natural shaft that goes through the rock to a tunnel below. One night when the Ohiats were having a great celebration, their rivals, the Clallams (from Cape Flattery) seeking vengence for an earlier incident, crept quietly up the rock and caught the Ohiats by complete surprise. Nearly the entire tribe was "executed" and thrown off the rock to the sea below. Four young Ohiats escaped by climbing down a rope into the tunnel below the house, and — as legend has it — later moved to Sarita and re-established their tribe's stronghold at that site.

Today you can take the path to the top of the rock where this gruesome event occurred and survey the sound from the vanished village of Keeshan. The tide rolls in and out of the tunnel below the rock and makes a haunting sound known as "the drums of Keeshan." Near the village site behind the rock a lone totem, whose features have surrendered almost completely to the elements, peers out over the scene of the massacre. On calm days boats sometimes anchor off the beach here, but overnight moorage is not recommended. Trails nearby can connect you to the lighthouse at Cape Beale, guardian of Barkley Sound's southeast entrance.

5 Cape Beale

The passage in Trevor Channel between Bamfield Inlet and Cape Beale is relatively free of dangers, and is the safest channel to take in and out of the sound in conditions of limited visibility. The main hazards to avoid are the Seapool Rocks (marked by a black buoy and named after the ship which struck the rocks in 1928), the patchwork maze of gillnetters (which can virtually block the whole channel) and the cape itself (which has a reputation for wild weather and rough seas). When an ebb current from a large sound meets the prevailing wind and current over a relatively shallow area in the vicinity of a cape, the result is a short, steep and sometimes confused sea.

Dangerous offshore rocks lie over ¼ mile from the high water mark, and these have claimed many unfortunate ships in their time. The first lighthouse on the west coast was built here because of the number of ships lost in the area. The lighthouse, built in 1874 today flashes its warning signal every 5 seconds, and its loud foghorn has moaned its mournful tune every 30 seconds to many a summer cruiser passing this way. Many heroic efforts have been undertaken by lightkeepers past and present who have operated the station here. The cape was named by Captain Barkley for John Beale, the purser aboard *Imperial Eagle* who lost his life a few weeks after it was named in a skirmish with the natives at Destruction Island near Cape Flattery. Much of the land between the cape, Pachena Bay (to the east), and Bamfield have been reserved for the "use, recreation and enjoyment of the public," commonly known as a U.R.E.P. Reserve, and some day may be added to Pacific Rim National Park.

A sigh of relief is usually heard after rounding the

Storm and current fraught waters off Cape Beale prompted the construction of the west coast's first lighthouse in 1874.

cape in either direction. Westbound cruisers have usually been pushing a large contrary swell all the way from Sooke, while eastbound travellers bucking the chop off Cape Beale usually find that the chop ceases and the slow motion roller-coaster ride begins. With the ragged coastline on one side and the smooth rolling blue on the other, the passage east can be a pleasant and exhilarating experience while, in contrast, the trek west can be a nauseous and sometimes frightening ordeal. In summer months, with the wind usually out of the northwest it is best to leave early in the morning when heading to Barkley Sound to reduce the time you would otherwise spend fighting the wind (and consequently the swells) which build throughout the day. Although the elements can create uncomfortable conditions and companion boats can be visually lost below the swells, there are very few

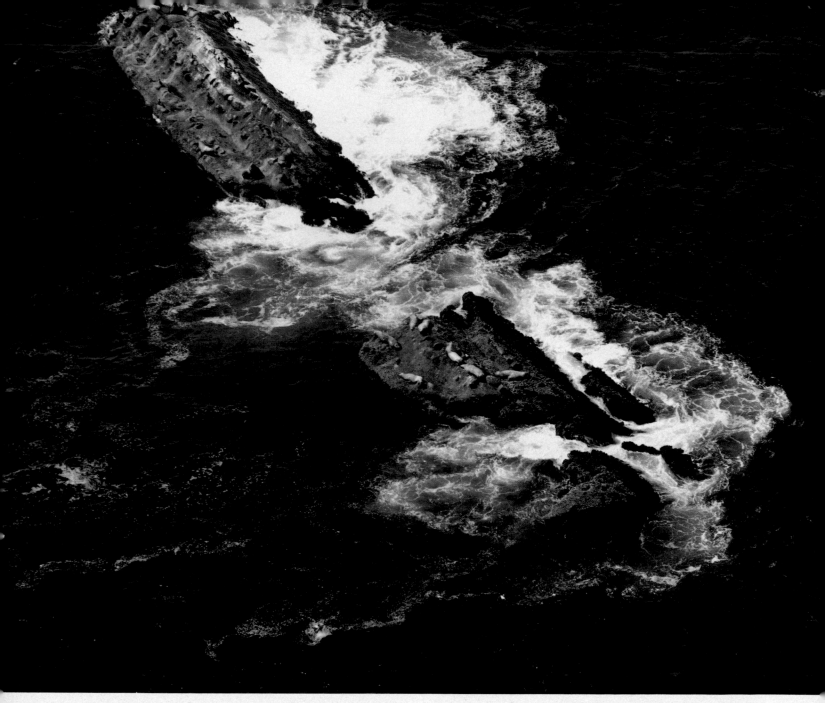

real hazards which need to be avoided. One of the few obstructions is located 3 miles southeast of Cape Beale, where a collection of rocks, reefs and islets appear on the rhumbline course between Cape Beale and Sooke. These are the well-marked Seabird Rocks lying off the entrance to Pachena Bay. They are often covered by herds of sea lions. Because this open bay is shallow and subject to a constant heavy swell, it is not recommended as an anchorage in any case. About 3 miles southeast of the bay is the Pachena Point light (built 1907) the next lighthouse guarding the coast, and the western terminus of the West Coast Trail Unit of the Pacific Rim National Park.

6   West Coast Trail

The stretch of coastline between Pachena Point and Port Renfrew is one of the most rugged and unforgiving shores anywhere in the world. It had such a grizzly record for shipwrecks (one for every mile of coastline) that it became known as "the graveyard of the Pacific". The wreck of the *Valencia* (on a stormy

Sea lions bask on foam-washed Seabird Rocks off entrance to Pachena Bay.

January in 1906) prompted the Federal Government to take action by erecting the lighthouse at Pachena Point, and constructing the lifesaving trail between the settlements of Bamfield and Port Renfrew. The *Valencia*, a well-found steel steamship bound for Victoria, overshot the entrance to Juan de Fuca Strait and, without warning, piled up on the rocks 3 miles southeast of Pachena Point. Although several heroic attempts were made, the shoreline was too rough and steep for safe landing or rescue, and 126 souls (who survived the crash) were lost trying to get to safety. That year work began on the trail, and bit by bit the lifesaving trail was completed.

Tales of shipwrecks on this coast have been well documented (see the Part I reading list) and make interesting historical reading. Most wrecks took place in an era when there were few good charts, no aids to navigation, and no radio communication. Con-

Lightstations such as this one on Pachena Point have reduced the risks along this coast once known as the "Graveyard of the Pacific".

A dangerous bar and numerous rocks make access into Nitinat Lake difficult even for those with local knowledge.

sequently, in recent years there have been substantially fewer incidents. However, certain conditions make your approach to this area more hazardous than it might otherwise be.

When the sky is obscured (stormy winters, foggy summers) celestial navigation is difficult, and days often go by with no clear sights being possible. (This is why Cook missed the Strait of Juan de Fuca, though he was seeking it.) In addition, an offshore current along the west coast is greatly affected by the prevailing wind and wave direction. This current, which runs southeast at 1½ knots in summer and northwest at 2 knots in winter, can cause great errors in dead reckoning calculations and greatly increase or decrease the time taken to transit this section of the coastline. When you add to this both the great effect of the tide rushing in and out of Juan de Fuca Strait and the strong net outflow of water caused by snow-melt and inland precipitation, it becomes understandable why so many sturdy ships have ended their days on these shores.

Today, the west coast trail is maintained as part of Pacific Rim National Park for more pleasant pursuits than lifesaving. It is a challenging hike for adventurers seeking to trek and camp on one of the wildest and remote shorelines in this part of the world. Along the 45-mile-hike are beaches, shipwrecks (still visible), sandstone shelves, and even an 80 ft waterfall called Tsusiat Falls which pours over the cliffs directly onto the beach. It is clearly visible from sea as a white band against the black cliffs 7 miles southeast of Pachena Point, as indicated on the charts. If conditions are favourable you can approach as close as ½ mile from the falls and get a good view of the cascading waters. Two miles east there is also a significant blowhole.

7   Nitinat Lake

About 3 miles southeast of Tsusiat Falls, a narrow split in the shoreline opens into a tidal lagoon called Nitinat Lake. Although marginally navigable, it is dangerous to enter, and seldom used, except by fishboats familiar with the area. The Lummi Bay Cannery was located here, and so much fish was taken between 1915-1920 that they completely depleted the resource. The "Sailing Directions" warn that: "A bar with depths of 5 to 7 ft lies between the entrance points; Saw Tooth Rocks, a local name, lie south of Tsuquanah Point and are the visible part of the bar. In Nitinat Narrows, a short distance within the entrance, the channel narrows to a width of about 140 ft. There is a large drying rock on the N.W. side of the entrance, and several rocks, covered less than 6 ft exist in the fairway."

If that's not enough to turn you away, there are numerous deadheads in the lake and when weather conditions are bad the bar breaks and is far too dangerous to cross. The large scale chart for this area (#3647) shows the bar and narrows in good detail, so each year a few curious helmsmen try their luck at entering, and the colourful array of different bottom paints on the rocks attests to their success. If caught by foul weather in the area and immediate anchorage is necessary, duck in behind the black buoy 1½ miles further southeast down the coast where some shelter is available off the deserted Indian village of Clo-oose.

8   Clo-oose

Shelter from northwesterlies is available in a tiny notch in the coast opposite what was once the village of the powerful Nittinahts. Their original village, Whyac, to the west, was considered impregnable, and remnants of their fortress still attest to the durability of its construction as many who hike the West Coast Trail have found. A significant petroglyph depicting a ship under full sail has been etched into nearby sandstone by some unknown Indian artist. Clo-oose was not the only area where villages occurred. Recent archeological research indicates that as many as 17 villages once occupied the eastern shores of Juan de Fuca Strait. As many as 3000 or 4000 natives made it

Rushing waters from Tsusiat Falls pour across the west coast trail near Clo-oose.

Looking north across Cape Flattery and the Strait of Juan de Fuca with Vancouver Island in the distance.

their home. There are 36 shell middens along this stretch of the west coast, located wherever there was a convenient place to launch a canoe.

Anchor close to shore to get out of the wind, but don't expect the swells to stop on your account — beam-to-beam rolling is common here as the lazy Pacific rolls on relentlessly into this bight and all down the coast.

The flood tides in this area are distinctively rotary — as shown on the Chart 3602 or 3607 — a result of tidal waters passing over the Swiftsure Bank south of here. The Swiftsure Bank, besides being a good commercial fishing area, is the turning mark for the famous Swiftsure Classic yacht race held every year. Watch for boats (day and night) engaged in fishing this area and take care to avoid their nets or trolling lines.

Southeast of Clo-oose are the lighthouses at Carmanah Point (182 ft high, built 1891) and two miles farther, the smaller one (56 ft) at Bonilla Point. Carmanah Point was once called Coal Creek with some of the black ore taken out in 1911. In a rather long and sometimes monotonous coastline, these bright buildings — a stark contrast to the dense green of the shoreline — are the prevailing measure of progress up or down the Strait. The fog signal at Carmanah Point (3 blasts every minute) gets a lot of use in late summer and early fall. A line drawn between Carmanah Point and Cape Flattery in Washington State marks the entrance to Juan de Fuca Strait.

9   Juan de Fuca Strait

In 1592 (almost 200 years before Cook's voyages) the Viceroy of Mexico sent a Greek pilot named Apostolos Valerianos (more commonly called by his Spanish name Juan de Fuca) on a voyage of discovery to the northwest coast of America. The pilot followed the coast until he came to the latitude of 47°, and "there finding that a broad inlet tended to the eastward between the latitudes of 47° and 48°" he sailed up it for more than 20 days. In "Purchas, his Pil-

grimes," de Fuca describes the many islands he found in the broad sea that opened up inside this entrance. He also noted "to mark the entrance of the great inlet that on the northwest coast, is a headland or island, with an exceedingly high pinnacle or spired rock, like a pillar thereupon." Today's charts would indicate the spired rock to be Fuca Pillar, a pinnacle of 150 ft standing a little offshore of Cape Flattery as a monument to this unlikely adventurer who discovered it exactly 100 years after Columbus stumbled upon the Americas. If Fuca Pillar is the pilot's "spired rock" (as seems to be the case), then surely the broad sea is the Strait of Georgia and the "many islands" are today's San Juan and Gulf Islands, indicating that he visited these areas as well.

Although Cook knew of Juan de Fuca's discovery and sighted and named Cape Flattery in 1778, he passed the entrance declaring emphatically that "no such passage existed hereabouts." It wasn't until 1787 that Charles Barkley sailed into the Strait, recognized it immediately from its description and named it Juan de Fuca's Strait.

Today the strait is a busy shipping lane with a major traffic separation scheme designed to prevent collision between the many ships going to and from the great ports of Seattle and Vancouver. For the yachtsman, the strait has a reputation as being either the best or the worst area on the coast to cruise, depending on the conditions at the time, and the direction headed. In summer months the prevailing northwest swells and winds make for a quick, pleasant, often exhilirating passage eastward. Consequently, the reverse direction consists of a long rolling slog against the current, usually under power. Storms can make the strait dangerous for small craft, and it is advisable to use discretion rather than valour when tackling this stretch of coastline. When conditions are good, the passage between Bamfield and Sooke can take just one day. The trip the other way, however, is best done in two days, with a layover in Port San Juan midway along the passage.

10   Port San Juan

Port San Juan — originally called Pachenaht by the natives, Hostility Bay by Captain Meares, and Poverty Cove by Manuel Quimper in 1790 — is a comparatively open bay, about 1½ miles wide which cuts into

Businesslike drum seiner (top) hauls its net in rolling seas off Port Renfrew. Above: The anchorages in Port San Juan are used most frequently as way points for yachtsmen en route to Barkley Sound.

Small headland and dock forms western side of anchorage known as Snuggery Cove at Port Renfrew.

the otherwise regular coastline of Vancouver Island for about 4 miles, terminating in a rough beach where two large rivers empty. Trolling in the area often rewards the angler with a fine salmon. Because the bay is completely open to the southwest, it has gained the reputation as a poor anchorage. Swells roll in unbroken from the sea in all westerly winds. However, small craft can find considerable protection by tucking in behind one of the headlands on the bay's southern shores.

11 Woods Nose

The first of these anchorages, known as Woods Nose (see inset map) appears on the south shore, about 1½ miles into the bay behind several small islets. The large scale chart (#3647) shows the anchorage quite clearly. Make sure your ground tackle is well set, because the bottom is rocky and covered by kelp, making anchorage more difficult. A stern line is also advisable here. Before logging defaced this little

209

Logging and surfing are mainstays of Jordon River between Sooke and Bamfield.

cove, it was a very pleasant and secluded anchorage. The shore has a gravel beach and the nearby caves, covered with moss and ferns, are worth exploring.

12   Port Renfrew

A mile farther into the bay, still on the south side, a public dock thrusts out into the shallow waters of the bay. The point of land upon which the dock appears forms the western end of an area known as Snuggery Cove. There is no public float on the dock, and mooring to the dock is not recommended for small craft because of the swell and the tide change. The dock is used mainly as a loading area for a small service station which provides fuel and water. You often have to walk up the dock to the head of the wharf in order to get service. In the town there are limited amounts of groceries and supplies but the port does not primarily serve yachtsmen. The most secure anchorage is ¼ mile to the east, behind the breakwater and ruins shown on the chart. Use your depthsounder to find the best spot, and avoid swinging onto the shallows that extend from the shore.

Booms and pilings fill much of the head of the bay, and though it rolls in calm weather, boats can anchor in depths that range from 17-24 ft over a pure sand bottom. In strong northwesterly winds, some boats even anchor in the mouth of the Gordon River, on the northeast corner of the bay, after crossing the shallow (3 ft) bar which blocks the entrance. This anchorage, however, requires a tidal lift over a shifting sandbar and, though very protected, this anchorage is not recommended. Port San Juan, where the West Coast Trail begins, is usually seen as more of a way-station on the trip north and not a cruising destination for the yachtsman.

13   Sooke Harbour

The coast between Port Renfrew and Sooke offers no refuge (at least on the Canadian side) or suitable anchorage for a cruising yacht. A passage westward

Cruising yachts steer close to shore as fog rolls through Strait of Juan de Fuca.

through the strait usually requires a determined effort because the beauty of Barkley Sound demands sacrifice. This is not to say that this part of the coast does not have its own attractions — Dall porpoises often catch a ride on a yacht's bow wave — but rather it is a fact of geography that there are simply no completely sheltered havens along this part of the coast for pleasure boats. (For kayaks and other small boats, the shoreline is relatively safe and quite interesting.) Each passing headland takes you closer to your destination — either homeward, or to the varied attractions of the west coast. Sombrio Point (Spanish for "shady point"), San Simeon Point and the conspicuous buildings of the logging camp at Jordan River pass by like roadsigns on this blue desert. Then, 4 miles east of Otter Point, lies the secure shelter of Sooke Harbour. Do not attempt to enter this harbour without the large scale chart (#3641 or #3430); the

extremely shallow, twisting entrance requires close observance to the chart and aids to navigation in the harbour. There is anchorage, a marina and a public float in this interesting and historic harbour, which is included in Chapter II of "Pacific Yachting's Cruising Guide to British Columbia", Volume I, Gulf Islands, by Bill Wolferstan.

Afternoon westerly speeds racing yacht on its way during annual Swiftsure Classic.

LOCAL CAUTIONS
- Overhead cable (Clearance 56ft) in Bamfield Inlet.
- Gillnet fishboats in Trevor Channel and in Juan de Fuca Strait.
- Fog lying in the channels of Barkley Sound, and Juan de Fuca Strait.

SELECTED BIBLIOGRAPHY

Abraham, Dorothy. *Lone Cone — Life on the West Coast of Vancouver Island*, fifth edition The Association of the Covenant People, Vancouver, B.C. 1961.

*Akrigg, G.V.P. and Akrigg, Helen B., *British Columbia Chronicle 1778-1846 Adventures by Sea and Land*, Discovery Press, Vancouver, 1975.

Carl, G.C., *Guide to Marine Life of British Columbia*, Handbook #21, Provincial Museum, Victoria, B.C. 1971.

Canada, Telecommunication and Electronic Branch, Canada Coast Guard, *Radio Aids to Marine Navigation (Pacific)*, Volume 29, Number 1-WE, April 4.

Canada, Ministry of Transport, Canada Coast Guard Aids and Waterways, *List of Lights, Buoys and Fog Signals*, 1984.

*Canada, Dept. of Fisheries and Oceans, *Sailing Directions British Columbia Coast (South Portion)*, Vol. I Twelfth Edition, Institute of Ocean Sciences, Patricia Bay, Sidney, B.C. 1982.

Chappell, John, *Cruising Beyond Desolation Sound*, Naikoon Marine, 4293 W. 13th Avenue, Vancouver, B.C. V6R 2T7, 1979.

Conner, Daniel and Miller, Lorraine, *Master Mariner Capt. James Cook and the Peoples of the Pacific*, Douglas and McIntyre, Vancouver, 1978.

Cullins, Warren and Laura, *Zeballos It's Gold It's People Yesterday and Today*, Cullins and Cullins, Slough House, California, 1982.

Drucker, Philip, *Cultures of the North Pacific Coast*, Chandler, San Francisco, 1965.

Duff, Wilson, *The Indian History of British Columbia*, B.C. Provincial Museum, Victoria, B.C. 1977.

*Efrat, Barbara S. and Langlois, W.J., *Nu'tka' Captain Cook and the Spanish Explorers on the Coast*, Aural History Provincial Archives of B.C., Victoria 1978.

Efrat, Barbara S. and Langlois, W.J., *NUT.KA. The History and Survival of Nootkan Culture*, Aural History Provincial Archives of B.C., Victoria 1978.

Geddes, Gary, *Skookum Wawa, Writings of the Canadian Northwest*, Oxford University Press, Toronto, 1975.

Hayes, Edmund, Ed., *Log of the Union, John Boit's Remarkable Voyage to the Northwest Coast and Around the World*, 1794-1796, O.H.S. MCMLXXXI, R.L. Spearing Collection.

Haig-Brown, Roderick, *Captain of the Discovery the Story of Captain George Vancouver*, Macmillan of Canada, Toronto, 1974.

Hill, Beth, *The Remarkable World of Frances Barkley*, 1769-1845, Gray's Publishing Limited, Sidney, B.C. 1978.

Ince, John and Kottner, Hedi, *Sea Kayaking Canada's West Coast*, Raxas Books, Orca Sound Publishers, Vancouver, 1982.

Jewett, John R., *Narrative of the Adventures and Sufferings of John R. Jewett While Held as a Captive of the Nootka Indians of Vancouver Island 1803-1805*, Robert F. Heizer, Ed., Ramona, California, Ballena Press 1975.

*Lillard, Charles, Ed. *Mission to Nootka 1874-1900*, Gray's Publishing Ltd., Sidney, B.C. 1977.

McDonald, Jim with Donna Pollack and Bob MacDermot, *Hot Springs of Western Canada: A Complete Guide*, The Labrador Tea Co., Vancouver, B.C. 1978.

Meares, John, *Voyages Made in the Years 1788 and 1789 from China to the Northwest Coast of America*, Israel Publishing Co., Amsterdam, 1967.

Middleton, Lynn, *Place Names of the Pacific Northwest: Origins, Histories, and Anecdotes in Bibliographic Form About the Coast of British Columbia, Washington, and Oregon*. Eldee Publishing Co., Victoria, 1969.

*Nicholson, George, *Vancouver Island's West Coast 1762-1962*, published by George Nicholson's Books, No. 4, 2222 Alma Street, Vancouver, B.C. V6R 3R3, 1965.

Pethick, Derek, *First Approaches to the Northwest Coast*, J.J. Douglas Ltd., North Vancouver, B.C. 1976.

Peterson, Lester R., *The Cape Scott Story*, Mitchell Press, Vancouver, 1974.

Ricketts, Edward F. and Calvin, Jack, *Between Pacific Tides*, 4th edition, revised by J. Hedgepeth, Stanford University Press 1968.

Rogers, Fred, *Shipwrecks of British Columbia*, Douglas & McIntyre, Vancouver 1973.

Rue, Roger L., *Circumnavigating Vancouver Island: A Cruising Guide*, Evergreen Pacific Marine Publications, Straub Printing and Publishing, Washington 1982.

*Scott, R. Bruce, *Barkley Sound a History of the Pacific Rim National Park Area*, Fleming-Review, Victoria, B.C. 1972.

Scott, R. Bruce, *Breakers Ahead*, Fleming-Review, Sydney, B.C. 1970.

Sharcott, Margaret, *A Place of Many Winds*, British Book Service (Canada) Ltd. Toronto, 1960.

Snively, Gloria, *Exploring the Seashore in British Columbia, Washington and Oregon — A Guide to Shorebirds and Intertidal Plants and Animals*, Gordon Soules Book Publishers Ltd., Vancouver 1978.

Stewart, Hilary, *Looking at Indian Art of the Northwest Coast*, Douglas and McIntyre, Vancouver, 1979.

Stooke, Philip, *Landmarks and Legends of the North Island*, North Island Gazette, Port Hardy, B.C. 1979.

*Thomson, Richard E., *Oceanography of the British Columbia Coast*, Department of Fisheries and Oceans, Ottawa, 1981.

Vander Ree, Frieda, *Exploring the Coast by Boat*, Vancouver, Gordon Soules, 1979.

*Walbran, Captain John T. *B.C. Coast Names 1592 — 1906 to which are added a few names in adjacent United States Territory their Origin and History*, Published for VPL by J.J. Douglas Ltd., Vancouver, 1971.

Wolferstan, Bill, *Pacific Yachting's Cruising Guide to British Columbia*, Vol. I — Gulf Islands, Vol. II — Desolation Sound, Vol. III — Sunshine Coast, Special Interest Publications, Maclean Hunter Ltd., Vancouver, B.C.

* Primary References

ILLUSTRATION CREDITS

All aerial photographs were taken by George McNutt. All photographs other than those listed below were taken by the author. The author wishes to thank the following individuals and institutions for contributing to this book:

Juergen Baumann — pages 'X', 5, 44, 61, 96, 202 (right); John Tincombe — pages 23 (right), 73, 74, 159 (top), 210; John M. Horton, CSMA, FCA — pages 2, 110 (bottom), 122 (left), 209 (top); B.C. Provincial Archives — pages 41, 101, 134 (top); Derek Gardner — pages XIV, 178; Parks Canada photo by B.I. Campbell — page 132 (left); Transport Canada satellite photo — page 4. Paintings on page 102 and 196 by John M. Horton CSMA, FCA.

All maps prepared by Carolyn Wells and Christiana K. Irving with the exception of: Wind Rose data map page 6 — Canadian Hydrographic Service; End paper map by George Vancouver courtesy of B.C. Provincial Archives.

INDEX

Acous Peninsula, 60
Adventure Cove, 135
Adventure, schooner, 135
Ahmah Cove, 189
Ahousat, settlement, 123
Ahous Bay, 127
Alberni Inlet, 182
Alma Russell Islands, 175
Amai Inlet, 73
Amphitrite Point, 141
Anchorage Island, 50
Apple Bay, 44
Arakun Islands, 135
Atkins Cove, 39
Austin Island, 172
Bacchante Bay, 120
Baeria Rocks, 178
Bajo Reef, 89
Bamfield, 199
Barkley, Captain Charles William, 147,170
Barkley Sound, 147-205
Barter Cove, 65
Bartlett Island, 126
Batley Island, 171
Battle Bay, 60
Bawden Bay, 123
Benson Island, 168
Beresford Island, 27
Bergh Cove, 39
Bligh, Captain William, 101
Bligh Island, 94,101
Boca del Infierno Bay, 97
Bordelais, trade ship, 196,199
Boston, trade ship, 12,98
Brabant Islands, 156
Brabant, Reverend A.J., 12,108
Brady's Beach, 203
Broken Group Islands, 153-173
Brooks Peninsula, 47
Browning, George Alexander, 34
Browning Inlet, 34
Browning Passage, 136
Bull Harbour, 5,19
Bunsby Islands, 63
Burlo Island, 202
Cachalot Inlet, 73
Cape Beale, 148,203,204
Cape Cook, 47,52,91
Cape Scott, 2,13,19,26
Cape Scott Provincial Park, 23
Captain Cook, trade ship, 25
Carmanah Point, 208
Carolina Channel, 144
Catala Island, 77
Catface Range, 122,129
Cayuse Creek, 41
Ceepeecee, settlement, 83
Chappell, John, 19
Checkaklis Island, 63
Checleset Bay, 57-66
China Creek, marina, 184
Cigarette Cove, 151
Clanninick Cove, 63
Clarke Island, 166
Clayoquot, settlement, 132
Clayoquot Sound, 117-139
Clear Passage, 74
Cleland Island, 127
Clerke Point, 53
Clo-oose, 207
Clutesi Haven, marina, 186
Coal Harbour, Quatsino Sound, 44

Coaster Channel, 169
Columbia Cove, 53
Columbia, trade ship, 55,136
Congreve Island, 195
Cook, Captain James, R.N., 11,52,91
Cox Island, 26
Coyote Cove, 114
Cuttle Islets, 60
Cypress Bay, 138
Deadman Passage, 133
Deer Group Islands, 189-194
Dempster Island, 160
de Roquefeuil, Camille, 196,199
Diana Island, 193
Dicebox Island, 172
Discovery, H.M.S., 11,91,102
Discovery Point, 102
Dixie Cove, 73
Dixon Bay, 117
Dodd Island, 161
Dodger Channel, 193
Drake Island, 38
Easy Inlet, 69
Ecoole, 180
Edward King Island, 193
Effingham Bay, 170
Effingham Inlet, 178
Effingham Island, 170
Ehatisaht, 81
Escalante Rocks, 105
Esowista Peninsula, 134
Esperanza Inlet, 77,81,91
Esperanza, settlement, 83
Espinosa Inlet, 81
Estevan Point, 5,105,106
Ewin Inlet, 102
Execution Rock, 203,204
Experiment Bight, 25
Experiment, trade ship, 25
Fair Harbour, 72
Fatty Basin, 179
Favorite Entrance, 66
Fisherman Bay, 24
Fleming Island, 192
Florencia Bay, 141
Flores, Don Manuel, 113
Flores Island, 113
Floyberg, schooner, 23
Folger Island, 194
Fort Defiance, 135
Fortune Channel, 137
Forward, gunboat, 34,141
Forward Inlet, 31,34
Friendly Cove, 94
Galiano Bay, 99
Galley Rock, 161
Gay Passage, 62
George Fraser Islands, 144
Gibraltar Island, 158
Gibson Marine Park, 124
Gillam, Captain E., 31
Gillam Channel, 80,86
Gillam Islands, 31
Gold River, 101
Goletas Channel, 19
Grant Bay, 31,34
Grappler Inlet, 199
Gray, Captain Robert, 55,135
Green Cove, 181
Grice Point, 133
Guise Bay, 25,27
Guise, Captain Henry, 25
Gunner Inlet, 137
Hand Island, 156
Hankin Cove, 71
Hankin, Lieutenant Philip James, 72
Hanna, Captain James, 29

Hanna Point, 28
Hansen Bay, 23,27
Hansen Lagoon, 25
Hanson, Rasmus, 23
Hayden Passage, 120
Hecate Channel, 83
Hecate Cove, 41
Hecate, settlement, 83
Hecate, survey vessel, 12,34,72,151,156
Helby Island, 193
Helen Islands, 28
Herbert Inlet, 122
Hesquiat Harbour, 108
Hesquiat Peninsula, 4,105
Hesquiat, settlement, 106
Hisnit Inlet, 99
Hohoae Island, 73
Holberg Inlet, 44
Holberg, settlement, 44
Holmes Inlet, 114
Hook Bay, 184
Hope Island, 19
Hot Springs Cove, 109
Imperial Eagle Channel, 178
Imperial Eagle, full-rigged ship, 147,170,178
Irving Cove, 136
Island Cove, 137
Island Copper Mine, 44
Island Harbour, 160
Jaques-Jarvis Lagoon, 158
Jarvis Island, 161
Jeune Landing, 40
Jewitt, John R., 12,98
Juan de Fuca Strait, 12,148,208
Julian Cove, 39
Julia Passage, 175
Kains Island, 29,31
Kakawis, village, 132
Kamils Anchorage, 66
Keeshan, 204
Keith Island, 160
Kennedy Cove, 136
Kildonan, 181
King David, cargo ship, 89
Kingfisher, schooner, 123,124
Klaskino Anchorage, 50
Klaskino Inlet, 50
Klaskish Anchorage, 51
Klaskish Basin, 51
Kokwina Cove, 43
Koprino Harbour, 36
Koskimo Bay, 37
Kyuquot, settlement, 64
Kyuquot Sound, 69-74
Lady Rose, freight and passenger vessel, 158,181,202
Lanz Island, 26
Lawn Point, 47
Lemmens Inlet, 135
Limestone Bay, 182
Lone Cone, mountain, 132
Loudoun Channel, 148
Louie Bay, 88
Lowrie Bay, 25,28
Lowrie, Captain Henry, 25
Lyche Island, 146
Mackenzie Anchorage, 193
Malaspina, Captain Alexandro, 77
Malksope Inlet, 63
Maquinna, chief, 12,85,98
Maquinna Point, 94
Marble Cove, 191
Marktosis, settlement, 124
Martinez, Estevan, 11,106
Marvinas Bay, 98
Mary Basin, 88

Matilda Inlet, 124
Matthews Island, 34
Mayne Bay, 151
McKay John, 25,148
McKay Passage, 97
McLean Cove, 74
Meares, Captain John, 95,170,204
Meares Island, 132
Mence Island, 157
Millar Channel, 120
Mills Peninsula, 203
Mission Group, 65
Mosquito Harbour, 137
Moyeha Bay, 122
Muchalat Inlet, 99
Nahwitti Bar, 19,22
Nahwitti Cone, 23
Nasparti Inlet, 55
Nels Bight, 25
Neroutsos, Captain C.D., 39
Neroutsos Inlet, 39
Nettle Island, 157
Nicholson, Major George, 73
Nissen Bight, 24
Nitinat Lake, 207
Nitinat Narrows, 207
Nootka, settlement, 97
Nootka Sound, 91-102
North Harbour, 34
Northwest America, schooner, 95
Nuchatlitz Inlet, 88
Nuchatlitz, settlement, 86
Numukamis Bay, 195
Obstruction Island, 120
O'Leary Islets, 57
Opitsat, settlement, 133,135
Ououkinsh Inlet, 61
Pachena Bay, 205
Pacific Rim National Park,
    136,139,147,203
Pamphlet Cove, 38
Peacock Channel, 161
Perez, Juan, 11,105
Perez Rocks, 105
Pinkerton Islands, 156
Pipestem Inlet, 151
Poett Nook, 195
Port Alberni, 5,185
Port Albion, 147
Port Alice, 40
Port Désiré, 199
Port Eliza, 80
Port Hardy, 22
Port Langford, 88
Port Renfrew, 206,210
Port San Juan, 208
Princesa Channel, 99
Princess Maquinna, steamship, 31,53
Quadra, Spanish Captain, 85,94,135
Quait Bay, 138
Quatsino Narrows, 43
Quatsino, settlement, 39
Quatsino Sound, 31-45

Queen Charlotte Sound, 25
Queen Cove, 80
Quineex Reef, 54
Rae Basin, 109
Raft Cove, 29
Rainy Bay, 180
Reeks Island, 157
Resolution Cove, 94,101
Resolution, H.M.S., 11,91,101
Richards, Capt., 12,34
Riley Cove, 113
Ritchie Bay, 138
Robber's Passage, 192
Rogers, Fred, 89
Rolling Roadstead, 77
Roquefeuil Bay, 196
Rugged Point, 74
Rumble Beach, 40
Rupert Inlet, 44
Russell Channel, 127
Saavedra Islands, 97
"Salal Joe", 161
Sandford Island, 192
San Josef Bay, 23,29
San Mateo Bay, 195
Santa Gertrudis Cove, 95
Santiago, corvette, 11,105
Sargison Bank, 148
Sarita, 195
Sartine Island, 27
Satellite, H.M.S. gunboat, 191,192
Satellite Passage, 192
Scott Channel, 23,26
Scott, David, 25
Scott Islands, 26
Scouler Entrance, 50
Sea Otter Cove, 28
Sea Otter, trade ship, 29
Sechart, 153
Seddall Island, 179
Shelter Inlet, 117
Shelter Shed, 53
Skirmish Islets, 60
Slocum, Joshua, 13
Smith Cove, 39
Snug Basin, 181
Snuggery Cove, 210
Solander Island, 53
Sooke Harbour, 210
Sooke, settlement, 2,205,210
Spencer Cove, 37
Spring Cove, 145
Sproat Bay, 195
Stamp Narrows, 185
Steamer Cove, 117
Stewardson Inlet, 114
Stopper Islands, 149
Strange, James Stuart, 25
Strange Rock, 25
Strathcona Provincial Park, 122
Stubbs Island, Clayoquot Sound, 132
Sulphur Passage, 120
Swale Rock, 157,175

Swiftsure Bank, 208
Swiss Boy Island, 191
Sydney Inlet, 111
Tahsis Inlet, 83
Tahsis Narrows, 83
Tahsis, settlement, 85
Tatchu Point, 75
Templar Channel, 138
Templar, cutter, 132
Thiepval Channel, 166
Tillicum, dugout canoe, 194
Tlupana Inlet, 99
Tofino, 5,7,129,133
Tonquin, trade ship, 129,138
Toquart Bay, 150
Tranquil Inlet, 137
Trevor Channel, 148,194
Triangle Island, 26,178
Trickett Island, 166
Tsowwin Narrows, 85
Tsusiat Falls, 207
Turret Island, 166
Turtle Bay, 161
Turtle Island, 161
Tzartus Island, 189
Uchuck III, freight and passenger vessel,
    95,101
Uchucklesit Inlet, 181
Ucluelet Inlet, 147
Ucluelet, settlement, 141,145
Useless Inlet, 178
Valdes Bay, 99
Valencia, passenger ship, 206
Vancouver, Captain George, 12,85,94,99
Vanlene, freighter, 172
Vargas Island, 126
Varney Bay, 43
Vernon Bay, 178
Volcanic Cove, 74
Voss Point, 193
Walters Cove, 64
West Coast Trail, 4,203,206
West Whitepine Cove, 123
Whitepine Cove, 122
Whitesand Beach, 125
Whittlestone Point, 204
Wickaninnish Centre, 147
Wickaninnish, Chief, 129,138
Wickaninnish Island, 138
Willis Island, 161
Windy Bay, 137
Winnifred Islands, 28
Winter Harbour, 34
Wolferstan, Bill, 211
Wood Cove, 71
Woods Nose, 209
Wouwer Island, 171
Yellow Bank, 138
Young Bay, 113
Yreka, 40
Yuquot, village, 94
Zeballos, 82

METRIC CONVERSION

Because of the conversion to metric, charts may be in feet, fathoms or meters, temperatures given in centigrade and wind speed in kilometers. For those unfamiliar with this system, the following conversion tables are provided.

C°	F°
− 15	5
− 10	14
− 5	23
0	32
5	41
10	50
15	59
20	68
25	77
30	86
35	95
40	104
45	113
50	122

Meters	Feet
1 m	3.28
2 m	6.56
3 m	9.84
4 m	13.12
5 m	16.40
10 m	32.80
50 m	164.00
100 m	328.00
1000 m	3280.00

TO CONVERT

meters to feet	multiply by 3.28
fathoms to feet	multiply by 6.0
kilometers to miles	multiply by 0.62
kilometres to nautical miles	multiply by 0.5399
litres to gallons	multiply by 0.22
centigrade to Farenheit	multiply C by 9/5 add 32
feet to meters	multiply by 0.305
miles to kilometers	multiply by 1.61
nautical miles to meters	multiply by 1,852.0
nautical miles to kilometers	multiply by 1.852
fathoms to meters	multiply by 1.828
gallons to litres	multiply by 4.55
Farenheit to centigrade	subtract 32, then multiply by 5/9

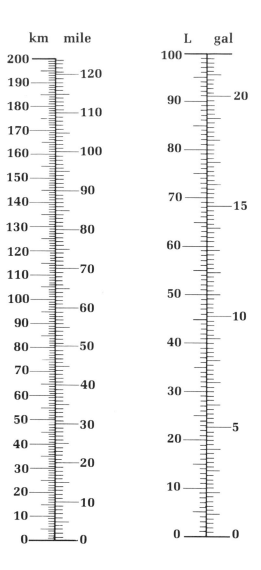

BEAUFORT SCALE

Force on Beaufort Scale	Nautical miles per hr.	Description	Height of sea in ft.	Deep sea criteria
0	0-1	Calm	—	Flat calm, mirror smooth
1	1-3	Light Airs	¼	Small wavelets, no crests
2	4-6	Light Breeze	½	Small wavelets, crests glassy but do not break
3	7-10	Light Breeze	2	Large wavelets, crests begin to break
4	11-16	Moderate Breeze	3½	Small waves, becoming longer, crests break frequently
5	17-21	Fresh Breeze	6	Moderate waves, longer, breaking crests
6	22-27	Strong Breeze	9½	Large waves forming, crests break more frequently
7	28-33	Strong Wind	13½	Large waves, streaky foam
8	34-40	Near Gale	18	High waves of increasing length, crests form spindrift
9	41-47	Strong Gale	23	High waves, dense streaks of foam, crests roll over
10	48-55	Storm	29	Very high waves, long overhanging crests. Surface of sea white with foam
11	56-65	Violent Storm	37	Exceptionally high waves, sea completely covered with foam
12	above 65	Hurricane	—	The air filled with spray and visibility seriously affected

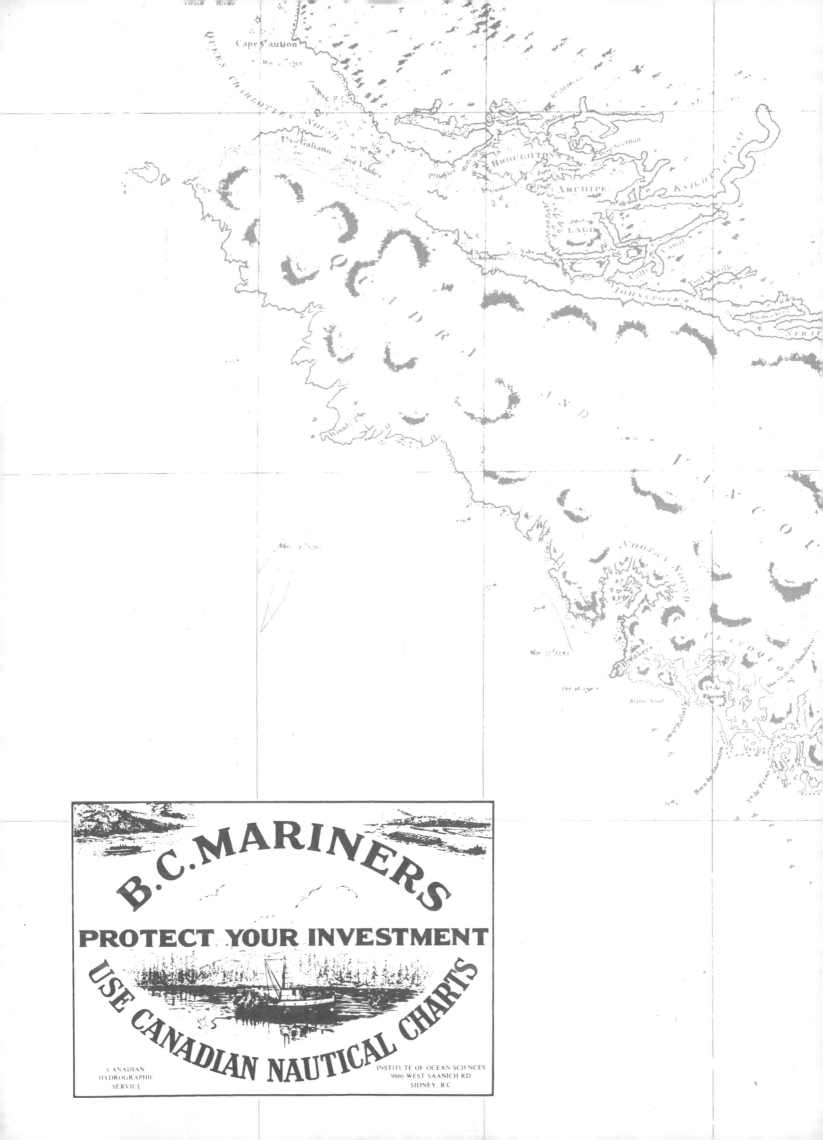